THE Writer's Guide to Creating a Science Fiction Universe

GEORGE OCHOA AND JEFFREY OSIER

Writer's
Digest
Books

CINCINNATI, OHIO

About the Authors

George Ochoa, author of reference books on many subjects, has been an SF fan since his days as president of his high school science fiction club. He studied English (and astronomy) at Columbia University, and received an M.A. in English from the University of Chicago. With his wife Melinda Corey, he is the coauthor of the New York Public Library Book of Answers series, including *The Book of Answers*, *Movies and TV*, and *Literature*. Ochoa's history books for young people include *The Assassination of Julius Caesar*. A New York native, he and his wife live in Brooklyn.

Jeffrey Osier is a life-long reader and fan of science fiction. He has published almost two dozen horror/dark fantasy stories and has finished his first novel. He is the writer, editor and/or producer of many educational science films, on topics ranging from plate tectonics to lunar and solar eclipses to the workings of the heart, immune system and kidneys. He is also an illustrator. Both his fiction and artwork will be featured in his upcoming collection, *Driftglider and Other Stories* from Montilla Press.

The Writer's Guide to Creating a Science Fiction Universe. Copyright © 1993 by George Ochoa and Jeffrey Osier. Printed and bound in the United States of America. All rights reserved. No part of this book may be reproduced in any form or by any electronic or mechanical means including information storage and retrieval systems without permission in writing from the publisher, except by a reviewer, who may quote brief passages in a review. Published by Writer's Digest Books, an imprint of F&W Publications, Inc., 1507 Dana Avenue, Cincinnati, Ohio 45207. 1-800-289-0963. First edition.

This hardcover edition of *The Writer's Guide to Creating a Science Fiction Universe* features a "self-jacket" that eliminates the need for a separate dust jacket. It provides sturdy protection for your book while it saves paper, trees and energy.

97 96 95 94 93   5 4 3 2 1

Library of Congress Cataloging-in-Publication Data

Ochoa, George.
    The writer's guide to creating a science fiction universe / George Ochoa and Jeffrey Osier.
        p.   cm.
    Includes bibliographical references and index.
    ISBN 0-89879-536-2
    1. Science fiction—Authorship. 2. Science in literature. 3. Technology in literature. 4. Literature and science. 5. Literature and technology. I. Osier, Jeffrey. II. Title.
PN3377.5.S3024   1993
808.3'8762—dc20   92-44258
                                                                          CIP

Scientific Consultant: Ronald J. Bonnstetter, Ph.D., Director of Secondary Science Education, University of Nebraska—Lincoln.
Edited by: Mark Garvey
Designed by: Paul Neff
Cover illustration by: Paul Neff

TO MELINDA, WHO BRIGHTENS MY FUTURE.

— *George Ochoa*

TO RACHEL AND GREGORY OSIER, WHO WILL SEE SO MUCH MORE OF IT THAN WE EVER WILL, AND TO ESTHER OSIER (1909-1992), WHO LIVED TO SEE THE WORLD REDESIGNED MORE THAN ONCE.

— *Jeffrey Osier*

ACKNOWLEDGMENTS

A book that aims to bring together all of science and science fiction is necessarily indebted to many people. We thank especially Dr. Ronald Bonnstetter, Director of Secondary Science Education, University of Nebraska — Lincoln, for his careful review of the manuscript. We thank also Jake Winemiller, physics instructor at Southeast High School in Lincoln, Nebraska, for his consultation. All errors and omissions are ours, not theirs.

From George Ochoa: Many thanks to Paul Wortel for taking us on "A Tour Through a Genetics Laboratory" (chapter 13). Thanks to the members of the Space Forum and SF & Fantasy Forum on CompuServe, for their knowledge, strong opinions, and readiness to help an author out. A special acknowledgment goes to my wife Melinda Corey, my collaborator in books, life and other endeavors.

From Jeff Osier: Special thanks to Sharon Johnson, who provided the initial link between the coauthors, and to Dr. Gary Lopez, for knowing how to say the right thing at just the right time. A special thanks to Yvonne Navarro, for all the love, support and clearheaded advice when it was needed most.

From both of us, thanks to our editors at Writer's Digest Books, Mark Garvey and Nan Dibble, and to our agent, Jane Jordan Browne.

Finally, we thank the scientists, teachers, science writers and science fiction writers who have helped all of us understand the universe and imagine what could be.

TABLE OF CONTENTS

Characteristics of stars in our galaxy. Supernovae. Neutron stars, pulsars and black holes. Intergalactic space.

IT SHOULD NEVER BE FORGOTTEN THAT WITHOUT SOME FOUNDATION
OF REALITY, SCIENCE FICTION WOULD BE IMPOSSIBLE, AND THAT
THEREFORE EXACT KNOWLEDGE IS THE FRIEND, NOT THE ENEMY, OF
IMAGINATION AND FANTASY.

— *Arthur C. Clarke*

The classic advice to writers is "Write about what you know." But if you're a science fiction writer, you must often write about what you do *not* know: things no one has seen, rooted in a body of knowledge no one person can thoroughly master. That means you are constantly asking yourself the strangest questions: When will the next ice age hit? What color is the Martian sky? How do you splice genes? Does a person exposed to the vacuum of space explode? What kind of ray could blow up a planet? However imaginative your answers will be, they must be at least scientifically plausible. *The Writer's Guide to Creating a Science Fiction Universe* will help you make sure that they are.

INTRODUCTION

The Writer's Guide to Creating a Science Fiction Universe is a handbook of science tailored to the needs of science fiction writers. By extension, it is also a companion for SF readers, designers of universes, and all those who speculate about the future. It provides scientific information for the kinds of stories SF writers tell — stories about space travel, life on other planets, future technology, apocalyptic disasters. Unlike most academic and popular books on science, which describe only what is known, *The Writer's Guide* also speculates about what is possible. It is fine to read in an astronomy textbook about the spectral class of blue giant stars, but what kind of spaceship can take you there? Could the star support life? How big would it look in the sky of one of its planets? These are the kinds of questions our book sets out to answer.

Necessarily, the scope of *The Writer's Guide to Creating a Science Fiction Universe* is enormous. To describe an alien lifebearing planet in plausible detail, you need to know something about biology, chemistry, geology, climatology. To describe the voyage there, you need to know physics, astronomy, engineering. To describe the civilization that commissioned the voyage, you need to know about energy sources and technology. No single book could possibly contain all that is known about these subjects. But we have sought to put in one place the facts about all these subjects that will be most useful to SF writers.

Do you really need to know these things? Yes — if you are serious about writing SF. Science fiction, by definition, is a literature based on science. That is what makes it different from fantasy. Readers of fantasy will accept a flying dragon, but SF readers want to know how the wingspan you describe could lift a creature with a dragon's mass. In fantasy, you are free to invent any natural laws you wish (though you must stick to them once you invent them). In science fiction, you must stick to the natural laws of this universe — unless you have some good explanation for changing them.

If your SF story contains a glaring misconception or is peppered with small errors, you will break the narrative spell you are trying to create. Your readers will become doubtful about the voice telling the story. More likely, you will not get that far: The editors you submit your work to will return it before anyone else can see it. Of course, mere accuracy does not guarantee that a story will be published or please its audience. But an inaccurate story does not even give itself the chance.

What about movie and TV science fiction? If they can have insects the size of houses and aliens crossbreeding with humans, why can't you? The answer is that literary SF has higher standards for scientific accuracy than most movies and TV shows. It also has higher standards than most comic books. As one SF editor used to say, it's fine to have a man leap tall buildings in a single bound, but, if you're writing SF, you'd better explain why he doesn't kick a hole in the sidewalk every time he does it.

Knowing enough science to make your science fiction plausible is a simple necessity of the art form. The good news is that it can also inspire you with new ideas. You may pick up this book to learn how to create a planet with high gravity, but, in browsing around, you may get interested in how meteorite impacts might affect the evolution of life on the planet, or in how the astronauts who traveled there were genetically retailored for the flight. The more science you know, the richer and more original your fictional world can be.

This does not mean that you have to put everything you have learned onto the page. Loading an SF story with jargon and technical information can be as damaging as inaccuracy. But a deep scientific understanding will let you construct your world more thoroughly, and allow you to select the details that are important to your story.

The Writer's Guide to Creating a Science Fiction Universe is organized with the SF writer in mind. The first nine chapters concentrate on the most popular of SF settings: the universe beyond Earth. Beginning with the basics about space, we talk about spaceships, space stations, the Solar System, starships and the galaxy. We explain step by step how you can design believable planets, alien life-forms, and galactic civilizations. The next five chapters (10 through 14) focus on Earth itself, from future technologies (fusion reactors, sentient computers, genetic engineering) to future political and ecological scenarios (corporate empires, global warming, the death of the Sun). The concluding chapter 15 considers alternate Earths and alternate universes. Throughout, *The Writer's Guide* offers examples from published authors of how science fact can be turned into science fiction.

The Writer's Guide to Creating a Science Fiction Universe is not confined to known science. Some of the favorite conventions of science fiction violate existing theory: faster-than-light starships, time machines, antigravity fields. This book does not discourage you from using such devices. It does, however, flag them as *imaginary science*. This kind of "science" is acceptable if handled plausibly and consistently—perhaps with the explanation that some unknown principle or process of nature is discovered in future centuries. You can, for example, say that hyperspace travel is based on some special case of Einstein's theory of relativity. But outside this special case, you will have to make sure that physical laws as we know them continue to operate. And you will have to be consistent about how the hyperspace drive works, and what it can and cannot do.

Imaginary science is not the same as *wrong science*. These are outright errors that will ruin the credibility of a story and can easily be avoided. If you explain that astronauts on their way to Mars are weightless because they are outside any gravitational field, or that Alpha Centauri is a single star, or that your alien monster is composed of a single giant cell, you are indulging in wrong science. *The Writer's Guide* will explain why.

There are several things *The Writer's Guide* is not. It is not a manual on how to create characters, develop plots, design alien languages, and do all the other things involved in writing science fiction. (Some excellent guides to these subjects exist, including Orson Scott Card's *How to Write Science Fiction and Fantasy*.) It is not a book on the social sciences: Although it contains some material on politics and culture, its focus is on the physical sciences. Nor is it a complete compendium of all the science you will ever need. It *is* a basic reference source for the kinds of science that lie at the heart of most SF stories.

As such, *The Writer's Guide to Creating a Science Fiction Universe* is meant to be used in whatever way serves you best. You can consult the sections you need when you need them. You can browse through it regularly for ideas. You can read it cover to cover. You can use it in combination with other sources, perhaps starting with those mentioned in the bibliography.

Who is this book for? If you have read this far, it is probably for you. It does not matter whether you are a beginning SF writer, an established writer, or a potential writer. For all those who love science and science fiction, this book celebrates the connections between the two. Perhaps, like many SF readers, you have a universe tucked away in your mind, a universe of planets and aliens and high technology, a history of the future that has never been told. If *The Writer's Guide to Creating a Science Fiction Universe* can help you imagine that universe fully and realize it in story, it will have served its purpose.

○

Space is the crown jewel of science fiction settings. Nearly every SF writer spends some time here, and some never leave it. It is a strange, hazardous and dazzling environment, where nothing moves or looks quite the way it does on Earth.

In writing about space, you may choose to stay inside our solar system or move outside it. If you stay inside, you are in a borderland between the familiar and the utterly mysterious. Current scientific knowledge provides a firm base for speculating about travel and colonization in the solar system. In contrast, the prospects for colonizing the stars are doubtful at best, and no definite evidence yet exists for planets outside our solar system. The stars may be tempting precisely because they are largely unknown. But whether you write about the solar system or the galaxy, you will want to be true to what *is* known.

This chapter tells you the basics about space: the extremes of heat and cold, the vacuum, the weightlessness. It will tell you about solar wind, cosmic rays, and the workings of gravitation. It concentrates on space as we encounter it in our solar system, but much of what is said here also applies to interstellar regions and to other star systems. The chapters that follow go on to discuss spaceships and space stations, the planets of the solar system, starships, the galaxy, and worlds not yet discovered.

CHAPTER ONE
SPACE:
THE BASICS

The Edge of Space

It is hard to say exactly where a planet's atmosphere ends and the region we call outer space begins. An atmosphere thins out rather than coming to an abrupt stop. At the top of Mt. Everest, Earth's tallest point (8.9 km or 5.5 miles above sea level), the air is too thin to breathe, but the sky is still blue from refracted sunlight. It isn't until about 160 km (100 miles) above sea level — 18 times the height of Mt. Everest — that what looks like space begins. Here air particles are too widely dispersed to scatter sunlight: about 10^7 atoms per cubic centimeter, compared to 10^{19} atoms at sea level. This would be considered an excellent vacuum by laboratory standards. This region, known as the ionosphere (50 km to 1,000 km), is the location for the low Earth orbit trajectories of the space shuttle and some satellites.

At about 1,000 km, the last vestiges of Earth's atmosphere dwindle to an end, blown away by the solar wind (see "The Contents of Space" below). Here interplanetary space may be said to begin.

Orbits and Gravitation

Having climbed above the atmosphere, your spaceship is orbiting Earth — that is, revolving around it without "falling." What is holding it up?

What keeps it up is its speed, or orbital velocity. This is a property shared by any celestial body — star, planet, satellite. The Moon moves at about 1 km per second relative to the Earth. In the same second, it falls about .14 cm toward Earth. However, because Earth's surface is curved, the surface of the Earth falls away from the Moon by the same distance of .14 cm. The Moon is never able to fall into the Earth because the Earth keeps "slipping" away from underneath. Every satellite we put in orbit follows the same principle: accelerate the satellite to just the right velocity so that it will fall *around* the Earth instead of *into* it.

So your spaceship has reached orbital velocity. You shut the engines off. What keeps it in motion? The answer is Newton's first law of motion — an object in motion remains in motion as long as no outside force is applied to it (see "Newton's Laws of Motion," page 7). On Earth, when you pitch a baseball, air resistance and the downward pull of Earth's gravity eventually bring the baseball down. In space, your baseball — or spaceship — may very well stay in motion forever at precisely the speed at which you pitched it. It will only alter its course if another force perturbs it — gravitational force from a passing asteroid, for example.

So your spaceship remains in motion. But Newton's first law also says that, in the absence of external forces, a moving body moves in a straight line. Why is the spaceship moving in a circle (or in a near-circle, an ellipse)?

The answer is that an external force *is* being applied: the gravitational force of the Earth. Gravitation is a force of attraction between any objects that possess mass. It increases in direct

---

Newton's Laws of Motion

The physical principles discovered by Isaac Newton in the seventeenth century are the same principles used to launch spaceships and plot orbital trajectories. Albert Einstein showed that Newton's system has its limits: It applies only to bodies moving at speeds relative to the observer that are small compared to the speed of light (300,000 kilometers or 186,000 miles per second). Space travel within the solar system is likely to remain well within that range. (For starships traveling near the speed of light, see chapter 4.)

The foundation of Newtonian mechanics are three laws of motion:

1. A body at rest stays at rest, and a moving body continues to move in a straight line at the same rate, unless acted upon by external forces. The property that causes a body to resist a change in motion is called inertia. Physicists define mass as a measure of inertia, or of resistance to acceleration.

2. This law has to do with momentum, the product of a body's mass and its velocity, its speed in a certain direction. When a force acts on a moving body, the rate at which its momentum changes is proportional to and in the same direction as the applied force.

3. When a force acts on a body, the body exerts an equal force, called a reaction, in the opposite direction.

---

proportion to mass and decreases rapidly with distance (in fact, it decreases as the square of the distance). The more massive the object, the greater its gravitational field: the region of space in which it can exert a "pull" on other objects. The Earth's pull tends to make the spaceship move closer to the Earth, while the spaceship's orbital velocity keeps it from falling in altogether. The same forces keep every object in the solar system in orbit: moons around the planets, planets around the Sun, the entire solar system around the galactic center.

A spacecraft's orbit can be unstable if it is too close to the planet, and there are enough particles of atmosphere to cause air resistance. This is what happened to the U.S. space station Skylab, which was orbiting about 300 miles above the Earth's surface before air resistance dragged it down. But as long as the spacecraft is placed in orbit well above the atmosphere and there are no other large bodies perturbing it, it will stay put until someone or something moves it. Hence, it is usually wrong science to have a spaceship's orbit around a planet begin to decay just because it has run out of fuel.

If a spaceship launched from Earth reaches orbital velocity, that means it has accelerated to a speed that enables it to orbit the Earth at a certain distance. In low Earth orbit (a few hundred miles above the surface), the speed is about 8.6 km/second. If it reaches escape velocity, that means it has accelerated to a speed (11 km/second, or about 25,000 mph) that enables it to escape Earth's gravity and enter an orbit around the Sun. Once a ship is in a desired orbit, it can turn off its engines. It does not need to turn them on again until it wants to change direction, move to a higher (or lower) orbit, or enter an orbit around a different body.

It is wrong science to say, "Our spaceship came to a complete stop." There are no complete stops in space. The Sun itself is revolving rapidly around the center of the galaxy. A spaceship either maintains its present orbit or changes it by firing thrusters. For more on spacecraft propulsion and navigation, see chapter 2.

The Contents of Space

Interplanetary space is a vacuum, but not a perfect vacuum. There is matter in the emptiest corners of the solar system, ranging from subatomic particles to boulder-sized rocks. (The larger objects called asteroids and comets are handled separately in chapter 3.) Here are the kinds of debris your spaceship will encounter in the space between planets.

Solar Wind. This is an invisible, very thin gas of charged subatomic particles, mostly protons and electrons, flowing outward from the Sun more or less continuously. It is like a wind on Earth because it consists of a flow of gaseous particles, but it is thinner than winds on Earth by several orders of magnitude. It is not the sort of thing that would "buffet" you on a spacewalk; normally you would not feel it at all.

The solar wind varies in density, becoming thinner the further you go from the Sun. Around Earth, it averages 2 to 10 protons per cubic centimeter, flowing away from the Sun at speeds of about 400 km/second. The solar wind increases dramatically during the explosive outbursts called solar flares. Individually, solar flares are unpredictable, but overall they follow a regular eleven-year cycle, rising to a maximum at the same time that sunspots (cool areas on the Sun's surface) proliferate.

The solar wind has been proposed as a possible method of propulsion for spacecraft (see chapter 2), but it also poses a danger to astronauts. High-energy charged particles are a form of radioactivity; reacting electrically with body cells, they can cause radiation sickness in the short term, cancer, sterility or birth defects in the long term. The symptoms of radiation sickness are fatigue, nausea, vomiting, loss of teeth and hair, decrease in red and white blood cells, and internal bleeding. In severe cases, it can kill within hours.

Shielded by Earth's magnetic field (see "Magnetic Fields"), most of us receive about one-fifth rem of radiation per year from all sources. In space, solar flares can produce radiation in fatal doses of hundreds of rems. Spacecraft on long voyages can protect against solar radiation with metal, synthetic and magnetic shields. When the ship's computers determine that a particularly violent solar flare has taken place, the crew might retreat to a "storm shelter" — a reinforced part of the ship.

Cosmic Rays. These are high-speed charged particles — considerably faster and deadlier than the charged particles that comprise the solar wind. The Sun emits some of them, but most come from outside the solar system, and they are everywhere in space. Cosmic rays reach Earth's surface every day, but the atmosphere breaks them into smaller particles of lower energy, so that they are generally not harmful. On long space voyages, strong shielding will be needed against them. A layer of rock or soil, harvested from the Moon or from asteroids, can protect space stations.

While cosmic radiation can cause cells to mutate, it is wrong science to think it can create the colorful mutations ascribed to it in pulp fiction (as in the origins of the Fantastic Four superheroes). Radiation sickness and cancer are the likelier results.

Meteoroids. These are bits of dust or rock that range in size from a few microns (invisible micrometeoroids) to several meters. Above a certain size — say, one kilometer in diameter — meteoroids are usually classed as minor planets or asteroids. Most meteoroids revolve around the Sun in highly elliptical orbits; relatively few orbit on the same plane as the planets (an imaginary disk called the ecliptic). Some are metal alloys such as iron and nickel; others are mostly silicates and other stony materials.

Meteoroid is the standard name for such an object when it is still in space. When a meteoroid enters Earth's atmosphere and burns up (as a result of friction), it produces a brief streak of light called a meteor (or, less accurately, a "shooting star"). If part of the meteor survives and falls to the ground, the resulting chunk of stone or metal is called a meteorite.

Many meteoroids travel in swarms — that is, they are denser in some parts of space than others. The meteoroids may be spread out more or less evenly throughout the swarm's entire orbit. Several times each year, Earth's orbit passes through such a swarm. This results in a meteor shower — an abundance of streaks of light in one region of the sky over the course of several nights.

In space — or on a body such as the Moon that has no atmosphere — it is wrong science to have your crew encounter a meteor shower in the form of streaks of light. The streaks of light are caused by friction with the air; in an airless environment, there are no "shooting stars." Seen from a spacecraft, a meteoroid would look like a black spinning chunk of rock. But since most meteoroids are small, sparse, and move at 12 to 72 km/sec, your crew is unlikely to see any at all.

The spaceship bombarded by a meteor storm is a standby of science fiction. It is also wrong science. Even in a meteoroid swarm, the particles are more than 100 km apart. Outside of such swarms (i.e., in most of interplanetary space), the distances between particles are even greater — making the chances of collision with a meteoroid extremely remote. Small meteoroids and micrometeoroids do sometimes strike spacecraft and leave unsightly pits, but usually fail to cause serious damage. Astronauts on spacewalks have a tough substance like Mylar in their suits to protect against micrometeoroids. As for large meteorites wreaking destruction on Earth, see "Killer Meteorites" in chapter 14.

Space Junk. Satellite remnants, booster rocket shells, and thousands of other bits of human debris (most fairly small) have been piling up in Earth's orbit since the dawn of the space age. More clutter can be expected on the most well-traveled orbits as humans fan out into the solar system. These can eventually cause damage: A window on the space shuttle *Challenger* had to be replaced when a stray flake of paint created a quarter-inch pit in the glass. Just as ocean dumping has become a matter of international concern, space pollution may be a hot issue in your future world.

Energy in Space

In addition to matter, your spacecraft will also encounter energy. It is commonplace in pulp fiction that this energy will take mysterious forms that do unexpected things to the crew. Unfortunately, energy is no different in space than it is on Earth.

Physicists define energy as a measure of the ability to do "work" — that is, exert force over a distance. Two forms of energy will be exerting force on your spaceship — gravitation and electromagnetic radiation. Gravitation has already been discussed. Electromagnetic radiation is energy caused by the acceleration of charged particles. It includes the whole spectrum of what we commonly think of as energy: everything from powerful gamma rays and X rays to weaker forms such as visible light and radio waves. (See "Electromagnetic Radiation.")

In the solar system, the Sun is a constant source of electromagnetic radiation across the spectrum. For your space travelers, this abundance of energy will be both a blessing and a curse. Your spaceship will use radio waves to communicate, and may use visible light as a power source. But your spacecraft will also need shields to protect against gamma rays, X rays and ultraviolet rays, all of which tend to damage human tissue.

Magnetic Fields

As any compass will show, Earth is a magnetized body with a magnetic field. This magnetic field extends far into space, but it will not prevent your spaceship from passing through. It does, however, trap charged particles in bands of rapidly moving electrons and protons called the Van Allen layer. The Van Allen layer surrounds Earth like a doughnut and helps to protect life on Earth against damage from cosmic rays. It also protects space shuttles and satellites in low Earth orbit (a few hundred kilometers). The inner region is centered about 3,000 km above sea level; the outer region is centered about 15,000 to 20,000 km above sea level. Both regions are areas of high radiation. Not all planets have magnetic fields; the phenomenon is believed to be

Electromagnetic Radiation

Electromagnetic radiation is energy in the form of waves created by the interaction of electric and magnetic forces. Like ocean waves, electromagnetic waves have peaks (crests) and valleys (troughs) and flow at a regular rate. If the flow is sped up by an influx of energy, the waves vibrate more quickly (at a higher frequency) and the distance between the crests (the wavelength) becomes smaller. Thus, high-energy waves have short wavelengths and high frequencies. Low-energy waves have long wavelengths and low frequencies.

In descending order of frequency, the spectrum of electromagnetic waves is comprised of gamma rays, X rays, ultraviolet (UV) light, visible light (from violet to red), infrared light, microwaves, and radio waves. These types of radiation differ from each other only in frequency; they all share a common structure. All move at the speed of light (about 186,000 miles per second). What we call "visible light" is simply the radiation that our eyes are built to monitor. Using different receptors, we can just as well pick up the other radiation.

Atoms can absorb radiation and reemit it. In the course of doing so, they generally make the radiation less energetic—degrading it, or decreasing its frequency. Gamma rays, for example, are generated by nuclear reactions deep inside the Sun. By the time the rays reach the Sun's surface, the journey through the solar mass has degraded the rays into visible light.

Electromagnetic waves do not possess mass, but they are sometimes thought of as particles so as to account for certain phenomena. Photons are "particles" of light: the smallest unit by which electromagnetic radiation levels can change. The light by which you are reading can be thought of as a steady rain of photons.

related to the planet's rate of rotation and the amount of molten iron at its core.

With powerful electromagnets, a ship or space station could generate a magnetic field of its own to protect against solar wind and cosmic rays. But it is wrong science to have a ship generate a magnetic force field that can repel laser beams or gamma rays. Unlike cosmic rays, laser and gamma energy are electromagnetic in nature, and electromagnetic radiation is not stopped by magnetic fields. The only effective shields against it are material ones—metal or rock.

If you do want to have a force field that stops lasers or other exotic weapons, you will have to use imaginary science to invent a force other than the four fundamental *known* forces that are described above. As with most imaginary science, it is best not to be too specific about how it works.

Conditions in Space

There are many differences between conditions in space and on Earth, but most can be boiled down to two factors: lack of an atmosphere and the complexities of gravitation away from a planet's surface. These two factors account for almost all of the weirdness, danger and peculiar beauty of space travel. Getting the details right will lend your story plausibility and may provide you with plot ideas.

Vacuum Effects. Earth's atmosphere is responsible for many things: long sunsets, the mild temperatures of a summer night, the sounds of city traffic, breathing. The vacuum of space affects light, temperature, sound, respiration and other phenomena.

Sound waves require an elastic medium like air to travel; in the vacuum of space there is no sound. An astronaut on an EVA (extravehicular activity) will not hear the ship's engines or hear his wrench tap against the hull. The movie spaceship roaring as it passes a planet is a simple case of wrong science. On the other hand, a spaceship's pressurized interior hums with all the white noise you might expect from the ship's systems.

Electromagnetic waves (X rays, light, radio, etc.) do not require a medium; air slows them down, and they are refracted or bent when they pass from one medium to another of different density. The scattering of light in air accounts for blue or red skies. In the vacuum of space, sunlight has a stark purity. Space is black; sunrises and sunsets are swift. Stars don't twinkle. There are many more stars, because there is no atmosphere to obscure them. Beams of light (including laser beams) are invisible until they strike a surface. Shadows are dramatic: The sunward side of objects are lit, the opposite side black (unless lit dimly by reflected light).

On Earth, temperatures are moderated by the atmosphere. Layers of air slow down solar radiation, preventing Earth's surface from heating up too quickly during the day or cooling down too quickly at night. In space, nothing mediates heat. Temperatures

13

Sunrise in Orbit

A space shuttle orbiting Earth at an altitude of 115 miles sees a sunset and sunrise sixteen times in a twenty-four-hour day. That is because the orbital velocity takes the shuttle around Earth every ninety minutes.

A sunrise from this perspective looks like this: The Earth is a curved body eclipsing the stars, perfectly black except for the scattered lights of cities. Then eight different bands of color appear on the horizon—refracted through the thin layer of Earth's atmosphere. The colors, says one astronaut, are "not like rainbows, which have the same color combinations no matter where you are on Earth. The colors change and the width of the bands is different every time."

The colors swiftly vanish. A blazingly white sun—brighter than it can ever be seen through Earth's atmosphere—obscures the stars. A blue-green crescent appears on the edge of the darkness below. The crescent grows until it becomes the daylit half of Earth.

---

on the sun side of a spacecraft can climb above a thousand degrees Celsius; on the dark side, or in the shadow of a planet, the temperature is nearly absolute zero. (Absolute zero is the lowest temperature theoretically attainable, the point at which all molecular motion stops. It is about −273° Celsius, or zero on the Kelvin scale.) Spacecraft and spacesuits have to be able to function under these extremes of heat and cold.

Finally, without air, there is no oxygen. A human exposed to the vacuum of space would die quickly from asphyxiation. Spacecraft and spacesuits must be pressurized to keep astronauts alive; airlocks are transition areas that can be filled with or emptied of air.

If your astronaut is exposed suddenly to the vacuum, it is wrong science to have him blow up like a balloon and explode. If the exposure is prolonged, the astronaut may get "the bends," in which dissolved gases in the blood, such as nitrogen, form bubbles; if rescued too late, he will suffer intense muscular pain and perhaps permanent damage. If the astronaut is not rescued at all, he will lose consciousness in about thirty seconds. His lungs may rupture from unequalized pressure. In a few minutes he will suffocate.

Weightlessness. At several hundred kilometers, your spaceship has climbed above Earth's atmosphere. Since it has escaped Earth's gravity, everyone inside is weightless. Right?

Wrong. A spaceship at several hundred kilometers has *not* escaped Earth's gravity: It is still well within Earth's gravitational field. Gravity, you will remember, is simply the attraction of matter for matter. A planet's gravitational field is the region within which it exerts an appreciable force on other masses. At a distance of 384,000 km, the Moon is well within Earth's gravitational field; otherwise, it would not stay in the sky.

The weightlessness of space, then, has nothing to do with lack of gravity. It is the result of free-fall — the condition that results when a spacecraft's engines are turned off and the vessel begins to "fall" in orbit. Because the vessel and all of its contents — including the crew — are falling at exactly the same rate (determined by Earth's gravitational pull at that distance), the crew and cargo experience weightlessness.

If you turn the engines on again, accelerating the spacecraft, weightlessness ends. The crew and every loose object inside begins to fall toward the "floor" — that is, toward whatever surface is opposite the direction of motion. This is because the spaceship has begun to move faster than the crew and the loose objects were moving. The force of acceleration and deceleration is measured in "g" or Earth gravity. (1 g is 9.8 meters per second, the acceleration due to gravity near Earth's surface; weightlessness is 0 g.) At launching and reentry, an astronaut may have to briefly withstand 3 g; forces of up to 11 g are possible. Intense g forces may result in bruises, black eyes from broken blood vessels, or death by hemorrhage of the brain.

Effects of Weightlessness. In older SF, weightlessness or zero gravity were considered a liberating prospect. Now that astronauts have spent up to a year in space, it is clear that it comes with a host of problems.

Space sickness, or space adaptation syndrome, affects about half of all space travelers. This is motion sickness (nausea and vomiting) that lasts three to four days as passengers adjust to zero gravity; it results from upsets to the balance mechanism of the inner ear. In the first weeks, faces will look puffy and nasal passages will feel stuffy, because of blood flowing freely to the head, unrestrained by gravity. Those feelings soon subside, but on long voyages astronauts may get dehydrated, because the unusually free flow of body fluids signals the kidneys to discharge more urine. Astronauts on long missions have to drink a lot of extra fluids to stay healthy.

Zero gravity leads to muscle wastage as the body gets less exercise. On long voyages, leg muscles wither and the heart shrinks by as much as 10 percent. Exercising several hours a day, on treadmills or pedal exercisers, may be part of the regimen for your astronauts. Electrical pulse stimulation for the muscles may be needed, or special suits that require full muscular exertion from the wearer.

A more serious problem is bone deterioration. On long flights, irreversible loss of bone calcium occurs that is not well understood. Most of the calcium comes from arm and leg bones, and is discharged in the urine. The long-term result could be brittle bones and kidney disease. No practical solution has yet been found; in the future, drugs may be developed that preserve or replace the calcium. In the more distant future, space colonists might be genetically altered to thrive in zero gravity conditions.

There is a bright side to zero gravity. To move across the cabin all you need is a gentle kick or push. Objects that are heavy on Earth weigh nothing here (though their original mass, or resistance to acceleration, is the same). On long-term voyages, aging processes due to gravity (such as sagging skin) would presumably be slowed. Orienting oneself can be tricky; some astronauts like to consider some part of the cabin as "up," while others enjoy the freedom from vertical direction. In cramped quarters, the ceiling can be used for extra space.

On the other hand, zero gravity can be a nuisance. Even with the most careful cleanup procedures, debris slowly builds up and floats around the cabin: screws, bolts, crumbs, hairs, spherical beads of sweat. On Earth, if you lose something you go back to where you last saw it; in space, it could be anywhere in the cabin. Drinks are taken in through straws; food is too, unless it is processed in such a way that it won't make too many crumbs. A problem little discussed is that you can't burp in zero gravity, because gas doesn't flow to the top of the digestive tract; gas is entirely expelled in the other direction.

Water won't drain away naturally, so showers are taken with vacuum hoses to collect the water. Zero gravity toilets require foot restraints and a seat belt; suction pulls the waste down, where it is shredded, vacuum-dried, or otherwise processed. Sleep takes place in sleeping bags clipped to the wall. Sex in zero gravity can only be imagined; it has not yet been clinically described.

The effects of zero gravity are so counterintuitive that writers who try to describe it can easily make mistakes. However, if you are careful, its strangeness may be an asset to your story.

This chapter describes the basic environment of space. The next chapter describes the machines that can get your characters into space, and allow them to travel, live and work there.

○

As far as we know, outer space is not a natural environment for living things. You may design exotic organisms able to live unaided in the vacuum, but humans are going to need a lot more help. Your characters will need technology to get them into space, to carry them around, to keep them alive, and to allow them to do the adventurous or dramatic things you have planned for them. This chapter is about these technologies.

Space technology can be broken into several categories. There are launch and reentry vehicles to get you into and out of a planet's atmosphere. There are craft designed to move you around space. There are space stations and space colonies, designed for long-term human habitation in space. These topics are applicable to space travel inside this or any other star system. However, this chapter does not touch the more difficult issue of getting a spaceship across the gulfs between stars. That issue, along with the imaginary science concept of "hyperspace," will be taken up in chapter 4.

CHAPTER TWO

SPACESHIPS AND

SPACE STATIONS

Launch Vehicles

In terms of energy expended, the hardest part of space travel is getting from a planet's surface to space. This is because a spacecraft has to work harder to climb out of the planet's gravity well — the region in which its gravitational field is said to "curve" space. From Earth's surface, a spaceship has to accelerate to a speed of 8.6 km/sec to reach low Earth orbit, but from there it only has to speed up about 3 km/sec more to escape Earth altogether. In engineering terms, the ΔV — Delta-V, or change in velocity — is lower in the latter case.

Here are some propulsion methods that your travelers can use to reach orbital velocities.

Chemical Rockets. This traditional method of getting spacecraft off the ground will probably be in use for a long time. A chemical rocket mixes a fuel (such as hydrogen) with an oxidizer (oxygen), burns them, and discharges the explosive exhaust gases out the back. In accord with Newton's third law, the force of the ejected gases is accompanied by an equal reaction force pushing the rocket forward. The gases don't have to push against the Earth; in fact, rockets work best in the vacuum of space.

The simplest and cheapest launch vehicles of this kind are solid fuel rockets, in which fuel and oxidizer are premixed and burned until they run out. Liquid fuel rockets are more controllable. Here fuel and oxygen are kept in separate cylinders and pumped into the rocket engine by pipes. Because hydrogen and oxygen are gases at room temperature, and gases waste space, these elements have to be kept in a liquid state at very low temperatures. (Kerosene may be used in place of hydrogen.) Like the gasoline in a car, liquid fuels give an astronaut control over the rocket's speed.

The U.S. space shuttle uses both solid and liquid fuel rockets. The shuttle consists of the winged orbiter, a liquid fuel external tank that fuels the orbiter's engines, and two solid-rocket boosters for extra thrust. The booster rockets are jettisoned two minutes after launch, parachuting to the ocean for reuse. After six more minutes, the empty external tank drops off and burns up in the atmosphere. The orbiter, all but empty of fuel, is now in low Earth orbit; upon completing its mission, it uses its wings to coast to a landing. (The wings are of no use in space, but in the atmosphere they provide the same aerodynamic lift that makes airplanes possible.)

In effect, the space shuttle is a multistage rocket: a rocket in which stages are successively emptied of fuel and jettisoned. Payloads carried aboard the space shuttle may come with their own upper stage to launch them into higher orbits or escape trajectories.

The space shuttle is not the ultimate spacecraft but a compromise among engineering, budgetary and political factors (as is any spacecraft built with taxpayer money). It is able to lift only about thirty tons of payload into low Earth orbit. The Russian Energia rocket, by contrast, is a 200-foot monster that, with up to six booster rockets strapped on, can lift up to 230 tons. To build space stations or deep space vehicles in orbit, heavy-lift vehicles like the Energia or the proposed U.S. Titan V rocket (which might lift up to 75 tons) will be needed.

A rocket's thrust or propelling force is sometimes measured in pounds or kilograms. The shuttle has 6.7 million pounds of thrust, the Energia 12.3 million. Thrust is sometimes measured in newtons: 10 newtons would support a mass of 1 kilogram (2.2 pounds) at Earth's surface.

Future chemical launch vehicles may be more diverse and streamlined. Solid fuel rockets may be phased out altogether; more powerful liquid booster rockets might become the norm. Booster rockets may be winged and land automatically, instead of coming down by parachute.

Scramjets. Passengers in the future may prefer to travel into space aboard scramjets (supersonic combusting ramjets). Also called an aerospace plane or a hypersonic transport, such a vehicle would take off from a runway like an airplane, and use oxygen from the atmosphere to burn its fuel. This would much reduce the spacecraft's weight, since one-third of the space shuttle's weight at launching is liquid oxygen. The scramjet would reach the speeds of Mach 25 (25 times the speed of sound) needed to enter orbit. At slower speeds, it could be used to take passengers halfway around the world in an hour or two, and would avoid creating sonic booms by flying above the atmosphere.

Coil Guns. Chemical rockets all share the same drawback: they have to carry fuel to lift the spacecraft, but they have to burn fuel to lift the fuel. Fuel is mass, and that mass itself slows the rocket down. The ratio of fuel to spacecraft mass (the fuel-mass ratio) is a limiting factor on how fast and how much the rockets can lift. Acceleration in a chemical rocket is further limited by the rate of gas expansion, which is related to the speed of sound.

Electromagnetic coil guns avoid these problems. Sometimes called a mass driver, a coil gun accelerates a projectile by pulling it through interacting magnetic fields created when electric currents flow through coils of wire. The fields pass a projectile from one stage of coil to the next, accelerating it more at each stage. The projectile reaches phenomenal velocities in a fraction of a second. It could be launched directly into orbit, or it could be launched above the atmosphere, where it would fire a small rocket to push it the rest of the way.

A coil gun launcher now proposed by the Sandia National Laboratories would consist of a long, tubular "flyway" aimed upward at a thirty-degree angle. It could launch satellites weighing up to 1,000 pounds. (Future coil guns may be even more powerful.) The projectile would be fitted with an aluminum girdle called an armature, which is pulled by the coils; a nose cone would provide a heat shield of carbon-fiber composite to protect against atmospheric friction.

The coil gun could not be used to launch people: acceleration forces of thousands of g's would crush a human. But unmanned spacecraft and supplies for a space station can be built to endure it. The cost could be as little as 1 percent that of chemical rocket launchings.

Rail Guns. These are similar to coil guns, but with a fatal flaw. A rail gun propels a projectile on two rails that conduct electricity and create plasma, an electrically charged, superhot gas that pushes the projectile forward. The trouble is that the sliding of the projectile burns and rips the rails so that they have to be replaced after one or two uses. In coil guns, there is no contact between the projectile and the coils — and therefore little wear.

Laser Power. This launch method, which has been studied at the Lawrence Livermore National Laboratory, depends on lasers, mechanisms that produce beams of intense coherent light (see chapter 11, "Designing a Future," for more details). A huge ground-based laser array is aimed at part of a spacecraft on its launchpad. The laser's intense heat vaporizes the target material, producing a reactive thrust. (The pressure of the laser light itself contributes to the thrust.) The spacecraft is launched — without having to lift the great amounts of fuel that chemical rockets require.

Laser power is limited by the wattage of the lasers, but a laser array of tens of millions of watts could provide a cheap method of launching small payloads (say, of 300 pounds). It is possible that space-based laser arrays will be built that are powered by the sun and reach billions of watts. Such an array could launch larger spacecraft from Earth to low Earth orbit, and from there to higher orbits.

Reentry

Reentry into the atmosphere of Earth or other planets presents special problems. A spacecraft entering a substantial atmosphere needs the thermal layers of a heat shield to protect it from the friction of air molecules. Materials that burn away in the process are called ablation shields; other materials are meant to be reused. Too steep a descent, and the spacecraft will burn up regardless of the heat shield; too shallow a descent, and the spacecraft will skip off the atmosphere like a stone off water. Once in the atmosphere, a spacecraft has to have wings to maneuver aerodynamically; otherwise, it drops like a rock (or like the Apollo capsules that used to parachute into the ocean).

Propulsion in Space

Because the atmosphere poses such problems, most SF writers foresee a space technology in which planet-to-space shuttles are sharply distinguished from spacecraft that remain permanently in space. The latter kind might be assembled in space and never enter Earth's atmosphere; they would be serviced by shuttles from Earth or a space station. Unhampered by aerodynamic considerations, these spacecraft could take whatever odd shape was required by propulsion, scientific or other considerations.

These spacecraft could be powered by chemical rockets, coil guns or laser power. But the environment of space also allows for several alternative methods of propulsion. Some of them may be in use in your future world.

Ion. Like chemical rockets, ion drives work on the principle of reaction: The force of ejected mass produces a reactive force in the opposite direction. In an ion engine, the ejected mass consists of ions. These are atoms that have become electrically charged by losing or gaining electrons (subatomic particles of negative charge). Ion drive technology is now available and has only to be applied.

An ion engine is powered by electricity from solar cells or, in larger vessels, nuclear fission. Its fuel consists of mercury or caesium, elements that are easily ionized by stripping them of their electrons. The ion thruster ionizes and then accelerates the positively charged particles with an electromagnetic field produced by magnetic coils. The ions flow out the back at very high velocities, pushing the spacecraft forward. A stream of electrons or negative ions is simultaneously emitted to neutralize the positive ions and prevent the spacecraft from itself becoming charged.

The thrust produced by ion drives is small, because the masses ejected are small. The high velocity of ejection is what propels the ship. On the other hand, the low rate of mass ejection means that fuel can be conserved for a long time. In everyday terms, ion engines get good mileage. Over a long period, an ion drive can accelerate a ship to high velocities while still conserving fuel, making it ideal for interplanetary voyages.

Nuclear. Nuclear engines could be used right now to launch a spacecraft from Earth, were it not for the dangers of setting a nuclear reactor on a launchpad in a public place and pouring explosive fuel into it. The risk of accidental release of radiation may keep nuclear drives from being used in launch vehicles any time soon. Space, however, is a natural hotbed of radiation. As long as the crew is adequately shielded, nuclear drives may become practical technologies for vehicles already in space.

A nuclear fission engine includes a nuclear reactor like those used commercially today (see chapter 11). It works by splitting the atoms of heavy elements like uranium and plutonium, converting some of the mass into energy. In a fission engine, liquid hydrogen is pumped into the reactor core. There the fuel is heated at high temperatures; the rapidly expanding gas is ejected, providing thrust. In principle, fission drives can propel a rocket much faster than chemical drives, but present-day reactors are too heavy to be efficient. Much of the gain in thrust would be used to propel the reactor and its shielding. In the future, more streamlined reactors may make fission drives an economical alternative.

Fusion reactors do not yet exist in economically viable form (again, see chapter 11). But the principle is clear: atoms of light elements such as deuterium and tritium (isotopes of hydrogen) are fused into heavier elements (in this case helium); part of the mass is converted into energy. If fusion reactors are developed, they may be adapted into fusion engines for spacecraft. In a fusion engine, thermonuclear fuel at high temperatures and pressures would fuse to form a superhot, high-velocity plasma of charged particles, channeled by electromagnetic coils and ejected from the ship to provide thrust.

The main problem is that deuterium and tritium fusion produce the subatomic particles called neutrons as a by-product. Neutrons are electrically neutral, and so cannot be controlled by magnetic fields; at high velocities, they are a dangerous form of radiation. The ship would have to carry heavy shielding (i.e., extra mass) to protect itself from them.

Alternatively, a fusion engine could use deuterium and helium-3 for fuel, a combination that does not produce neutrons. However, helium-3 is very rare on Earth, and would have to be mined from the atmosphere of gas giants such as Jupiter. Once the solar system has been more thoroughly colonized, helium-3 collecting at Jupiter might become a profitable industry.

Antimatter. Antimatter drives require more imaginary science than any of the drives yet discussed, but they are based distantly on accepted science. An antiparticle has the same mass as another particle but opposite values on other properties, most notably electric charge. An antiproton is negative while a proton is positive; an antielectron or positron is positive while an electron is negative. (Antineutrons differ from neutrons in properties called spin and baryon number.) When antimatter encounters matter, they *annihilate* each other: They are completely converted to energy. Where a fusion bomb releases only about ½ percent of the exploding mass as energy, an antimatter explosion can release up to 100 percent.

Antiparticles have been produced in particle accelerators: very long tubes that accelerate particles to high velocities with electromagnetic fields, then smash them together to create other particles. The quantities of antimatter produced are tiny, and there is at present no known way to produce quantities large enough to serve as fuel (natural antimatter has never been discovered). If a way was found, the antimatter fuel would have to be kept separate from matter with magnetic fields, since any contact with matter would produce a violent explosion.

The reaction of charged streams of matter and antimatter could produce enough power to propel large ships. The reactive thrust would come from unspent matter ejected at high velocities, or perhaps from photons themselves (units of electromagetic radiation).

Solar Sails. Most of the propulsion methods discussed in this chapter depend on reactive force from the ejection of mass. Solar sailing, like wind sailing on Earth, depends on the application of force from *outside* the craft. A standby of SF, though not yet tried in real life, solar sailing relies on the pressure of photons of light from the Sun; the charged particles of the solar wind may also be a factor. The pressure is exerted on a huge, thin, reflective sheet of a light material like Mylar or Kevlar. The pressure is small, but over a long period can accelerate a spacecraft without expending rocket fuel. The sail (or sails) can be oriented to travel toward the Sun as well as away from it.

Solar sailors (and their computers) would have to be extremely handy in controlling the sails, and the intense energy of solar flares, if unprepared for, could wreck a ship. This method may remain the favorite of small pleasure craft; Arthur C. Clarke's "The Wind From the Sun" describes a race among such craft. Theoretically, it could also be harnessed for large-scale use on space "galleons."

Plotting a Course

As noted in chapter 1, every object in the solar system is orbiting something: the Sun, a planet, a moon. Choosing a course in space is a matter of choosing an orbit. Orbits become more complex as they involve more celestial bodies. A spaceship's computers (or the computers of mission controllers on the ground) are therefore essential to plotting orbits and making course corrections.

Remaining in an orbit requires no fuel. Changing an orbit does—and at least in the near future of space travel, fuel is precious. Mission planners and spaceship captains will be exceedingly careful in planning what they want at the beginning, and very stingy in making changes later on. One wrong move, coupled with inattention to the fuel gauge, may cause the ship to race millions of miles in the wrong direction, perhaps beyond rescue.

To rise from low Earth orbit to a higher orbit requires a change in velocity. (By the way, be careful how you use the term "velocity." It is technically not just speed, but the speed of a body in a particular direction.) One special orbit is geosynchronous orbit. About 36,000 km above Earth's surface, this is the orbit at which a spacecraft's period of revolution around the Earth exactly matches Earth's rotation. A spacecraft in a geosynchronous orbit stays above one fixed longitude of Earth at all times. In a geostationary orbit, it stays above one point at all times.

An escape trajectory takes a spacecraft out of orbit around the Earth and into an orbit around the Sun. To reach another celestial body, such as Mars, the spacecraft plots a trajectory that intersects with the orbit of Mars around the Sun—a course known as a transfer orbit. In essence, the course is laid so that the spacecraft will reach a certain point in space at the same time Mars does. The orbit of Mars and the orbit of Earth together determine when the spacecraft should be launched. The time frame in which it is feasible to launch a spacecraft into a transfer orbit is known as the launch window.

Navigation. Spacecraft usually have to make "mid-course corrections" near the beginning and end of their journeys. They use small thrusters to adjust the ship's orientation (so that the engine's exhaust gases will flow the right way), then they do a "burn" of the main engine, pushing the ship into a slightly different orbit. For the unmanned interplanetary missions of recent years, these maneuvers have been directed by remote radio control from Earth. In the future, they may be run by remote control from space stations or be entirely controlled by the spaceship's crew.

Whoever corrects the course will need to know exactly where the ship is in relation to its objective. A method called radiometry calculates a ship's position by analyzing radio waves transmitted between the ship and a base of known position (at present, Earth). Optical navigation involves measuring the angles between a planet and some of the stars against which it moves (the principle behind the sailor's sextant). The more measurements taken the better; computers allow for quite a few. Space travelers will probably use a combination of optical and radiometric methods to be sure.

As for orienting the ship (that is, pointing it in the right direction), the spinning wheel of a gyroscope, corrected by star sightings, can keep the ship's attitude stabilized.

Note that as far as trajectory goes, the ship's orientation only matters when the engine is burning. When the ship is in orbit with the engines off, it can be pointed any way at all. In fact, one of the most common images of movie SF — the spaceship turning around on a dime and heading the other way — is wrong science. A spaceship that reverses its orientation in orbit will keep heading the same way — but facing backward. To turn around, a spaceship would have to first reverse its orientation, then fire its main engine, slow to a relative halt ("retrofiring"), and then accelerate in the opposite direction. This spoils the dogfighting maneuvers popular in the *Star Wars* movies, but your fiction can probably survive without them.

Gravity Assists. Interplanetary voyages can take advantage of boosts from the planets themselves. In such an orbit, a spacecraft "swings by" a planet to take advantage of its gravitational influence. A planet is moving around the Sun at tens of thousands of miles per hour. By quickly dipping into the planet's gravitational field and then escaping, a spacecraft receives some of that extra speed. It may be launched into an entirely different direction at much higher velocities. NASA's Galileo probe used a roundabout trajectory past Venus and Earth to send it speeding toward Jupiter.

Aerobraking. To be "captured" by a planet's gravity—that is, to enter into orbit around it—a spaceship has to decelerate by retrofiring (firing its engines in the opposite direction). This process burns a great deal of fuel. A more economical method, as yet untried, is aerobraking. In this procedure, a spacecraft plunges into a planet's upper atmosphere, where air friction slows it down. After several minutes, it climbs out again into the desired orbit. As in any atmospheric entry, angle is everything: If the angle is too steep, the craft burns up; if too shallow, the craft skips away. Even when done correctly, a spacecraft designed for aerobraking will need heat shielding to keep from being incinerated.

Artificial Gravity

Weightlessness has enough long-term ill effects (see chapter 1) that planners of long voyages or permanent space stations must consider a way of providing a substitute for gravity. No spaceship likely to be built will be massive enough to generate a substantial field of real gravity. Some SF writers employ an "artificial gravity" field that is switched on and off, like central heat. Presumably it is an energy field that somehow does the work of gravity without requiring mass. Since no such field is known to exist, you will need imaginary science to postulate it.

If you prefer to stick with known science, then there is only one practical way to simulate gravity: centrifugal force produced by rotation. As many carnival rides demonstrate, a person on the inside surface of a rotating cylinder feels a force pushing him or her against the wall of the cylinder. The degree of centrifugal force depends on the speed of rotation and how big the cylinder is. The faster you spin, and the further you are from the center, the heavier you feel.

There is a physiological limit to how fast you can rotate a cylindrical space vessel. Rotate it too quickly and the fluids of the inner ear are affected, causing motion sickness. The solution is to make the vessel large enough so that a relatively low rate of spin is possible. A cylinder 1.6 km in diameter would require 1 rpm (revolutions per minute) to supply Earth gravity. A cylinder 6 km in diameter would only have to spin at about ½ rpm. Smaller cylinders would have to spin faster, or could be built to provide only a fraction of Earth gravity.

To cut building costs, the cylinder can take the form of a torus: a doughnut- or wheel-shaped disk, with the enclosed rim and the central hub connected by spokes (as in the movie *2001*). Artificial gravity would operate within the enclosed rim. Or, the spaceship can be shaped like a dumbbell or a cross; "artificial gravity" would exist in cabins at the ends of the spinning arms. Alternatively, spaceships can be built as rotating spheres. Gravity would be strongest at the equator; it would gradually decrease to zero at the poles as you walked "north" or "south." If you looked directly over your head, you would see other people walking on what appears to be your ceiling.

Whatever the shape, space travelers who want to avoid motion sickness will have to move slowly and carefully in passing from zero gravity sections to those with simulated gravity.

Spacecraft Design

The spacecraft of the future will come in many shapes and sizes to serve a variety of functions. Think of the diversity of watercraft: canoes, life rafts, barges, yachts, speedboats, tugboats, cruisers, warships, tankers. The analogy between space and ocean is helpful in filling out the "ecology" of spacecraft, with all its possible niches. But space is not water, and other considerations will also affect your spacecraft design.

Aerodynamics. Aerodynamic design — wings, stabilizing fins, streamlining — are only needed if your spacecraft is intended to enter the atmosphere. For such craft, heat shields are needed to withstand the friction of reentry. Landing gear is needed for touchdown: either wheels like an airplane's or legs like the Apollo lunar module's. A "biconic" craft (a design that looks like a bent cone) is designed for maneuverability in the air; it would touch down basefirst, slowed by parachutes and retrorockets.

Unmanned probes that are used to explore the thick atmospheres of "gas giant" planets may lack landing mechanisms;

they may be designed to burn up or be crushed in the atmosphere.

Propulsion. The ship's engine design will determine much about its shape. Rockets of any sort — chemical, nuclear, ion — consist basically of a tank from which fuel is fed; a cylindrical chamber where combustion or reaction take place; and a funnel-shaped exhaust from which gas or plasma is emitted. Tank and chamber can be contained together in one cylinder, or the components can be kept separate. The reaction cylinder can be short and thick, long and thin, multiple or solitary; there can be many exhaust funnels or a few. The fuel containers can be arranged in a belt of spherical tanks around the engine. The ship may carry very little fuel, if it depends mostly on refueling stations along the way.

Solar sailcraft will be dominated by large reflective sails, probably circular. The body of the craft will be tiny compared to the sails. Spaceships powered by external lasers will need surfaces — perhaps sails — to receive the laser beams.

Low-Propulsion Craft. A spacecraft launched to travel in one specific orbit, with only minor adjustments, does not need powerful engines at all. All it may need are thrusters for attitude adjustment and perhaps a small main engine for course corrections. Space stations designed to provide long-term habitation are an example of spacecraft that never vary in their orbit. Interplanetary probes such as Voyager and Galileo are launched on a fixed, if complex, orbit, for a single mission. Satellites and platforms (unmanned orbiting structures used for communications, research, surveillance or manufacturing) are other examples of this class of spacecraft.

Manned or Unmanned. Unmanned spacecraft are free of all kinds of headaches that plague manned spacecraft: the need for heavy life-support equipment, extra radiation shielding, insulation from vibration, very high reliability. As robots become more versatile and intelligent, robotic spacecraft will become more and more popular: for exploration, industry, perhaps war. They will also become smaller. NASA's Galileo orbiter, launched in 1989 to explore Jupiter, weighs 2.5 tons; a separate atmospheric probe weighs 760 pounds. In the future, microspacecraft weighing only two pounds, looking something like insects, may be able to perform the same kinds of experiments.

Manned spacecraft need living and working quarters that are

pressurized, well ventilated and temperature controlled. These quarters will be more or less cramped (since every cubic centimeter of pressurized space represents mass that must be lifted). The crew compartments, oblong or cylindrical, may have several decks and small private cabins not much bigger than a phone booth; rotation may provide artificial gravity for long voyages. The compartments can be kept separate from the heat and radiation of the engines — perhaps in a rotating wheel at the end of a long connecting arm.

Unless the spaceship has a sustainable ecology, life-support systems will depend on stored supplies. Oxygen and nitrogen tanks will provide air; exhaled carbon dioxide and water vapor will be filtered out and jettisoned, or stored in waste tanks. Human waste products will also be jettisoned or stored. Ejecting anything in space produces a reaction force that may affect the ship's orbit; jettisoning will therefore happen in a carefully regulated way.

The average astronaut needs about ten pounds of "consumables" per day to stay alive: 1.3 pounds of dehydrated food, 6.3 pounds of water, 1.8 pounds of oxygen. Supplies for long voyages or large crews will quickly add up to huge masses. In an advanced space civilization, spacecraft will depend on resupply vessels that may be unmanned.

Self-Sustaining Life Support. As an alternative to constant resupplying, spaceships and space stations may develop bioregenerative or self-sustaining life support. Green plants will use the Sun's energy to provide oxygen and food, recycling human and animal urine, feces and carbon dioxide — just as they do on Earth. An array of crops — wheat, soybeans, rice, peanuts, fruits and vegetables — may become part of large ships, along with fish ponds and chicken farms.

Maintaining a viable shipboard ecology is theoretically straightforward but technically difficult. Humans are hard enough to care for; more living things to sustain may be the last thing a crew needs. Growing methods will have to be sophisticated. In zero gravity, plants do not extract nutrients from the soil as they do on Earth. Nutrients and water have to be fed to the roots through tubes, a thin film of solution, and a porous membrane. The method is called thin-film hydroponics. On a ship with artificial gravity, both hydroponics (growing plants in water) and soil farming can be used to grow plants.

Generators. Any spacecraft will need electricity to power its systems. The on board generator will produce electricity from solar power (collected by mirrors or purplish photovoltaic cells), chemical-fuel combustion, or nuclear sources.

Equipment. In addition to navigation and propulsion systems, spacecraft will need instruments for a variety of other kinds of work. They will need sensors to detect fields, radiation and particles: infrared and UV sensors, visible light cameras, magnetometers, plasma detectors, cosmic-ray and charged-particle sensors, spectrometers, radiometers. Some instruments, such as magnetometers, will be mounted on booms away from the ship to avoid its interference. Spacecraft sensors will need "imaging systems" to convert invisible radiation into visible light on monitors.

Instruments may be geared to scientific purposes (lots of very delicate research instruments), or to commercial, transportation or military purposes. A commercial craft will need cargo bays and processing plants; transport craft will provide space and life support for large numbers of people.

Warships. Military craft will need surveillance equipment, high maneuverability, and perhaps stealth capability (some way of baffling people when they bounce radio or other waves off it in an effort to establish its position). A warship's weapons would include solid missiles, perhaps accelerated in coil guns, perhaps built to work as "smart" robotic suicide craft. The ship may also carry laser beams and particle beams (beams of high-velocity charged particles). To defend itself, the ship will need thick body shields to slow projectiles and laser beams and perhaps magnetic fields to protect against charged particles. For lasers that operate in or near visible light, mirrors might be the best defense. The ship may also be able to draw in delicate systems and extend protective armor during a battle.

Communications and Computers. For communications, a spacecraft needs radio dishes to collect radio and television waves, and transmitters to send messages to other ships or bases. For nearly everything, the ship needs computers. Self-sufficient vessels with generalized missions will need state-of-the-art supercomputers. However, probes that depend primarily on radio control from Earth or another base, and whose missions are highly specialized, can do with smaller computers. Their main computing power comes from outside.

A ship's radio antennae, perhaps using steerable bases, have to be kept oriented toward home base to stay in touch. The home base will be out of touch when it is eclipsed by the rotation of the planet on which it is situated. But a network of listening bases across the planet surface allows continuous contact with the spacecraft (the principle behind NASA's "Deep Space Network" of stations scattered across Earth).

As spacecraft travel further out into the solar system, they will have to contend with the speed of light. Electromagnetic waves, including radio, move at a fixed speed (about 186,000 miles per second). This is virtually instantaneous for short distances, but over astronomical distances it means delays. It will take more than an hour for a message from Earth to reach a spacecraft near Saturn, and the same period again for a reply to be received on Earth.

EVA Capability. Like any machine, spaceships break down. They will need airlocks so that astronauts can go outside on EVA (extravehicular activity). Astronauts will need pressurized spacesuits, tethers (ropes) to hold them to the spacecraft, suit radios to communicate with the ship, maneuvering gear with jet packs to allow them to move around.

EVAs are dangerous and time-consuming and will be avoided. Robots with cameras, arms and jointed "fingers" will do much of this work. They may be teleoperated: controlled by a human operator inside the ship, using radio or wires.

Large ships will have launch vehicles to use as shuttle craft, repair craft or lifeboats. Astronauts can use them to fly off from the ship and return. These craft don't have to be kept in a space-wasting "shuttle bay" as in "Star Trek"; they can be linked by docking collars to the ship's exterior.

The ship will need additional docking collars to link itself to other ships or to space stations. The docking mechanisms contain airlocks through which crew members can pass from one craft to another.

Size. A ship's size is determined by its function and its propulsion capability. NASA's space shuttle Orbiter is 122 feet long and 78 feet across the wings; its cargo hold or payload bay is 15 feet wide and 60 feet long. But there is no theoretical limit to how large a spaceship can be. Asteroids many miles long may someday be hollowed out, equipped with engines and used as spaceships. On the other hand, microspacecraft may become the preferred means for planetary research. Showers of microspacecraft may be used in terraforming—remodeling planets to make them more Earthlike (see chapter 3).

Space Stations

Space stations are spacecraft that are built to remain permanently in a fixed orbit. They can be used as refueling stops, launch bases, research centers, factories and colonies. The U.S. Skylab project of the 1970s was an early test of a space station; the Mir space station has been in orbit around Earth since the then-Soviet Union launched it in 1986. The American space station Freedom will probably be completed early in the twenty-first century. Science fiction, however, has always thought bigger, and envisions space stations spread across the solar system: some big, some small, some automated, some heavily populated.

Because they are basically spacecraft, many of the design issues already discussed apply equally to space stations. Power, shielding, sensors and life support all have to be provided. Here are a few special issues related just to space stations.

Design. The simplest space station design, used by Skylab, is a single module: a cylinder with solar power panels like wings, radio antennae and sensors. However, single modules have to remain fairly small. Mir and the proposed Freedom space station share a multiple-module design. In this design, a core module is launched first. It has several docking ports where other modules can be connected, along with extra ports for resupply craft, transport craft, and perhaps lifeboats. Added modules may themselves become "core" modules for new pieces.

The modular design allows very large space stations, looking like "Tinkertoy" structures, to be built up bit by bit. The disadvantage is that such a space station will probably remain at zero gravity, since it is difficult to set spinning. New modules will be limited by the technology of the old modules, which may quickly become dated. One can imagine a modular station that resembles an expanding city hospital in yoking together old wings and new, up-to-date wings.

Instead, space stations may be built as spinning spheres, cylinders, toruses, dumbbells or crosses to provide artificial gravity. Visiting spacecraft would dock at a point of zero gravity—say, the hub of the torus. Visitors would then ride in elevators down the "spokes" of the torus. Strapped into their seats, they would gradually feel their weight return as the elevator approached the outer rim, where full gravity would be in effect.

Space stations would be constructed in space with material launched from the Earth or the Moon. The Moon's low gravity makes it a much more economical base from which to launch building supplies. Any other celestial body — Mars, for example — can also serve as a base and a source of raw materials. Slabs of lunar rock would be especially useful as shielding from solar radiation and cosmic rays.

Space stations will probably be surrounded by a cluster of associated platforms and satellites traveling in the same orbit. The unmanned platforms can serve as factories, laboratories and generators.

Location. The first space stations will be built in low Earth orbit. Orbital transfer vehicles can transport cargo from these space stations to higher orbits, where more space stations can be built. Fuel tanks floating near the station can serve to refuel these orbital transfer vehicles as they come and go.

Outside Earth's orbit, one wants to place space stations where they are easy to find — that is, where they will follow predictable orbits that are convenient to some desired location. Space stations will probably be placed in orbit around the planets and in the asteroid belt.

One favored location for space stations is the Lagrange points. These are five points in the plane of revolution of a two-body system, such as the Earth and the Moon, where a third body can remain in equilibrium with respect to the other two bodies. Two of the five points are exceptionally stable: If you put a space station at one of these, you will always know where to find it. The most stable Lagrange points in the Earth-Moon system are called L-4 and L-5. They are located in the Moon's orbital path around the Earth, 60 degrees to either side of the Moon. A space station at one of these points would revolve around the Earth just as the Moon does, at a fixed position relative to the Moon.

Another useful location is an interplanetary orbit. An unmanned station could be launched to revolve around the Sun on a transfer orbit between Earth and Mars. It would "visit" Earth and Mars at regular intervals. (Its designer John Niehoff calls it VISIT — Versatile Station for Interplanetary Transport.) A series of four or more such stations could provide a kind of permanent escalator or shuttle system between Earth and Mars. When a

VISIT station was near Earth, a spacecraft would dock with it. The crew would move into the station and live there for nine months, until the station arrived near Mars. The crew would then leave the station, taking a biconic craft down to the Martian surface. When they were ready to leave, the astronauts would rocket up to another VISIT station passing by, and hitch a ride back to Earth.

Transfer stations could work anywhere in the solar system, providing a cheap means of regular interplanetary transport while colonies were being established.

Uses. Space stations may not be economical in the early years of their development, but over the long term the investment may pay off handsomely. Zero gravity and microgravity (very low gravity) allow for the manufacturing of materials that cannot be produced on Earth. On Earth, light fluids rise to the top of denser ones, but in zero gravity the two mix. This means that strong flexible alloys may one day be mass-produced in space. Certain pharmaceuticals can be made faster in zero gravity. Perfect crystals can be grown for use in electronics and solar power cells. So can perfect spheres of plastic and metal, useful for many applications.

Space stations will also be used for astronomical observations and scientific experiments. They will be important in repairing satellites and in constructing and maintaining spacecraft. They could service solar power stations directing energy toward Earth, or control laser power arrays that propel spacecraft. Near the Moon or asteroids, they could serve as mining outposts.

As space technology spreads, the planning and building of space stations will increasingly become an international activity. NASA, Japan, the European Space Agency, the Commonwealth of Independent States, and other public and private players will all be competing or cooperating in space station activities.

Space Colonies

For a long time, space stations will probably remain outposts like those in Antarctica, where specialists come to work for a while and then leave. But in time, some space stations will develop into space colonies or space habitats: places where generations of people live, have children and die. To these people, their colony will be their home. They may develop a political identity and think of themselves as separate nations, allied more or less closely with Earth nations or with colonies elsewhere. They may develop distinct cultures and countercultures, as varied in temperament and habits as any cultures on Earth.

One of the most famous proposals for a colony is that envisioned by physicist Gerald O'Neill. An O'Neill colony would be placed at L-4 or L-5. In one version, it would consist of a giant rotating torus with a radius of 0.8 kilometers. Along the inside edge of the outer rim, the gravity would be close to Earth's. Ten thousand people could live there, with forty-nine square meters of residential area per person. This is more space than Manhattanites have: They get only thirty-eight square meters per person.

Electricity for such a colony would be supplied by floating mirrors reflecting sunlight onto banks of solar power cells. Sunlight would be directed through mirrors into windows in the outer rim. When people looked "up," they would look up into a glass ceiling bright with sunlight. The mirrors could be angled away to simulate twilight, night and dawn. Radiator systems would radiate away excess heat, keeping the temperature comfortable. Crops could be grown on terraces, in a self-sustaining ecology.

Space colonies can be built to simulate any environment: tropical, European, Pacific Northwestern, arctic. They can reach large sizes, though it is cheaper and easier to maintain several small colonies rather than one huge one. One of the proposed O'Neill colonies is spherical, about 1.8 km in diameter with a population of 140,000.

Dyson Spheres. This is a far-future variation on the space colony, first imagined by physicist Freeman Dyson. Pushing the envelope of imaginary science, a Dyson sphere would be built at Earth's present radius from the Sun. It would completely enclose the Sun, making use of *all* the Sun's energy, instead of the tiny percentage we now use. The raw materials for the huge sphere would come from dismantling planets, asteroids and moons. The inside surface area, where people would live, would be about 1 billion times that of Earth. People would live on the inside surface.

The stresses of such an enormous construction would probably rip it apart, but a million or more smaller structures could be built to make up a stable spherical shell of the same dimensions. Larry Niven's *Ringworld* describes a ring-shaped variation on a

Dyson sphere. Niven has also written on Dyson spheres in his collection *A Hole in Space*.

Large or small, the space colony is one of the most powerful images in science fiction. Arthur C. Clarke, Robert Silverberg, John Varley and William Gibson are just a few of the SF writers who have described space colonies and their inhabitants. The best way to start imagining new variations, as with all the other spacecraft described in this chapter, is to see what some of these writers have done.

○

The Sun and the planets, their moons, the asteroids and comets that orbit around the Sun, make up our solar system. Depending on how advanced the space technology is in your stories, the solar system can be seen in different ways: the stepping-stones of humans just learning to break free of their home planet; a wealth of raw materials for the creation of a human empire; real estate to be used in massive terraforming projects that will fill the solar system with Earths and mini-Earths; a base of operations for interstellar travelers; or the ancient, perhaps mythical, homeland of space travelers who have spread throughout the galaxy but are no longer sure of their place of origin.

SF writers have built-in advantages and disadvantages writing about the solar system. One advantage is that nearly all of the planets and their moons have been studied close up by spacecraft. We now know their surface temperatures, atmospheric makeup, topography and geologic histories. An SF writer now has a wealth of concrete information on which to build stories set in the solar system. This is also a major disadvantage, since some of the mysteries have been solved and are no longer open to wild speculation.

CHAPTER THREE
THE SUN AND THE
PLANETS

Great SF writers in the past, such as H.G. Wells, Olaf Stapledon and Edgar Rice Burroughs, imagined a solar sysem populated with all kinds of wondrous creatures. It is no longer possible to imagine civilizations thriving on a tropical Venus, or intelligent arthropods living beneath the surface of the Moon. Great alien civilizations have been moved to more inaccessible regions—planets orbiting other stars. SF writers now usually look at the solar system as a frontier to be populated and transformed by human beings.

Origins

The solar system began as a vast cloud of gas and cosmic dust. About 4.6 billion years ago, something—perhaps shock waves from the explosion of a nearby star—caused the cloud to begin contracting, gradually forming into the shape of a swirling disk.

Planets of the Solar System

Data	Mercury	Venus	Earth	Mars
Equatorial Diameter (in km)	4,878	12,103	12,756	6,794
Mass (Earth = 1)	0.055	0.81	1.0	.107
Gravity (Earth = 1)	0.39	0.88	1.0	0.38
Period of Rotation (in hours)	1,407.6	5,832.2	23.9	24.6
Major Atmospheric Gas	—	carbon dioxide	nitrogen	carbon dioxide
Known Moons	0	0	1	2
Mean Distance From Sun (in millions of km)	58	107	149	228
Period of Revolution (Earth Years)	0.24	0.62	1.0	1.88

As more gas and dust spiraled inward, the center of that swirling disk grew hotter and denser. Within a hundred thousand years of that initial shock wave, the cloud of dust and gas was already beginning to differentiate into the cast of characters that would eventually make up the solar system as we see it today. At its center was an infant sun. The increasing gravitational pull of infalling matter kept raising the temperature until it was hot enough to vaporize light materials (such as water, methane and ammonia) for a distance of about 400 million miles, leaving only denser particles in a solid state. Beyond 400 million miles, however, temperatures were cold enough to condense large amounts of water vapor into ice and smaller amounts of ammonia, meth-

Jupiter	Saturn	Uranus	Neptune	Pluto
142,800	120,660	51,400	50,950	3,500
317.8	95.26	14.5	17.2	0.00198
2.34	0.93	0.79	1.09	0.0637
9.8	10.2	17.2	16.1	6.4
hydrogen	hydrogen	hydrogen	hydrogen	methane
16	17	15	8	1
774	1,472	2,685	4,486	5,914
11.86	29.46	84.01	164.79	247.7

ane and other gases that coated and mingled with the small rocky particles.

While the sun continued to condense, the particles surrounding it were also condensing. Gravitational attraction caused them to collide and coalesce into larger and larger clumps, and to fall into more compact orbits — creating a wide, thin sheet of matter circling the sun along its equatorial plane. A stellar system at this stage might appear to a space traveler as one vast asteroid belt swirling around a sun that is still a dull, hazy orange mass, its temperature rising as the gases continue to contract.

Gradually the orbiting particles began to differentiate into bands dominated by the gravitational pull of the largest planetesimals (small orbiting bodies that grow as they collide with and stick to other small orbiting bodies). These bands coalesced into nine planets. Those closest to the Sun — the inner or terrestrial planets — were small and rocky: what we now call Mercury, Venus, Earth and Mars. Most of the outer planets — beyond that 400-million-mile range — were large, cold and gaseous: Jupiter, Saturn, Uranus and Neptune. The outermost planet Pluto, a rocky world smaller than Earth, is a puzzling exception. The band of rocky particles between Mars and Jupiter never managed to coalesce into a planet because of the disruptive influence of the tremendous gravitational pull of Jupiter — already the second largest object in the solar system.

Once the sun reached sufficient temperature — 6 million degrees Fahrenheit — to cause hydrogen atoms to fuse, it triggered a self-sustaining nuclear reaction. This infant sun was not as bright, but was far more active than the sun we see today. Solar winds consisting of charged particles blew through the solar system at speeds of up to 2 million miles per hour and, along with ultraviolet rays, cleared away nearly all the remaining traces of the nebulous cloud from which the sun and planets had formed. Chunks of matter too massive to be swept away by the solar winds then bombarded the planets. Rocky fragments and icy particles began to hurl inward, leaving scars upon Mercury, Mars and the Moon that are visible today.

These icy particles also brought something else. It is from them that the Earth, and perhaps Venus and Mars, received water in the form of melting or vaporizing ice.

The Sun

The Sun is the dominant body in the solar system. Not only do all other objects in the solar system orbit around it, but in itself the Sun comprises 99 percent of the solar system's mass. It has a diameter of 1,392,000 kilometers (864,950 miles). Compare this with the diameters of the planets in the table on pages 40-41. Even the sunspots (dark, cooler areas) that appear regularly upon the surface of the Sun can be as big as 31,000 miles in diameter, easily large enough to swallow Mercury, Venus, Earth, Mars and Pluto. Yet the Sun is only an average star in size and temperature, one of 100 billion stars in the Milky Way galaxy. (For more information on stars, see chapter 5, "Around the Galaxy.")

Seen from the galactic perspective then, the Sun is no big deal, but it is the single most important factor humans will have to consider as they colonize the solar system. It is the one body in the solar system we are unlikely ever to colonize or mine. However, even a negligible percentage of the energy it releases is enough to power all human endeavours in space, provided that energy can be tapped effectively.

Less than a billionth of the Sun's energy output reaches the Earth. Even that small amount is enough to heat the equatorial regions and stimulate the circulating air currents that control our weather patterns. It is enough to trigger photosynthesis in the plants that have been the foundation of the food chain for hundreds of millions of years. The fossil fuels we rely on today are remnants of those ancient plants and animals whose existence depended totally on the energy from the sun. In space, the constant unfiltered radiation from the Sun will be the most useful resource in colonization of the solar system.

How the Sun Works. At the Sun's core, matter is compressed so much by gravity that it is hot enough to trigger nuclear fusion. The intense heat causes the protons of hydrogen nuclei to collide and combine to form a stable helium nucleus. The helium nuclei are slightly less massive than the hydrogen nuclei that combined to form them. The rest of the mass is released as energy in the form of gamma rays. Every second, the Sun converts 4 million tons of matter into energy. It has been doing this for 4.5 billion years and is expected to continue doing it for at least that long.

The gamma radiation undergoes many interactions over the course of its next few hundred thousand years, when it finally emerges from the photosphere — the 200-mile deep "surface" of the Sun. The appearance of the photosphere is constantly changing. The motion of the photosphere reveals that the sun rotates at an uneven rate — a revolution taking thirty-three days at the poles but only twenty-five days at the equator.

Strong magnetic fields in the photosphere cause sunspots, which appear darker because they are thousands of degrees cooler than the surrounding areas. The magnetic fields also cause jets of gas in the chromosphere (the Sun's inner atmosphere) and in the corona (the outer atmosphere).

The solar wind consists of charged particles (along with ultraviolet, gamma and X-ray radiation) that stream outward from the Sun at speeds of up to 2 million miles per hour and spread

Terraforming

Terraform means to artificially transform a planet to a condition that is capable of supporting terrestrial life-forms. The term was coined by Jack Williamson in the 1940s for a series of stories (collected and released as the novels *Seetee Ship* and *Seetee Shock*) about "spatial engineers" who terraform the Moon, Mars, Venus, the moons of Jupiter, and even some of the larger asteroids. While some of the techniques employed in these novels appear dated today, the idea caught on quickly among SF writers. Thanks to the spacecraft that have examined the planets and moons of our solar system, we now know a great deal about the conditions on these worlds. And along with this new knowledge, SF writers and scientists now have clear ideas on how the planets really could be transformed into Earthlike worlds.

For a detailed look at the complex interactions of living and nonliving systems that created the atmosphere and weather conditions so important to life on Earth, see chapter 4. It would take millions or billions of years to completely mimic these conditions on another planet. Terraformers would take shortcuts whenever possible.

Genetic engineering would be used to design plant and animal species capable of surviving harsh environments. Blue-green algae can survive and sometimes flourish under hostile conditions, and can be found on freshly cooled lava beds devoid of all other life. Widespread beds of blue-green algae would convert carbon dioxide into oxygen as a waste product of their photosynthesis. Some species can digest nitrogen directly from the atmosphere, and so over time they will create a nitrogen-rich soil.

Lichens could be introduced next, helping to prepare the soil and process the atmosphere. On a planet with high winds and dusty, desertlike conditions, grasses could be introduced into the new soil, intertwining and forming a net that would keep the soil from blowing away. Specially engineered plants with deeper roots could be planted once the soil was rich and stable enough, and their photosynthesis would speed up the conversion of the atmosphere.

Next, small burrowing animals would open and aerate the soil. Earthworms are continually processing and reprocessing decomposing tissue in the ground. New species of worms could be designed and introduced into the terraforming plan, paving the way for larger, more complex organisms: genetically engineered arthropods, mollusks and finally vertebrates.

Icy asteroids could be set on trajectories toward planets that have no water. Even planets could theoretically be pulled out of their present orbits and moved to more hospitable sectors of the solar system. You would need to set off explosives or create magnetic fields powerful enough to counteract the mutual gravitation of the Sun and the planet, yet controlled enough not to destroy the planet. Or else you'd need to maneuver other large masses into positions where they could perturb a planet's orbit. After a few thousand years of such tinkering, the entire solar system could be reshuffled and terraformed into a handful of Earthlike planets, each with its own unique ecologies and histories, but all of them with breathable air and edible life-forms.

Obviously, these are engineering feats on a scale beyond anything humans have ever tried, just as the Great Pyramid of Giza, the Great Wall of China, and the original Suez Canal were in their time. Still, it's unlikely that other planets would be terraformed to relieve the burden of overpopulation on Earth; the process is too slow to be a practical solution. And while it appeals to the pioneering spirit of human beings, it is also evidence of the hunger to destroy natural order for human benefit. It might never happen at all. An endeavour as expensive as terraforming would require enormous wealth — only a prosperous society with longevity would be able to afford such a project. In the future, asteroid mining tycoons or zero gravity industrialists might have the wealth and materials to invest in terraforming. But more than anything else, terraforming projects would need a visionary, someone whose energy and imagination might stir the enthusiasm of large numbers of people at just the right moment in history.

---

throughout the solar system, extending at least as far as the orbit of Neptune. Wherever astronauts travel in the solar system, they will need protection from the dangerous radiation levels of the solar wind.

How close will we ever venture to the Sun? It seems likely that solar research outposts will exist on Mercury once effective heat shielding is developed. Nuclear fusion technology will probably require the development of controlled magnetic field shielding, and offshoots of this technology might allow explorers to venture even closer to the Sun. However, the Sun's gravitational attraction will be so powerful that tidal forces might rip apart a ship that ventured too close. See David Brin's *Sundiver* and Jeffrey Carver's *From a Changeling Star* for stories of explorers who do venture very close to stars — even into the photosphere.

Mercury

Because Mercury is so close to the Sun (and because, as seen from the Earth's surface, it appears to rise within two hours of the Sun), it has been difficult for scientists to make detailed observations of it. It wasn't until the Mariner 10 spacecraft made several flybys in the mid-1970s that detailed maps could be made of its surface. The picture they presented is not promising for colonization.

Not only is the surface of Mercury sometimes extremely hot (only Venus is hotter), but the temperature varies dramatically. This is because of its orbit (which is more elliptical than most) and its slow rotation: It takes fifty-nine Earth days for Mercury to make a single rotation about its axis, thus completing one Mercury day. While it is facing away from the Sun, surface temperatures can be as low as −173 degrees C (−96° F) just before dawn and as high as 402 degrees C (723° F) at noon.

A crew of well-insulated astronauts might use Mercury as a base from which to study the Sun. If their research station were mobile, they could keep a steady course just in front of the line of dawn, where the ground beneath them would still be cool. For them, the Sun would always remain in the sky. They would circumnavigate the planet every two months.

Because of the planet's slow rotation and highly elliptical orbit, the researchers would note some interesting effects. At aphelion — the point when a planet is farthest from the Sun — the researchers would see a Sun that appears twice as large as it would on Earth. At perihelion — when a planet is closest to the Sun — the Sun would appear four times as large as it does on Earth. The Sun would also appear to change speeds as it moved across the sky, and would even appear sometimes to reverse its course. Also, even though Mercury rotates on its axis every fifty-nine days, sunrise would only occur in the same part of the sky once every 176 days, the length of time it takes Mercury to orbit the Sun twice (Mercury's year, its period of revolution around the Sun is eighty-eight Earth days). By the time Mercury finishes one rotation, it's one-third of the way around the Sun, which would therefore appear in a different part of Mercury's sky.

Some parts of Mercury are heavily cratered. Because there is almost no atmosphere to weather the surface, many of these craters record impacts on the planet's surface from 4 billion years ago, when the planet was newly formed. Separating these cratered regions are rolling plains that are also about 4 billion years old, but whose surfaces were smoothed by lava flows or from an accumulation of fine materials ejected from the impacts. Other parts of Mercury's surface are even smoother, revealing few impact craters. These lava flows are probably not nearly as old. There are also long, steep cliffs called scarps that may have been caused by a shrinking of Mercury as it cooled, buckling its crust.

Mercury is very dense, with a core that is probably made of nickel and iron. Gravity is about one-third of Earth's. There is an atmosphere on Mercury, composed of hydrogen, helium, potassium and sulphur, but because of the weak gravity, it is very thin.

Could Mercury be colonized? A better question would be: Why should it be? When it is closest to the Sun, Mercury receives more than ten times as much solar radiation as does Earth. Even with atmospheric pressures similar to those of Earth's surface, the change in albedo (the reflectiveness of a planet's surface) would only cut the absorption of solar energy in half. Giant parasols, artificial rings and shadow-casting dust clouds are some other techniques that might be used to reduce solar heating.

While Mercury might make an ideal research outpost — or even a penal colony — it doesn't hold much promise for terraformers. Its orbit needs to be smoothed out, and it would need a tremendous amount of ice to provide it with liquid water and atmospheric oxygen. James Edward Oberg, author of the terraforming manual *New Earths*, suggested that Callisto, one of the moons of Jupiter could be forced to collide with Mercury, providing water and readjusting its orbit. Mercury might then be pulled out of its orbit entirely, perhaps becoming a moon for Venus. Without such farfetched engineering, Mercury is unlikely to become more than an outpost for solar research.

Venus

Named after the Greek goddess of love, Venus is one of the brightest objects in the night sky — surpassed only by the Moon. Because it is the planet closest to Earth, and because of its similarity in size, mass and density, Venus has been called Earth's sister planet. Thirty years ago conditions on the surface of Venus were still a mystery because of its impenetrable cloud cover. SF writers as diverse as Olaf Stapledon and Edgar Rice Burroughs imagined it as a watery planet choking with strange life-forms.

We now have a clearer, more comprehensive view of Venus. It has probably the harshest, most nightmarish surface of any planet in the solar system. Not only is it inhospitable to life, it has quickly destroyed every spacecraft that has ever landed there. It may yet see colonies of human explorers and pioneers, but consider the obstacles they will have to overcome.

The atmospheric pressure on the surface of Venus is about ninety times higher than Earth's: The atmosphere is denser than the water at the bottom of Earth's deepest oceans. There are traces of nitrogen, argon and even some water vapor. But the atmosphere is primarily carbon dioxide, laced with sulfuric acid stronger than that from a car battery. The winds are gentle and slow-moving — more like ocean currents than wind. The thick sea of gaseous carbon dioxide is a perfect heat trap. Sunlight penetrates the atmosphere and part of it is absorbed at the planet's surface, while the rest is reradiated off the surface in the form of heat. But carbon dioxide absorbs heat, so the reradiated heat never reaches space. Because of this greenhouse effect, Venus has the highest surface temperatures of any planet in the solar system, 477° C (890° F), hot enough to melt lead and even make some of its rocks glow faint red.

A human being suddenly forced unprotected out onto the surface of Venus would die a swift ugly death. The atmospheric pressure would instantly crush the chest, cracking ribs and rupturing the diaphragm. Meanwhile the body fluids would boil, explosively shaving off the flesh a layer at a time. Within moments there would be no more than small body fragments, searing and charring in the heat as they floated off on the air currents.

Venus is slightly smaller than Earth (see "Planets of the Solar System," pages 40-41) and slightly less dense. Surface gravity is 90 percent of Earth's. Venus completes an orbit around the Sun every 224 days and rotates on its axis once every 243 days, turning in the opposite direction of the other planets. Explorers on the surface would experience a sunrise to sunrise "day" of 118 Earth days. Because of the dense cloud cover, however, little light reaches the surface, so the days are overcast. At night, the cloud cover refracts — or bends — light, so that light would extend from the day side around to the night side. There is probably little difference between day and night on Venus.

The highest mountain on Venus is Maxwell Montes, which rises some 7½ miles (12 kilometers) high. There are many lava flows on Venus's surface and relatively few impact craters, so the planet's surface may be younger than that of the other planets. Some of its volcanoes are probably still active. Two continents have been discovered on Venus, both of them about the size of North America — Ishtar and Aphrodite. In addition, folds and fractures on the surface could be caused by some kind of plate tectonics.

Terraforming Venus. The three greatest obstacles to settling upon and terraforming Venus are its heat, air mass and spin.

Unlike Mercury, the excessive heat on Venus can't be entirely blamed on its closeness to the Sun. In fact, Venus's cloud cover reflects so much sunlight, that the amount of solar energy reaching the surface is about equal to that on Earth. To cool Venus's atmosphere and its glowing-hot surface one would have to stifle its greenhouse effect. Even if sunlight could be blocked out entirely, it would take hundreds of years to cool.

For Venus's surface temperature to drop, the "surplus" air would have to be disposed of. Even if blue-green algae could convert *all* the carbon dioxide to oxygen, atmospheric pressure would still be sixty times Earth's. Somehow, the atmosphere would have to be thinned. Could the oxygen be locked into the unoxygenated rocks? If the rocks weren't already oxidized, they could be selectively exposed to the atmosphere and absorb the excess oxygen. However, to lock all the excess oxygen, the entire surface of the planet would need to be gardened — churned for maximum exposure — at depths of more than 100 kilometers.

Perhaps the excess atmosphere could be pumped off the planet's surface, and ejected at escape velocity using a mass driver (also known as a coil gun, as described in chapter 2). The sun could provide the energy necessary to tank or freeze the gas, and ship it up a skyhook (which is like a very thin powerful freight elevator). But if we tried to remove 98 percent of the mass of Venus's atmosphere in 100 years, 300,000 tons would need to be hauled up *every second*.

One way to dispose of the surplus oxygen is to *import* hydrogen. The hydrogen in water weighs only one-eighth as much as the oxygen, so to tie up the oxygen on Venus in water, only one-eighth as much hydrogen would be needed.

Saturn would be a good candidate for a ready source of hydrogen. Two-mile long "scoopers" could gather up cargoes of atmospheric hydrogen on Saturn, use part of it as the reaction mass to escape Saturn's gravity well, ship it across the solar system and hurl it into Venus, where it will burst into flame, absorb oxygen, and produce water. Fusion technology (using part of the hydrogen cargo for fuel) could provide the energy source for this scooping operation.

Even though Venus would seem too hot to allow for the formation of open bodies of water, water can be kept in a liquid state at very high temperatures if enough pressure is applied (as any pressure cooker will demonstrate). If Venus could be shielded from enough sunlight to drop the temperature 190 degrees C, water vapor in the atmosphere would condense and rain down onto the surface. There it would be converted into steam — most of it returning to the atmosphere as vapor once more, but cooling the surface rocks in the process.

The oceans that would eventually begin to form would be lifeless at first. The oceans would support rainfall, dissolve harmful salts, and help the formation of soil deposits. The blue-green algae that have been converting the carbon dioxide to oxygen could later be joined by genetically engineered forms that can survive in the scalding-hot oceans. The temperature would have dropped enough to allow machines to prepare Venus's surface for later inhabitants: damming rivers, crushing rocks, and digging canals. The first colonists would probably live at altitudes where the air pressure was most similar to Earth's; just as the first terraforming sites on Mars will be at the bottom of canyons and craters (where the air pressure is greater), the first true vegetation introduced on Venus will probably be at high altitudes, where the air is thinner and the temperature cooler. Perhaps the top of Maxwell Montes, near the north pole, would be the ideal site for the foothold colony. Gradually, vegetation and animals could inch their way down the mountain sides.

Would Venus's slow rotation be an obstacle to the establishment of stable ecosystems? Life-forms could be engineered to cope with the 118 day sunrise-to-sunrise cycle. What kind of psychological effects might it have on human beings?

The task of terraforming Venus could only be accomplished by a civilization with a well-established presence in space. It might take as long as a thousand years to turn it into another Earth. In the meantime, the settlers would probably need protection from pressure and high temperatures. The potential threats to those attempting to settle, explore, and transform Venus can inspire all kinds of interesting story ideas.

The Moon

The Moon is second only to the Sun in its domination of the sky. It is not only our nearest neighbor but our satellite, one hundred times closer to the Earth than the nearest planet, Venus. Human beings first stepped on the Moon in 1969, only twelve years after the space age began with the launching of the Sputnik satellite. The Moon is many things to us: brightest light in the night sky, the subject of many superstitions, one of the gravitational influences that powers the tides of Earth's oceans, the subject of many song titles, and the first step on humankind's ascent into space. As a first step, the Moon will have a number of practical uses: a laboratory-colony, a gigantic observatory, a mining operation, one-third of a trading-manufacturing triangle that would also include the Earth and the space colonies that will orbit both the Moon and the Earth.

The Moon orbits the Earth from west to east at an average distance of 239,000 miles (384 km). It is less than one-third the size of Earth, with a surface gravity about one-sixth that of Earth. It completes an orbit around the Earth once every 29½ days, exactly the amount of time it takes for it to rotate once on its axis, so that the Moon always shows the same face to observers on Earth.

The far side of the Moon, which we never see from Earth, has often been called the "dark" side of the Moon, although it spends as much time in daylight as the near side. Because it never receives Earth's reflected light, its two-week-long nights are darker than nights on the near side (and four times darker than nights on Earth). It is also free of the radio noise from Earth that bombards the Moon's near side. This makes the far side an ideal location for sensitive astronomical instruments.

With the Moon's low gravity and tranquil surface (500 gentle moonquakes a year compared to 10,000 powerful earthquakes a year), engineers could build telescopes far larger than any on Earth. Giant radio dishes could fill entire craters, gathering faint radio whispers. Giant gamma ray and X-ray detectors would pinpoint sources of radiation. Optical telescope arrays, consisting of up to forty domed telescopes arranged in two concentric circles, would be so powerful that they could detect planets around other stars.

Lunar Bases. But before telescopes are constructed on the Moon, before mining operations and terraforming begin, the first lunar bases will need to be set up. The first lunar bases could be constructed early in the twenty-first century, after a space station is set up in Earth-orbit. Construction facilities on the space station would be the ideal location to build the lunar spacecrafts: a transfer vehicle using conventional chemical propellants to travel from Earth-orbit to lunar-orbit, and a heavier cargo ship. To save on rocket fuel, the unmanned cargo ship could be powered by a small nuclear fission reactor, departing from the space station before the transfer vehicle and reaching lunar orbit first. The two ships will then meet up, and the crew will transfer to the cargo ship, which will carry them to the Moon's surface.

Most of the construction could be done by remote-controlled robots. Within two years the lunar base could be fully functional. It would be made up of a hemispherical living structure (a habitation module), perhaps fifty feet in diameter, that also extends down into the lunar surface. The dome would be covered in up to nine feet of lunar soil to provide protection from radiation and micrometeroids. There would also be the first oxygen mine and processing plant, which would produce liquid oxygen to be used as propellant.

As the cargo ship continues its runs between lunar orbit and the surface, more habitation modules could be constructed, along with laboratory modules, greenhouses to provide food, medical facilities, and resource plants for equipment like power and life support. The base would grow in population and in mining and scientific capabilities. A solar power station would collect sunlight during the two-week lunar "days" while a nuclear power station could remain in operation continuously.

Beyond geological studies of the Moon itself, astronomical studies and the mining operations, the Moon might slowly become domesticated. People might work there, grow food there, raise families — less an isolated scientific outpost like Antarctica and more like a frontier, the first step in humankind's colonization of the solar system.

Mining the Moon. Analysis of moonrocks brought back by the Apollo astronauts has shown that 40 percent of the rock is composed of oxygen bound up in mineral compounds. There is also silicon, iron, calcium, aluminum, titanium and magnesium, along with traces of hydrogen and helium. The metals can be refined into building materials; oxygen and hydrogen can be used in rocket fuel. They also combine to form water. There appears to be no surface water on the Moon, unless it is frozen in the interior of craters at the Moon's north and south poles. Astronauts would be able to supply their own water by extracting its ingredients from the soil itself.

The biggest advantage to mining on the Moon is that it would be a far more practical and affordable place than Earth from which to launch the fuel and building materials needed for space exploration. The Moon's escape velocity is 5,400 miles per hour compared to the Earth's escape velocity of 25,000 miles per hour.

Oxygen may be the element in the biggest demand from lunar mining activities. To extract it from the minerals in which it is bound, its chemical bonds with other elements must be broken. One-quarter of the basaltic rock on the Moon's surface is ilmenite, which contains oxygen. The highest concentrations of ilmenite are in the sealike lunar maria—low-lying areas of meteorite craters. Oxygen mining will probably begin here.

Robotic excavators and haulers operated by humans from remote control haul the basaltic rock from quarries. They transport it to the processing plants, where the rocks are crushed and ground to a fine powder and then run through magnetic separators that isolate the grains of iron-bearing ilmenite. The ilmenite then goes to a cylindrical chamber called the "oxygen extraction reactor." The ilmenite enters the top of the reactor, where it meets rising two-atom hydrogen molecules. In the middle chamber of the cylinder, the intense heat (1,800 degrees F) causes the oxygen in the ilmenite to react with the hydrogen, forming water vapor. The water vapor then moves on to an "electrolysis cell" where the hydrogen atoms are separated from the water vapor by cathodes, negatively charged electrodes that emit electrons. The oxygen is cooled to about −150 degrees F and stored in liquid form.

Terraforming the Moon. Is the Moon a likely candidate for terraforming? In spite of its weak gravity, the Moon could probably hold an atmosphere. But a moon base would be one of the first achievements of the colonization of space, whereas the technologies necessary for the terraforming of a planet—transporting asteroids across the solar system, altering planetary spin—are much further in our future. By the time human technology is ready to terraform a nearby world (Mars is the most likely candidate) the Moon might already have a sizable population and industrial base. Whether or not terraforming the Moon is possible, its long-range advantages would probably be overridden by its immediate disadvantages. It would hinder astronomical observations. An earthlike atmosphere would raise the escape velocity and therefore the expense of transporting materials from the Moon's surface. And finally, hurling large chunks of ice into the Moon's surface could damage delicate astronomical instruments or industrial equipment and endanger the lives of what might by that time be a population of several million.

Mars

Mars, like the Moon, is the stuff that dreams are made of. In the stories of H.G. Wells, Edgar Rice Burroughs, Ray Bradbury and many others, it was a sister-world of Earth, a place of ancient civilizations, a place where humans might settle on the shores of the canals. More recently, SF writers have recognized it for what it is—a barren world that most likely has never had life and cannot, in its present state, support human life. Still, it continues to fascinate, and plans for its manned exploration are part of official U.S. policy. Unlike Venus, it has a surface that is visible and relatively hospitable. Any SF writer writing about humanity's near future in space would do well to consider Mars as a possible locale.

From orbit, Mars looks like an enormous scarred citrus fruit. It is mottled in shades of red and orange with white caps at the poles. There is not enough atmosphere to present the haze that Earth or Venus offer. With brilliant clarity, orbiting astronauts would see dark molelike spots representing huge volcanoes; mazes of lines that are actually vast canyons; light-colored plains and craters like the Moon's.

With a mean diameter of 6,787 km, Mars is about half the size of Earth and twice as big as the Moon. The surface gravity is 38 percent that of Earth, so that a 150-pound man would weigh only 57 pounds on Mars. The Martian year lasts about 687 Earth days, but the Martian day is almost the same as Earth's — 24 hours and 40 minutes.

Mars is tilted on its axis twenty-five degrees. With the presence of an atmosphere, this means that Mars has annual winters and summers just as Earth does. Its atmosphere is thin, with the surface pressure less than 1/100th that of Earth. Even if it were thicker, it would be unbreathable: mostly carbon dioxide, with some nitrogen and argon, traces of water vapor, and almost no oxygen.

Because Mars is farther than we are from the Sun, and because the atmosphere is thin, the surface temperatures are colder than ours and vary more widely in the course of a day. During summer near the equator, the temperature may climb to 15 degrees C at noon, but fall at night to −80 degrees C — about as cold as it ever gets anywhere on Earth. In winter at high latitudes at night, the temperature may drop to −125 degrees C. At such temperatures carbon dioxide freezes and turns into dry ice. The polar caps that form during the Martian winter and dissolve in the summer are made of carbon dioxide, not water. Underneath these caps, however, are small residual polar caps that do contain water ice.

There is no sign of liquid water on Mars's surface; because of the lack of atmosphere, any water placed there would evaporate explosively. But there is evidence that water once ran over this desert world: extensive systems of channels that look like dry riverbeds and streambeds. No one knows for sure if erosion by water formed these channels, or, if so, where the water came from. Some scientists believe that water is frozen under Mars's surface, perhaps in a layer miles thick, analagous to permafrost. Periodic warming by volcanoes or colliding meteorites might release this water in torrents onto the surface, where it would carve out streambeds before evaporating away.

The Viking missions to Mars found no organic substances, but they did not visit the poles. It's possible, but not likely, that organic molecules might be trapped in the permanent polar caps of water ice.

One major obstacle to life on Mars is the absence of an ozone layer in the atmosphere. Without that layer, there is little to block the Sun's ultraviolet radiation, which is harmful to organic molecules. Human visitors to Mars will have to wear pressureized spacesuits that provide them with oxygen, heating and protection from UV rays. Even so, long-term visitors might risk abnormally high rates of leukemia and other radiation-induced cancers.

Mars has two moons, Phobos and Deimos: dark cratered lumps of rock that are irregularly shaped. Phobos is 27 km across — about the length of Manhattan Island. Deimos is only 15 km across. From Deimos, Mars looks about thirty times the size of our Moon as seen from Earth. From Phobos, Mars looks about eighty times the size of our Moon. Surface gravity on these moons is only about a thousandth that of Earth. An astronaut who jumps on the surface of these moons will rise several hundred feet and have to wait a few minutes to drift down.

Terraforming Mars. Mars is not what humans expected it to be, but it is a place of great beauty (see "A Tour of Mars," page 58). Like the Moon, it may be colonized someday — either underground or in enclosed self-sustaining cities on the surface. Or, like Venus, it may be terraformed. The process has been imagined by many SF writers, including John Varley in "In the Hall of the Martian Kings" and Ian Watson in The Martian Inca.

Here is one possible approach to terraforming Mars. The first step is to warm Mars's surface from its present subzero temperatures. Dark dust, perhaps mined from Mars's moons, could be sprinkled across the surface. Like the asphalt in a parking lot, this blackish layer would absorb heat and warm the surface. Then, giant mirrors would be placed in orbit to concentrate sunlight on the polar caps, melting them and providing gaseous carbon dioxide.

The best place to start colonies would probably be inside deep craters, where the atmosphere is already denser than at the surface (Mars's canyons, since they exist on fault lines, might be considered too unstable to serve as dwelling places).

Existing craters could be used, or craters could be added by steering asteroids from the nearby Asteroid Belt into collision courses with Mars. If some of the asteroids were made of ice, they would provide water vapor. Water vapor could also be released from the thick layer of permafrost under the Martian surface (if such a layer exists). The combined water vapor and carbon dioxide would represent the beginnings of an atmosphere.

The next step, as on Venus, is to seed the atmosphere with thousands of shiploads of blue-green algae. Through photosynthesis, the algae would release oxygen (O_2) from carbon dioxide (CO_2). Over the course of perhaps thousands of years, the atmosphere would become thick enough, warm enough, and oxygen-rich enough — at least in the craters — to support all the creatures necessary for a self-sustaining food chain. The sky would turn blue, though perhaps with a pinkish cast. Storm systems would form and rain would fall. Bacteria, trees, grass, vegetables, insects, animals and people would gradually be introduced.

An SF story would not have to cover the entire process. It might be set at any point along the way: with the crews in space-suits seeding and tending the algae, or with the first settlers at the bottom of a crater, surrounded by walls of rock, their bodies as light as children, the air around them as thin as in the mountains of Tibet.

The Asteroid Belt

Ninety-five percent of all the asteroids in the solar system are part of the asteroid belt that orbits between Mars and Jupiter. This collection of rocks is in roughly the same general configuration as it was during the earliest formation of the solar system. The enormous gravitational influence of Jupiter hindered the gradual clumping together of larger planetesimals. Jupiter's influence more likely caused the materials to crash and break apart. Even if all the rocks in the asteroid belt were to coalesce into a single body, many scientists believe it would probably be no larger than the Moon or one of Jupiter's moons. The individual asteroids are generally very small: Only thirty known asteroids have diameters greater than 200 km (124 miles). Ceres, the largest of the known asteroids, has a diameter of 940 km (584 miles). There are probably millions of asteroids of boulder size in the solar system.

Spectroscopic analysis indicates that many of the asteroids are very rich in metals such as iron and nickel. Some contain water in the form of permafrost and many contain carbon-rich terrestrial materials — possibly even an oil-like substance. Many of the minerals in the carbonaceous (carbon-rich) asteroids are oxidized (they contain oxygen).

The asteroid belt could be one of the richest resources in the solar system. It isn't likely that they'll be exploited until after orbital space colonies are built and the Moon has been settled, possibly not until after Martian colonies have been established. In reaching and exploiting the asteroid belt, space travel will

A Tour of Mars

The sky, first of all, is a light pink or peach, the result of fine dust particles suspended in the air. White clouds of carbon dioxide ice may be floating 45 km from the surface. Oxidized, iron-rich clays at the surface give the ground a salmon pink or rust color. The southern hemisphere is heavily cratered, so your landing craft might set down in the north. If so, you might choose to set up a base in the Chryse Planitia, a moderately cratered low-lying plain. Here you will come across Viking Lander I, covered with red dust and no longer operating. It has been sitting here since 1976. The view from the lander is not unlike the deserts of the American Southwest—strewn with rocks of many sizes and colors, covered with dust. In the distance you see windblown dunes.

Wind is an important factor here. Normally, the winds course at 10 to 15 km/hr, but in the spring and summer they gust at speeds of 150 to 300 km/hr. These winds form dunes and flame-shaped hills called Crater streaks. They also create violent dust storms unlike anything seen on Earth. Once or twice a year, the yellowish storms may envelop entire regions and possibly the entire planet.

It is winter now; the storms are over. On the camp instruments you note a light layer of frost—only a few hundredths of a millimeter thick. You get into the airplane that was assembled upon landing. (Airplanes are possible on Mars because air exists to lift the wings— though the plane would have to be specially designed for the thin atmosphere.) You are off. Embedded in the plain are craters 2 km or less across. The craters are streaked with dark areas—places where bright surface dust has been blown away and left patches of under-lying rock.

You come to a region called the Tharsis Bulge, centered on the equator at an elevation 1 km higher than the surrounding plains. Tharsis is a continent-sized area as large as the entire United States, including Alaska. Here you find enormous volcanoes—great mountains whose height is difficult to comprehend. Olympus Mons, the largest volcano in the solar system, is 26 km high and 600 km across—almost as tall as three Mount Everests. If you fly over its summit, you will see a crater 90 km in diameter. Clouds of water ice sometimes condense around its summit.

Cliffs surround Olympus Mons—steep cliffs nearly 5 km high, draped with lava flows. Farther away are three other volcanoes almost as large—Arsia Mons, Pavonis Mons and Ascreus Mons. Eruptions must take place rarely—perhaps every few thousand years—but the volcanoes are not extinct.

Below the high plateau of the Tharsis region are canyons hundreds of kilometers long and several kilometers deep. Some of the canyons are parallel; some, such as those in the Noctis Labyrinthus, form a maze of intersecting valleys. To cross the canyons on foot, you would have to climb down one wall of a canyon, up the facing wall, across the intervening plateau, and on through canyon after canyon. These deep valleys have been formed not by river action, as on Earth, but by the shifting of ground along fault lines. However, there is some evidence of water sedimentation, suggesting that frozen lakes might have formed here in the past, and that groundwater still lies locked behind the walls of the canyons.

Moving east over the canyons along the equator, you come to the Valles Marineris—a huge rift in the planet surface, 4,000 km long, 700 km across, more than 8 km deep. Seen from the bottom of the valley, the walls would be as high as the Himalayan mountain ranges. In the deepest section, the atmospheric pressure is two and a half times what it is on the rim.

There is more on Mars—"chaotic terrain" to the east of the canyons, consisting of long, wide channels cut by river action; craters standing rim to rim, common in the southern hemisphere and reminiscent of the Moon. A vast dune field surrounds the northern polar ice cap—a sand sea of parallel ridges each a few hundred meters across.

---

finally become not only a profitable venture but one of the most lucrative of all human endeavors. Most of the asteroids are small, so their mineral riches are easily accessible. Asteroids are not as tightly packed as many people imagine, and they have stable, predictable orbits, so the risk of collisions is very minimal. Asteroids could provide the materials with which humans build gigantic space colonies, Martian cities, and water for terraforming projects.

While much of the dangerous mining work could be handled by robots, the mining operations would probably be supervised by humans. Colonies could be established in the belts themselves, and entire societies could eventually build up around mining operations. Asteroids could be partially hollowed out and self-contained cities built within them. Carbonaceous asteroids would be ideal for this because of their ready supplies of water and carbon materials. Large solar mirrors could be constructed, surrounding the asteroid colonies like gigantic, shimmering wings. Smaller asteroids could even be hollowed out and turned into spaceships as suggested in chapter 2.

Eventually, populations in the asteroid belt could grow so large and so independent that it might no longer be possible to even keep track of them. It would be far easier for a breakaway colony to use their robots to hollow out a chunk of rock than to build a cylindrical or torus-shaped space colony. This might encourage the formation of all sorts of strange isolated populations. As a frontier, the asteroid belt could be mysterious and fragmentary, full of legends about small rogue colonies in their microworlds, lost among the many settled and unsettled chunks of rock within the belt.

Not all asteroids remain within the main belt. Some have eccentric orbits that bring them very close to the Sun. Evidence suggests that asteroids have actually crashed into the Earth at certain points in our prehistory. Thousands of tons of rock (meteors) fall toward Earth every year, but they are burned up as they pass into our atmosphere. The fragments that survive are called meteorites. In 1908 a meteorite struck near Tunguska in Siberia. It was and is a largely uninhabited area, and the devastation of the crash is visible today.

Eros, a slab-shaped piece of rock 18 miles (30 km) long has come within 13 million miles (22 million km) of Earth. Scientists estimate that three asteroids with a diameter of 0.6 miles (1 km) could collide with Earth every million years. An object this size crashing into the Earth would produce an explosion with as much force as several hydrogen bombs and leave a crater 8 miles (13 km) across. This could be catastrophic for all life on Earth. It is suspected that just such a collision might have destroyed the dinosaurs. (See also chapter 7, "A Case Study of a Lifebearing Planet.")

Jupiter

Jupiter is the largest planet in the solar system—larger than all the other planets combined. It is estimated to have a rocky core that in itself could be ten times the mass of Earth. Other than that, Jupiter has no true "surface," only layer upon layer of gaseous clouds. Because the gases are under enormous gravitational pressure, the atmosphere at deeper levels is in a fluid state. About 99 percent of the atmosphere is comprised of hydrogen and helium, in roughly the same proportion (three to one) as in the Sun.

In fact, Jupiter is almost like a mini-Sun. It gives off 70 percent more infrared radiation than it receives from the Sun and has sixteen known moons orbiting it—almost like a miniature solar system. Had Jupiter been several dozen times more massive than it is now, the heat at the core (which is already 25,000 degrees C) would have been great enough to cause nuclear fusion. Jupiter might then have been a true star, though small and dim in comparison to the Sun. Carl Sagan has referred to Jupiter as "a star that failed." In the novels 2010 and 2061, Arthur C. Clarke has a mysterious alien intelligence pumping more matter into Jupiter until nuclear fusion begins, turning our solar system into a binary star system.

Jupiter's banded appearance is due in part to the difference in wind speeds at different latitudes. The colors within those bands—yellow, brown and gray—are caused by the various ammonia-sulphur compounds in the atmosphere. The Red Spot so prominent on Jupiter is a cyclone larger than Earth and Venus put together. This cyclone is still going strong after more than 300 years of observation and shows no sign of diminishing its fury. In addition, there have been many other, smaller cyclones observed on Jupiter.

Jupiter's influence in SF has been in several directions. In the two Clarke novels mentioned above, the author also speculates that the core of Jupiter might be made up of carbon, and, that under the enormous pressure, the carbon has compressed into a diamond larger than the Earth.

While no indications of life have been found on Jupiter, a gas giant such as Jupiter could harbor forms of life that, while quite different from those we know on Earth, could be advanced and even intelligent. Terraformers might actually seed Jupiter's atmosphere, creating life-forms suited to those vast seas of gas. See chapter 5 for a closer look at these types of life-forms.

The hydrogen and helium in Jupiter's atmosphere could be seen as an almost unlimited supply of fusion fuel. This would be particularly beneficial if it didn't have to be shipped halfway across the solar system but used by colonists close by.

And that could very well be the case. SF writers' biggest

fascination with Jupiter centers around its many moons, which could be exploited not only for their mineral resources, but as potential terraforming projects. It is within the farthest fringes of imaginary science to speculate that humans might ever be able to induce a self-sustaining fusion reaction within Jupiter's core. But if it happened, space travelers could transform the Jupiter system into a mini-solar system.

The Moons of Jupiter. Jupiter has sixteen satellites or moons. Four of them would be of particular interest to explorers. In order of their closeness to Jupiter, they are: Io, Europa, Ganymede and Callisto. These four Jovian satellites were discovered by Galileo in 1610 — the first objects in the solar system to be discovered through a telescope.

Io. Because of its great size, Jupiter has a far-ranging gravitational effect, causing gaps in the asteroid belt and changing the trajectory of comets. But perhaps its most dramatic effect is on its innermost moon, Io. During its highly elliptical orbit, Io undergoes an effect known as tidal fluxing, as it is squeezed in and out like an accordion. This causes friction and heat within the satellite, which in turn stimulates volcanic activity. Io is more volcanically active than any planet or moon in the solar system. Voyagers I and II, during their brief flybys of Io, recorded ten erupting volcanoes and fifty active gas vents. As no craters were found in the Voyager photographs, it is estimated that volcanoes can resurface the entire satellite in less than a million years.

Io is about the size and density of our own Moon. There appears to be no trace of water or carbon dioxide on Io. Sulphur compounds account for the rich array of colors on the moon's surface: reds, yellows, blues, blacks and whites.

Io is an uncertain candidate for terraforming. It would be difficult to introduce an Earthlike atmosphere, because it would probably lead to the formation of sulphur dioxide and rainfalls of sulfuric acid. And while the amount of sulphur belched into the atmosphere by volcanoes is not great, there is so much sulphur on the surface that it would poison any body of water formed there. However, a layer of crushed rock several kilometers thick could be imported from one of Jupiter's outer moons or from the asteroid belt. The one advantage Io has as a potential candidate for terraforming is that it has its own internal heat source.

Callisto. On the other hand, Callisto, the outermost of Jupiter's great moons, is a cold inactive satellite. With a radius of 2,400 km, it is nearly one and a half times the size of our Moon. Its surface is covered with impact craters and appears to have no smooth plains whatsoever. As these craters are mostly records of impacts in the first half billion years of its existence, the surface of Callisto has undergone almost no seismic activity since that time, nearly 4 billion years ago.

Callisto, like Ganymede and Europa, is a watery world, and its water-ice crust might contain frozen oceans hundreds of kilometers deep. This water ice might be a valuable resource in terraforming Mars or Mercury.

Ganymede. Ganymede, of all Jupiter's moons, has been the most popular among SF writers. It is the largest Jovian moon, with a radius of 2,600 km (about one and a half times the size of our Moon). Robert Heinlein used it as the setting of his 1950 novel about terraformers, *Farmer in the Sky*. While the scientific basis of the novel has been dated by what we now know about Ganymede, it still offers insights into the social issues surrounding terraforming. Poul Anderson described a terraforming project in "The Snows of Ganymede" in 1955, and Gregory Benford's novels *Jupiter Project* and *Against Infinity* also detail the terraforming of this moon. Many of Philip K. Dick's novels take for granted that Ganymede would have thriving colonies.

Ganymede's icy surface is mottled with dark regions that are heavily cratered, like Callisto's surface. The light regions are dominated by grooves: parallel sets of ridges and troughs that run for thousands of kilometers across the surface. The sets sometimes intersect and form elaborate patterns. The grooves are several kilometers wide and perhaps hundreds of meters deep. They seem to indicate tectonic activity early in Ganymede's history: the breaking up and moving of crustal blocks in response to tensions under the surface.

Insights by Voyagers I and II indicate that the layer of water ice covering Ganymede might be thousands of kilometers deep. Even if it could be warmed to temperatures suitable for Earthlike life-forms, there would be no dry land on the entire world. The density of Ganymede is so low that half of its mass is probably water ice. Would humans terraform Ganymede into a totally aquatic world?

Europa. Europa is the only one of Jupiter's four largest moons that is actually smaller than Earth's moon. It too is covered by a layer of water ice, probably about 100 kilometers deep. Mass drivers could hurl chunks of ice into space, to provide water for colonies orbiting Jupiter or living in the asteroid belt. Of the three watery moons, its low mass (and therefore its lower gravity) make it most suitable for this purpose.

Europa is crisscrossed by dark ridges and its surface is very smooth, with very few impact craters. In fact, Europa has the smoothest surface of any solid body in the solar system. Because it is the second closest of Jupiter's great moons, tidal effects similiar to those on Io could cause the opening of volcanic vents at the bottom of Europa's world-ocean. This would melt the bottom-ice and cause the shifting of the ice plates above it, which would account for Europa's smooth youthful appearance.

In Clarke's *2010*, life evolves on Europa. Colonies of strange aquatic creatures congregate in the warmth near the volcanic vents, their survival dependent on a continuous source of warmth from below. Clarke's powerful alien intelligence observes these life-forms and determines that they are doomed to eventual extinction because of the unreliability of this heat. Therefore, Jupiter is transformed into a small star to give the life-forms on Europa the chance to achieve their evolutionary potential.

The colonization of Jupiter's moons and the orbital space surrounding Jupiter is dependent on a plentiful energy source, probably hydrogen and helium from Jupiter's atmosphere. Solar mirrors might still be used, but because of Jupiter's great distance from the Sun, they would have to be gigantic to collect enough light to fuel a thriving colony. The arrays of mirrors would have to be nearly as large as the moons themselves. As we move outward, this problem will only increase.

Standing on any of Jupiter's four major moons, the largest thing in the sky would be Jupiter. (It would be particularly enormous viewed from Io.) Other moons would also pass through the sky in complex orbits. The tiny Sun would be only one-twenty-seventh as bright as it is viewed from Earth.

Saturn

Saturn is easily the most recognizable of the planets. While Jupiter and Uranus have minor rings, Saturn has a system of rings that is in a class by itself. These bands of icy particles are so prominent that they were first observed through telescopes in

1655, more than 100 years before William Herschel discovered the planet Uranus. There are three main rings, each with an orbit independent from the others. Each of these rings is composed of thousands of smaller rings (or "ringlets"). As wide as they are, however, the rings are very thin, so that when viewed edge-on from earthbound telescopes, they nearly disappear.

The sixth planet from the Sun and the second largest in the solar system, Saturn never comes any closer than 1.9 billion kilometers to the Earth during its orbit around the Sun. Like its nearest neighbor Jupiter, it is a gas giant, consisting of a (relatively) small iron and rock core surrounded by layers of gas, mostly hydrogen and helium. It too is banded though these bands tend to have a milky appearance, not like the sharply divided bands that run parallel to Jupiter's equator. Voyager discovered cyclone activity on Saturn, similar to that on Jupiter, but nothing to rival Jupiter's Red Spot, and the haze in the upper atmosphere makes the cyclones less conspicuous.

The two most valuable resources Saturn offers are the hydrogen in the atmosphere and the water ice in the ring system. Because it has a far lower escape velocity than Jupiter, Saturn might be a better source for collecting hydrogen for fusion fuel and terraforming activities. If mineral resources are imported from the asteroid belt, orbital space colonies could thrive in the Saturn system. While water and gaseous hydrogen are plentiful, most of Saturn's moons are so icy that their rocky cores might be inaccessible.

Should the rings of Saturn be exploited for water ice? If a thriving, populous string of space colonies were created in orbit around Saturn, this ice would be a ready resource. Eventually, however, this exploitation would thin the rings. One day, this most beautiful ring system might disappear altogether. This thought might seem abhorrent to us. How would the colonists themselves see it, or those segments of humanity at a distance from Saturn, watching the destruction of the rings?

Many people object to the idea of terraforming and other intrusive space activities because they would destroy the natural beauty of places that have so far escaped the hunger and ambition of human presence. The rings of Saturn could be a perfect example of this. Instead of being polluted or purposely altered or colonized like the larger asteroids, the ring might simply thin out and eventually disappear altogether.

Moons. Saturn has at least twenty moons, most of them small icy worlds. Some, like Phoebe, the outermost moon, may be captured asteroids. Many show excessive cratering. One of them, Mimas, has a crater that covers more than one-third its surface.

The largest of Saturn's moons is Titan, which is nearly as large as Mars. Titan is most notable for its dense atmosphere, which is mostly nitrogen, with smaller amounts of methane and cyanide; it may be one and a half to two times as dense as Earth's atmosphere. Voyager photographs show that Titan's surface is obscured beneath an orange-colored "photochemical smog." Many scientists believe that its extremely cold surface might be partially covered by oceans of liquid methane.

Uranus and Neptune

Olaf Stapledon, in his novel *First and Last Men*, postulated that billions of years in the future, the last remnants of humanity would be living on a terraformed Neptune, made habitable by an increase in solar activity. As the dying Sun expanded, humans were able to adjust the orbit of the planet to maintain temperate climates, widening and then contracting the orbit as the aging Sun's energy grew less ferocious.

It is now clear that terraforming gas giants, even smaller ones like Neptune and Uranus, would be impossible. The interiors of Neptune and Uranus are under so much gravitational pressure that even if the gaseous outer layers of hydrogen and helium could be removed, it would take a million years for the molten rock cores to cool into planets roughly the size of Mars.

Uranus is the seventh planet in the solar system, and the third largest. It has fifteen moons in a compact orbit on a plane roughly the same as Uranus's equator, like the moons of most planets. But the rotation of Uranus itself is odd. Most of the planets rotate at a slight tilt from their orbital axis around the Sun. Uranus, however, is tilted 98 degrees from its orbital axis, so that the planet, its moons and its faint ring system are in an orientation perpendicular to that of all other planets.

Neptune is only slightly smaller than Uranus. Up until the discovery of Pluto in 1930, it was believed to be the outermost planet. In fact, occasionally Pluto's orbit does bring it closer to the Sun. In 1979 Pluto's orbit brought it closer to the Sun, and it will remain that way until 1999, making Neptune the outermost planet in the solar system — if only temporarily.

Neptune has eight moons, the two largest of which are Triton and Nereid. Triton is an icy world similar to Ganymede or Callisto and, like Titan, is nearly as large as Mars.

The usefulness of the moons of either Neptune and Uranus is doubtful. There are many other sources for water ice not nearly as distant. Only if space colonies using fusion technologies settle near these worlds will these moons be exploited even for this plentiful resource.

Pluto

Less is known about Pluto than any other planet in the solar system. In its very eccentric orbit, it takes about 248 years to complete one pass around the Sun. Pluto's orbit is also highly inclined, about seventeen degrees to the mean plane of the solar system. At its closest, it is 4.4 million km from the Sun; at its farthest, it is 7.4 billion km away. From this distance, the Sun would appear as an unusually bright star, perhaps several hundred times as bright as the full Moon seen from Earth.

Pluto has a single moon, Charon. Before Charon's discovery in 1978, it was estimated that Pluto could be anywhere from one-fifth to seven times the size of Earth. Now it is estimated that the combined mass of the two worlds is only about 1/400th that of Earth. Their individual masses, diameters, chemical compositions, origins, and the physical nature of their surfaces can only be guessed. Figures in the "Planets of the Solar System" chart in this chapter are far more speculative for Pluto than for any other planet. Best guesses suggest that Charon is no smaller than 1,200 kilometers in diameter, and Pluto no larger than 6,000 kilometers in diameter. Because of its large relative size, Charon would be a giant presence in Pluto's sky.

Telescopic images of Pluto, which resemble those of faint stars, are actually composite images of Pluto and Charon. Spectroscopic and infrared analyses indicate that Pluto is composed of mostly methane frost and ice. Temperatures on Pluto are estimated at about −213 degrees C on the sunlit side and −253 degrees C on the dark side. At these extremely low temperatures, nearly all materials are frozen or at least liquefied, except for hydrogen and helium, which are too light to be held by a body

THE WRITER'S GUIDE TO CREATING A SCIENCE FICTION UNIVERSE

with as weak a gravity as Pluto's. If Pluto has any kind of atmosphere at all, it is probably a low-density methane haze on the sunlit side. Pluto's period of rotation is estimated at about six and a half days.

Pluto is so different from the other outer planets — massive bodies with extensive atmospheres — and its orbit so inclined and eccentric, that its origin may be different than all other planets. It has been suggested that Pluto and Charon might be runaway satellites of Neptune.

Because so little is known about Pluto, SF writers are free to invent stories around it that are far more speculative than for any other known planet. These ideas will be limited by its small size and extreme distance from the Sun, which limit its potential usefulness in terraforming or colonization.

Pluto may not even be the farthest planet from the Sun. It was discovered only sixty years ago, and it is still such an unknown quantity, that other equally small and enigmatic worlds might exist even farther from the Sun.

In addition to the planets, moons and asteroids that orbit the Sun, there are additional objects — such as meteoroids (see chapter 1) and comets — that are bound by the gravitational attraction of the Sun and the planets.

A comet is an irregularly shaped mass made up mostly of dirty water ice surrounded by a crust of sootlike dust material. Most comets are too small to be detectable by telescopes until they near the Sun. Then they begin to warm. As the crust heats up, the ice thaws. The tail of a comet appears only at this time, and is composed of dust and vaporizing gases, 80 percent of which is water. The rest is made up of carbon monoxide, carbon dioxide, methane and ammonia.

The nucleus of a comet may range from a few hundred meters to ten kilometers. As it approaches the Sun, it actually emits two tails. The dust tail, composed of microscopic particles of silicate minerals, appears yellow from reflected sunlight, and may extend from 1 to 10 million kilometers. The plasma tail, composed of ionized gases, appears blue from ionized carbon monoxide. Its length may reach an astonishing 100 million kilometers or more — even as far as the distance from the Earth to the Sun.

The plasma tail points straight out, away from the Sun. The dust tail is more arc-shaped. Both are produced by interactions with the Sun's radiation and the solar wind.

The elongated orbits of comets indicate that they might originate in vast clouds out near the edge of the solar system. These
clouds extend nearly two light-years from the Sun — almost halfway to the nearest star, and their fringes can safely be called the
edge of the solar system. The Oort Cloud is the name given to
the area in which these comets originate. This collection of dust-
laden chunks of ice is as old as the solar system itself.

The most famous of all comets is Halley's comet, because it
has been viewed with such regularity throughout human history.
SF writers have sent scientists to land on and study Halley's
comet. Clarke's *2061* details such a journey. *Heart of the Comet*
by Gregory Benford and David Brin postulates a team sent to
inhabit Halley's comet for the duration of one orbit through the
solar system — seventy-six years.

O

The solar system is a fertile ground for science fiction, but even more fertile are the stars. In the solar system, a host of hard facts constrain you — nine well-documented planets; little likelihood of life outside of Earth: But in the far reaches of the galaxy, most of the facts are waiting to be known. You design the stars and planets that will be the theater for your drama; you decide where and in what form life exists.

But be warned: Enough is known about the galaxy to derail your story unless you take the trouble to learn the basics. If you talk about interstellar distances as though they were only ten or twenty times those between planets, if your starship reaches twice the speed of light simply by accelerating, if you recount a visit to Alpha Centauri without realizing that this system contains three stars, you will in indulging in wrong science.

This chapter outlines the science — accepted and imaginary — that you will need to design a starship. It explains the problem of interstellar scale and presents the plausible alternatives SF writers have used to get vehicles out there. It tells you what kind of equipment your crew will need, how to calculate their travel time, how they can survive the long voyage, and

CHAPTER FOUR
STARSHIPS

how they can stay in touch with Earth while they are traveling.

The chapters after this will say more about what your voyagers will find among the stars, and what kind of planets you can create for them. For now, the priority is to get them there.

Scale

The most important thing to understand about the galaxy is that it is big — so big that our minds cannot comprehend it intuitively. It is easy to say that the star Aldebaran is 300 trillion miles away from Earth, but what can that possibly mean in human terms? Here is one way to think about it: On a ship traveling at the speed of current spacecraft, how many generations would live and die before reaching Aldebaran? If the ship travels at the smart clip of nine miles per second, the answer is 40,000 generations over the course of a million years — the length of time it took for *Homo erectus* to evolve into modern man. The travelers who stepped off the ramp at Aldebaran might not even be the same species that left.

These distances are mind-boggling because they are not just greater than earth distances, but several orders of magnitude greater. A billion miles is not the same as two million miles, though our minds tend to think of it that way. To get to a billion, you multiply a million by ten, then multiply the result by ten, then multiply *that* result by ten. To reach a trillion, you do the same thing by three *more* orders of ten. To put this in human terms, consider that it would take eleven and a half days for you to count to a million at the rate of one numeral per second. For you to count to a billion, it would take thirty-two years. Neither you nor your grandchildren would ever reach a trillion. That would take 32,000 years — about the length of time since Neanderthal man became extinct.

An appreciation for scale will add an essential quality to your science fiction stories: respect. You will not portray travel across galactic distances without some understanding for what they mean.

Light-Years and Parsecs

One aid to working with galactic distances is to talk in terms of light-years or parsecs. The distance between the planets in our solar system may seem great, with Pluto at its maximum distance more than 4.5 billion miles from the sun. But this distance can be covered by light in a mere five and one-half hours. Once we leave the solar system, we refer to light-years. A light-year is the distance that light (moving at about 186,000 miles per second) travels in a year — about 6 trillion miles. Our nearest stellar neighbors are those in the Centauri system, three stars that lie 4.3 light-years away (26 trillion miles). There are about twenty-five stars within thirteen light-years of the sun.

For very long distances, parsecs are sometimes used as units of measurement. One parsec equals 3.26 light-years. The Centauri system is about 1.3 parsecs from Earth. Aldebaran is sixteen parsecs (52 light-years) from Earth.

Do not make the elementary mistake of talking about light-years and parsecs as if they were units of time ("We cut our

Scientific Notation

Galactic distances are so great that it is difficult to talk about them in ordinary language. Scientific notation is one aid to exactness. In this notation, a number is expressed in terms of 10 raised to a certain power—that is, 10 multiplied by itself a given number of times. 100 is 1×10^2; 1000 is 1×10^3; 1/100, or 0.01, is 1×10^{-2}. The rule is that the exponent, or power, of 10 is the number of places that the decimal point is to be moved to the right (if the exponent is positive) or to the left (if the exponent is negative). In the case of 1.5×10^6, you move the decimal right six places to get 1,500,000.

To multiply two numbers expressed in scientific notation, you add the exponents. To divide two such numbers, you subtract the exponents. Multiply 3×10^6 times 2.2×10^9, and you get 6.6×10^{15}.

This notation is useful in calculating your own answers to problems like the Aldebaran one above. To write the distance to Aldebaran in ordinary notation, you would have to write 300,000,000,000,000 rather than 3×10^{14}. In that case, you would run a high risk of dropping or adding a zero while you were figuring out how many years it takes to get there.

While doing such calculations, remember that *Distance = Rate × Time*. Also, realize that the number of seconds in a year is 31.5×10^6. Thus, if your ship travels at nine miles per second, it travels $9 \times 31.5 \times 10^6$ miles per year, or approximately 3×10^8 miles per year. With that knowledge, the travel time to Aldebaran is easy to figure out:

Distance to Aldebaran = Rate of Travel × Time to Get There

$$3 \times 10^{14} \text{ mi.} = 3 \times 10^8 \text{ mi./yr.} \times t$$

$$\frac{3 \times 10^{14} \text{ mi.}}{3 \times 10^8 \text{ mi./yr.}} = t$$

$$1 \times 10^6 \text{ yr.} = t$$

traveling time down to three light-years"). Light-years and parsecs are ways of measuring distance, not time. This minor point accounted for one of the biggest gaffes in the movie *Star Wars*, when Harrison Ford's character boasted that his ship was so fast it made the Kessel Run in less than twelve parsecs.

It is clear that travel to the stars would require methods of propulsion far beyond what is needed to hop from planet to planet. Most likely, it would also require great amounts of time. Finally, it would require a strong sense of purpose. The rest of this chapter will help you determine what kind of vehicle might take your characters to the stars.

Basic Starship Planning

There are two basic obstacles to interstellar travel: getting a ship to go near the speed of light, and going faster than light. As far as we know, the speed of electromagnetic energy in a vacuum (better known as the speed of light) is an absolute limit. Nothing moves faster. Nothing can move as fast without becoming energy itself. And, as will become clear, it is highly improbable that a spacecraft could go very near that speed. But for the kinds of galactic voyages most science fiction writers envision, even light speed is not fast enough.

The trouble is that just sending a spacecraft to a star is not enough for most SF writers — or most space mission planners. If it were, NASA would have aimed one of the Voyager probes at Proxima Centauri and been content to have it arrive there safely in about 100,000 years. The mission planners want to be around to see the results — or at least have their near descendants see them. And the imaginations of most SF readers require in addition that a human be aboard the spacecraft to colonize the star's planets, send back reports, and even complete a round trip home. (For a possible unmanned starship, see "The First Starcraft," page 76.)

There are two ways of handling the problem. The first and most popular method is to find a way around the speed of light — usually some variation on what is called hyperspace. The second is to accept the speed of light as a limit, but get the spacecraft to travel near that speed. Which way you choose will determine the type of story you tell. If you want to have frequent round trips in a far-flung galactic civilization, you will need hyperspace. If you are willing to accept the speed of light as a limit, then your characters will not be making short, routine trips between stars.

It is wrong science to assume that one day the speed of light will be broken, as the speed of sound was, and that ships will travel at two, three or four times the speed of light. Einstein's Special Theory of Relativity postulates that as the speed of an object comes closer to the speed of light, its mass becomes greater, and more energy is required to move it. If an object were to travel at light speed, its mass would be infinite, and infinite fuel would be needed. You cannot have a spacecraft move at or above light speed, unless you — and your readers — are willing to dispense with Relativity. Hyperspace is generally a less drastic alternative that achieves the same end.

Hyperspace

Hyperspace, subspace or alternate space is a bit of imaginary science that has been used by SF writers since at least the 1940s. It can be visualized in two ways: as another dimension or as another universe.

Hyperdimensions. We perceive space in three dimensions (with time as the fourth). Within those dimensions, we think of distances as fixed: The distance between Earth and the Moon, for example, is 240,000 miles. But what if, from the point of view of another dimension, space were crumpled or folded, so that Earth and the Moon lay on opposite sides of the fold? In normal travel, we are actually going up and down these folds. If a ship could travel through the fifth dimension, it would cut directly through the fold and appear at the Moon in virtually no time at all. In the same way, two countries on opposite sides of the Earth's surface may appear separated by 12,000 miles as the crow flies. But if the crow could fly through a tunnel in the Earth's interior, the distance between the two points would be only 4,000 miles.

Hyperspace requires some way to cut beyond the four dimensions we already know in the same way that a tunnel cuts through rock. The exit and entry points of the hyperdimensional tunnel are sometimes known as wormholes.

Alternate Space. Hyperspace can also be thought of as a different universe — in the sense that the Earth's interior is a different "universe" from its surface. In that universe, points that seem far apart lie close together. Perhaps this alternate universe is structured like a map of our universe — a model where the distances between points are only a fraction of what they are in ours.

The Problems. Whichever way you think of hyperspace, you are thinking of something for which there is no hard evidence. The only basis for hyperspace travel offered by existing science lies in the speculations of some physicists concerning black

The First Starcraft

Because most SF writers prefer to focus on humans rather than machines, starships tend to be manned. But it is likely that the first interstellar vehicles will be robotic — descendants of planetary probes like Pioneer and Voyager. If they were sufficiently intelligent, robot starcraft could not only explore, but colonize a planet revolving around a distant star. They could also terraform it and prepare it for human habitation.

Robot starships can serve as decor for your story, or they can be the focus. A starship with artificial intelligence and a human personality could easily be the main character.

Because these craft would not need to carry humans, they could forgo all of the heavy extra mass of life-support equipment. They could also be extremely small: microspacecraft perhaps no bigger than a hummingbird, with circuits and mechanisms of microscopic size. They might also be organic rather than mechanical, engineered genetically, grown in a vat. They might be cybernetic organisms with computer chips for brains. Later chapters will say more on microminiature machines (nanotechnology), computers and cyborgs.

The great advantage of smallness is that the less the vehicle's mass, the faster it can go. A relatively small ion drive or laser-propulsion system could take the craft to speeds much higher than those of a starship carrying humans. That is one reason why robot craft are almost certain to serve as scouts for any human expedition.

Physicist Robert Forward has already proposed a starcraft using these principles: *Starwisp*. Weighing about an ounce, *Starwisp* would consist principally of metal mesh pushed by microwaves beamed from a solar power station orbiting the Earth. *Starwisp*'s maximum velocity would be 20 percent light speed. It would reach the star Alpha Centauri in twenty-one years. At that point, a solar power station near the Earth would aim microwaves at the Centauri system, activating the electronic circuits in the mesh. Light detectors in the mesh would form images of the Centauri system, and the mesh, serving as an antenna, would beam the signals to Earth. Traveling at light speed, the signals would reach Earth in less than five years, presenting the first close-up images of another star.

Because the technology to produce *Starwisp* is already close at hand, such a vehicle could be launched within the next twenty-five years. If it were, it would be remembered years later in your future universe as the first step to the stars.

holes. These are objects so massive that not even light can escape their gravity (see chapter 5). Because powerful gravitational fields can curve space and time, the black hole may contain wormholes. But their use in interstellar travel depends on a starship technology capable of surviving the immense tidal stresses of black holes. If that technology is not available in your universe, you will need some other basis for hyperspace.

There are also a few logical problems. Why should alternate space, if it exists, be so conveniently structured as to allow for shorter distances between stars? Why shouldn't it entail longer distances? Why should the geography of alternate space bear any maplike correspondence to ours? What possible mechanism could open both entry and exit gates into hyperspace, or control a ship's course inside it? Why shouldn't the ship be destroyed by the forces that propel it into hyperspace?

Possible Solutions. These are not insuperable problems for the SF writer. Since the science is imaginary, you can make assumptions, design mechanisms, and establish limits any way you choose — as long as you are consistent and plausible. It may be that your ship generates powerful fields that somehow crumple or warp space in the vicinity, allowing the ship to pass instantly from one point to another. Maybe space is only crumpled from the ship's hyperdimensional point of view, so that stay-at-homes don't notice what is happening.

If hyperspace is more like a universe than a dimension, there may be a definite number of preexisting gates into that universe. These tunnels through hyperspace may have to be mapped by explorers before they can be used. Most may land in interstellar space; some may land in dreadful places like the interiors of stars. It is a little hard to believe that they all land conveniently on or near "Earthlike" planets, but you are the boss.

Perhaps the "jump" through hyperspace can only occur near the gravity wells of stars and planets. The jump may need to happen at a precise point of balance between gravitational fields, such as the Lagrange points (see chapter 2). Perhaps the opposite is true: the jump can only happen far away from a star to avoid distortion. In that case, hyperspace would reduce but not eliminate travel time, since travelers would have to handle the long journey from their home star to the "jump" point at sublight speeds.

You will have to decide how easy or hard it is to get through hyperspace. It can't be that easy to hit on the mechanism, or else humans would have been using it for a long time (unless they have been using it in some limited way without knowing it — perhaps in their dreams; perhaps in drug-induced or psychotic states). That means the scientific principles and the technology must be developed some time in the future. Once it has been developed, it could turn out to be a risky voyage.

Most jumps through hyperspace may disintegrate the ship in the process, or thrust the ship into lethal destinations. Perhaps at the beginning of exploration, death is a frequent occurrence, and only the bravest astronauts or most desperate colonists go. Perhaps after many generations it becomes safer, as routine as air travel between American cities. Perhaps the jump through hyperspace is always or usually an unpleasant event, resulting in vomiting, disorientation, even things like cancer or insanity. Or perhaps the traveler notices nothing more than a shudder.

Hyperspace and Light Speed. If you do work with hyperspace, bear in mind that you will in effect be traveling faster than light. This may lead to some odd situations in dealing with radio or visual messages traveling at normal light speed, or with ships traveling slower than light. Here's a simple example: In the year 2000 you send a radio message to Planet X, ten light-years away. In the year 2010, you develop a hyperspace drive and visit Planet X in person. You are there to receive your own radio message just coming in. Here's a more complex example: A galactic civilization built on sublight-speed travel encounters an alien civilization that has discovered and mastered hyperspace. What effect does such a dramatic inequality have on their relations — in peace and in war?

Some scientists believe such a conflict would be not only difficult but impossible. They argue that hyperspace — or any other kind of faster-than-light travel — violates causality by allowing people to get news about a distant star before light from the star could transmit the information to their home planet. However, quantum physicists have laid open the possibility that causality is not necessarily an absolute. In your universe, it may generally be accepted that causality, like Newtonian mechanics, is something that applies in everyday situations, but not in hyperspace travel.

Interestingly, hyperspace may also work as a form of time travel. If a starship can travel through a higher dimension to land at a different point of space, why could it not choose to land at a different point in time? One of the perils of hyperspace might be that the crew might never know if they will land in the time frame they are aiming for, or in some distant future or past.

If you do choose to use hyperspace, you can feel free to call it by that time-honored name, or you can invent your own terminology. In William Gibson's short story "Hinterlands," a version of hyperspace is discovered near Earth that drives travelers to suicidal insanity. It is called by the lonely and evocative name "the Highway."

Propulsion at Sublight Speed

Building a universe without hyperspace eliminates some of the adventure: no quick round trips to distant planets; no five-year missions to explore strange new worlds; no space pirates zipping off to distant stars and making the jump to hyperspace just ahead of the police. It can also eliminate some of the worst clichés, and open the way for equally entertaining stories rooted firmly in known science.

It is not known how close you can get to light speed: just that it becomes harder the closer you get. Any of the space drives discussed in chapter 2 – chemical, ion, fusion, laser, antimatter – can produce a steady acceleration. A continuous acceleration of just 1 g (Earth gravity) will propel a ship half a light-year in a little less than a year. When the ship reaches its top speed, it can turn off its engines and coast. It will cover most of the distance at that coasting velocity, then turn its engines back on to decelerate.

The trouble is that the ship must carry enough fuel for acceleration, deceleration and maneuvering. If it is going to return home, it also needs an equal amount of fuel for that voyage. And fuel is mass. The bigger the ratio of fuel mass to ship mass, the more energy is needed just to propel the fuel tanks. Worse, the Special Theory of Relativity predicts that as the ship approaches the speed of light, its mass increases. Unless the engines are very efficient or the fuel very light, travel at near-light speeds will not be practical – a casualty of the law of diminishing returns.

Clearly, your starship will need the lightest fuel possible. Chemical fuels are out of the question. Your ship will have to be propelled not by huge masses ejected from the ship, but by small masses ejected at very high velocity. The British Interplanetary Society's Project Daedalus is a proposal for a starship that would use helium-3, harvested from Jupiter's atmosphere and burned in a fusion reactor. Other starship planners prefer ions of mercury in an ion drive. In your future, a relatively light system could be found for manufacturing, storing, and harnessing antimatter. Finally, the pressure of laser beams aimed from the solar system at a thin rigid metal sail would work — if computers could keep the beams focused on the sail throughout its long journey.

Ramscoops

Another alternative, now somewhat discredited, is the ramscoop, a ship that collects its own fuel while it hurtles through space. The ramscoop starship is first accelerated to about 1 percent light speed using ordinary fusion power. At that velocity, the loose particles of hydrogen scattered throughout space begin to pile up in front of the ship, just as an airplane encounters air resistance as it flies faster. The ship uses a huge funnel-shaped device — a ramscoop — to scoop up the hydrogen in front. The scoop is composed of superconducting coils that generate an electromagnetic field with a diameter several times larger than Earth's. The ramscoop ionizes the hydrogen atoms and funnels them back into the engine, where the fusion reactor burns them as fuel.

There are several problems with the ramscoop. It is doubtful that the fusion reactor could use mere hydrogen as a fuel; the rarer isotope deuterium is needed. It might not be possible to build a funnel device that is both light and sturdy enough to generate planet-sized fields. And the hydrogen piling up in front of the ship would increasingly slow the ship down as the ship reached faster speeds. It is unlikely that ramscoops will ever be favored in real life over more conventional propulsion methods, but it may still appear in your story if you suggest plausibly how the technical problems were solved.

Starship Design and Equipment

Design. The shape of your starship will depend on its propulsion system: sails for a laser-propelled ship; a cylindrical reactor core with a funnel-shaped exhaust for a fusion-powered ship; an enormous latticework scoop for a ramscoop; anything you like for a hyperspace drive (booms, hooks, funnels, sails, multiple cylindrical engines — whatever it takes to enter hyperspace). If you plan to use centrifugal force to create artificial gravity, then the living quarters will be placed inside a rotating torus, dumbbell, sphere or cylinder.

Equipment. The life-support cargo — food, air, water, medicine, climate control system — will be very similar to that used for long missions inside the solar system. There will be a laboratory to conduct tests, a sick bay, computer systems, an exercise area, and a factory to construct needed materials — from medicines to new uniforms. Scientific equipment will lean heavily toward the study of stars: an optical telescope to measure visible light, telescopes at higher and lower wavelengths (X ray, infrared, radio), a spectroscope to view the spectra of stars, a stellar interferometer to measure the diameters of stars, a magnetometer to measure magnetic fields. If the ship aims to explore planets, it will need robot craft to serve as atmospheric and landing probes. It may also need terraforming equipment and shuttle craft capable of carrying humans from the starship to the planet and back.

Communications. You will need communications equipment: one or more radio dish antennas on steerable bases, aimed at Earth or its colonies, to serve as receivers; a transmitter to send out messages. Radio waves are perfectly suitable for communication over interstellar distances — that is why radio telescopes are even now searching the skies for radio messages from extraterrestrial civilizations. But they travel only at the speed of light. If you want something faster, you will have to use some form of instantaneous communicator. Whether it is called an ansible (the term coined by Ursula K. LeGuin), subspace radio, or something else, such a form of transmission is pure imaginary science, but it is just as common in SF as hyperspace travel. It allows radio energy (and the information it carries) to travel just as fast as hyperspace carries your starships.

You may decide to have a universe where hyperspace travel is not possible, but subspace communication is. Earth could exchange detailed information with star colonists and extraterrestrials at faster-than-light speeds, but still be forced to send its starships at sublight velocities.

Subspace communication may actually be a little more plausible than hyperspace travel. Quantum physicists have suggested that subatomic particles may be able to communicate instantly across any distance, perhaps through quantum wormholes in space. It is at least theoretically possible that submicroscopic quantum wormholes could be harnessed to transfer information through faster-than-light channels.

Weapons and Shields. Whether your starship carries weapons depends on the likelihood of a ship-to-ship fight. Weapons are extra mass, and extra mass means more fuel and slower travel: Explorers and colonists are unlikely to bother with them. But if your story takes place in a developed galactic civilization where war is a fact of life, lasers, missiles, particle beams, or whatever imaginary weapons you invent may be a necessity.

Whether war is a problem or not, you will need to give your starship extra shielding if it is to travel at any substantial fraction of light speed. At such high velocities, hydrogen particles will hit the ship with the force of gamma radiation. Force field generators or a thick coat of crushed asteroid will protect the ship — and represent further mass that will limit the ship's top speed.

How Long Will It Take?

Once you have decided just how fast your starship can go, you will be able to calculate how long it takes to get to a given star. For example, travelers headed for Barnard's Star, about six light-years from Earth, will get there in twelve years if their top velocity is 50 percent c (the speed of light), or twenty-four years if it's 25 percent c. The travel time is found by dividing the distance in light-years (l.y.) by the top speed (expressed as a fraction of c):

$$\text{Travel time} = \frac{6 \ l.y.}{.5 \ c} = 12 \text{ years}$$

You will have to add however long it takes to accelerate and decelerate from top speed. The distance traveled during the acceleration and deceleration periods will not be very great, but the time will most likely be measured in months or years. Thus, the ship with the top speed of 50 percent c may actually take fourteen years, not twelve, to get to Barnard's Star.

It is clear that interstellar travel at these rates will not produce close-knit civilizations. Travelers who spend fourteen years getting to their destination are not likely to make a return trip. If they do, even if they travel in suspended animation, the people they left behind will be twenty-eight years older. How many personal relationships could survive that kind of break? How might the culture have changed in twenty-eight years?

Barnard's Star is relatively close. A civilization that tried to stay in contact with colonies around the forty closest stars would face communication gaps of up to thirty-two years while waiting for signals to travel out to the frontier and back, and sixty-seven years waiting for round trip voyagers to go out and back.

Still, a civilization of this kind can be imagined. John Barnes, in an article called "How to Build a Future" in *Writing Science Fiction and Fantasy*, imagines a system of colonial outposts on the terraformed worlds of the twenty-five closest star systems, all within thirteen light-years of the sun. Each colony is self-sufficient in terms of material and energy resources, but there is a trade in ideas communicated by radio — designs for new technologies, works of art, even genetic descriptions of newly engineered life-forms. The only individuals who travel between stars are "visiting scholars" who help distant colonies interpret data — intelligent young people willing to abandon their home planet and work abroad.

If your voyagers want to travel farther — out to stars hundreds or thousands of light-years away — they will have to be prepared for voyages that last at least that many years. How could space travelers survive on voyages that lasted more than a human lifetime? There are three possible ways: time dilation, cryonics and generation starships.

Time Dilation

This phenomenon, predicted by Relativity, is a fortunate side effect of traveling at speeds close to the speed of light. It means that time slows down for the people inside the fast-moving starship, while it continues to pass at the "regular" rate for those of us left at home.

Suppose your ship accelerates at the rate of 1 g, or 1 Earth gravity. That means the ship increases its velocity by 9.8 meters (32 feet) per second, every second that it travels. Once in space, the space travelers could maintain a constant acceleration of 1 g and experience pressures no more intense than they would feel standing on the Earth. They might even use the acceleration to provide artificial gravity — since the force of the tug toward the rear of the ship would be identical to Earth's surface gravity. At the end of a year, the ship would be traveling at close to the speed of light.

Imagine a year as the time it takes to reach 99.99 percent of light speed. Then add another year to decelerate at a steady 1 g as the travelers approach their destination. In between those two years, the travelers would be moving at near light speed. If they traveled for five years at that speed, they would have covered nearly five light-years.

During this period, relativistic time dilation would affect the ship's crew. According to Special Relativity, time would pass at a far slower rate for those on the ship than for those left behind on Earth. The longer the journey, the move extreme these effects would be.

Let's say your ship is on an exploratory mission to the center of the Milky Way, a journey of 30,000 light-years. From the crew's point of view, twenty years would have passed. However, 30,000 years would have passed on Earth during that same expedition. Traveling at 99.99 percent of light speed, the crew of an intergalactic craft could reach the galaxy of Andromeda in thirty shipboard years, during which two million years would have passed on Earth. It could also circumnavigate the known universe in sixty shipboard years — within the span of a single human lifetime. By the time they reached their original starting point, however, tens of billions of years would have passed, and their sun and their home planet would be no more.

Of course, it may be impossible to propel a ship to 99.99 percent of light speed, because of the practical problems discussed earlier. But in your universe, these practical problems may have been solved. Even if they haven't, time dilation will become important at only about 10 percent of light speed. Shipboard time goes slower the more the ship continues to accelerate.

Theoretically, then, you can travel to anywhere in the universe within the lifetimes of most of your characters. But if they visit the same planet twice, far more time will have passed on the planet than your characters will have experienced. It would be wrong science to have them leave a planet, travel some great distance at near-light speed, and have them return three of their years later to find that only three years have passed on the planet while they've been gone.

Traveling at relativistic rates is a form of time travel into the future, and a classic SF device. Much of its poignancy derives from its limitations, because it is strictly a *one-way* form of travel. When you leave for what may seem like a five- or ten-year stint exploring other star systems, loved ones left on Earth will age and die, society will change and eventually grow unrecognizable. And there is no way back—unless you choose to invent a way of traveling back in time. Joe Haldeman's novel, *The Forever War*, is an excellent example of the ironies and inconveniences time dilation can cause space travelers.

In Poul Anderson's classic *Tau Zero*, a starship crew actually watches the universe age and contract and become born again all within a single human lifetime.

These themes have been explored many times in SF and it would be a good idea to check out existing variations before trying out what might seem like a new twist. It is one of the most popular themes in SF, because it combines—in ways quite plausible to known science—travel into the future, and travel to the farthest edges of the galaxy and beyond.

Cryonics

In your universe, it may turn out that starships cannot accelerate much beyond 10 percent of light speed. In that case, time dilation will not help much, and a journey of only ten light-years will take 100 years. Even if ships do travel at faster top velocities, acceleration may be slow—taking five, ten or twenty years instead of one year. In any of these situations, you may find it useful to place your crew in a state of suspended animation.

For the most part, this technology (called cryonics or cryogenics) is still imaginary science. There is no evidence that a deep-frozen mammal can be thawed and brought back to life— even if it is alive at the time of freezing. Your imaginary cryonics, however, need not depend on something as crude as freezing. In your universe, drugs may have been developed that can place a human into a state resembling hibernation, where metabolic processes are virtually stopped. Nanoagents—microscopic machines—might be able to do the job (see chapter 10).

Cryonics is such a staple of SF you hardly have to explain it. But remember: If the technology is in use on starships, it is probably also used at home. You will have to consider the social implications on Earth as people use cryonics to slow down aging, extend their lives, and wait out incurable diseases until cures can be found.

Another possible form of cryonics is the freezing of embryos (in liquid nitrogen at −196° C). Animal embryos have been kept alive this way, then thawed and placed in wombs to develop normally. On your starship, a whole bank of human embryos could be kept frozen until the end of the voyage. Adult female colonists, who have themselves spent the time in suspended animation, could then receive the embryos and bear them to term. The embryos would not have to be their own; thus "brothers" and "sisters" from one womb would have different genetic compositions, and could mate without fear of inbreeding.

Alternatively, a way may have been found in your universe for hundreds or thousands of embryos to be brought to term in artificial hatcheries. In that case, a large number of women to bear the children would not even be a requirement. A few attendants (human or computer) could do the job—and serve as "parents" for the new brood on the distant world. To say the least, child rearing in the world would be very different from ours. How would the handful of attendants nurture, teach, guide and control their charges? How would such a childhood affect the thoughts, hopes, rebellions and nightmares of those who became adults?

Generation Starships

The final way that a crew could survive a journey of hundreds or thousands of years is if they regenerated themselves. They would do it in the normal way—living, conceiving, giving birth, and dying—aboard a ship big enough to serve as an artificial world.

This generation starship—sometimes called a space ark—has much in common with the space colonies described in chapter 2. It would be a cylinder, torus or sphere, spinning to provide artificial gravity. It would have a self-sustaining ecology, with plants providing oxygen and food, animals providing food and fertilizer, and human wastes recycled. Unlike a space colony in the solar system, this space ark would also have a stardrive capable of accelerating it to whatever the maximum practical velocity is for its mass. And unlike a space colony in the solar system, it would be virtually out of touch with Earth.

For that reason, the space ark's ecology would have to be almost perfect—no slow leaks; no gradual accumulations of carbon dioxide; no wearing down of the food supply. There would be no way to resupply the ship with the things it needed, and over the course of centuries even tiny defects would become deadly. On the other hand, a "perfect" ecology may be impossible. The second law of thermodynamics, and common sense, predicts that the disorder of an isolated system will increase with time. (See chapter 11 for the other laws of thermodynamics.) Your story might be set at a crisis point as the inhabitants of the space ark begin to realize their days are numbered unless a solution is found.

Matter Transformers. If you prefer not to face this problem, part of your space ark's equipment might be a matter transformer — a chemical system allowing any needed compound (such as water or carbohydrates) to be synthesized as long as the necessary elements (carbon, hydrogen and oxygen) are around. This is at least theoretically possible, though complex. Chemical processes form compounds by manipulating the outer electrons of atoms — through heating, mixing, freezing, whatever. The difficulty is to know and execute the right process for each kind of compound.

Compounds differ from elements because they can be chemically decomposed, while elements cannot. The smallest unit of an element is an atom; the smallest unit of a compound is a molecule, a combination of atoms.

It is imaginary science to have a shipboard machine that can readily transform one element (such as hydrogen) into any other (such as iron). According to known science, creating the full range of elements out of simpler ones requires thermonuclear fusion at temperatures and pressures found only in supernovae, or exploding stars. If your society can create any element at will, it is hard to know why it would ever send a ship anywhere to obtain anything.

Space Ark Society. The space ark would need a self-sustaining culture as well as a perfect ecology. Life would have to be varied and rewarding enough for the inhabitants not to succumb to boredom or despair. Of course, the starship could communicate with Earth by radio, exchanging art and ideas, but the delays in transmission would grow by years, decades or centuries as the ship moved farther out. The ship would have to leave the solar system with its own renewable supplies of the intangibles that make human lives meaningful — art, recreation, science, philosophy, religion.

Over the centuries, the space ark's culture would evolve in its own unpredictable directions. Generations who live and die aboard the ark would probably have no more concern for the starship's destination than we have for the Virgo cluster, which our galaxy is heading for at about 1.5 percent light speed. Eventually, they might "forget" they were on a space ark. The world of the ark would be the only world they knew, or cared to know. There might be no reason at the end for them to leave their space ark for whatever star system they finally reached. By that point in their culture's development, they might not even be interested in studying it.

So many stories have been written about generation starships that it may seem the concept is outworn. Yet humans never tire of telling stories about Earth, though that too is a space ark. As with all stories, the freshness of your story will ultimately depend on how well you imagine your characters and their conflicts — not on their propulsion system.

O

Once you have figured out how to get your characters to the stars, you will have to imagine what the stars look like. The only star we have ever seen close up is our own Sun; the others, even in the most powerful telescopes, have forever been points of light. Some of the universe's contents, such as black holes and cosmic strings, have never been seen at all, except in theory. Yet the ingenuity of astronomers over the centuries has built a dazzling detailed base of knowledge of what lies beyond the solar system. Your stories will benefit by being true to that base of knowledge and drawing on its resources.

An Overview of the Galaxy

This chapter gives an overview of the Milky Way galaxy and its contents: stars, gas and dust, black holes. It ventures outside the galaxy to consider the structure of the universe, exotic entities such as quasars and jets, and questions about the universe's origin and future. It does not take up the issues of extrasolar planets, alien life, intelligence and civilization, which will be handled in the chapters that follow. Indeed, you may find you

CHAPTER FIVE
AROUND THE
GALAXY

are able to write an interesting story about the stars without ever taking your characters to a lifebearing planet. If you do land on such a planet, it will help to know all you can about what lies on the way there.

The first thing to understand about the galaxy is what it is not. It is not the whole universe. It is not a star system. It is a collection of star systems. It is one among many such collections in the universe.

Do not talk about "aliens from another galaxy" as though this were roughly the same thing as aliens from another star system *within* our galaxy. It is not even close. The star Betelgeuse is 150 parsecs away. The Andromeda galaxy is 680,000 parsecs away.

As astronomers currently understand it, the universe is a vast expanse peppered with superclusters of galaxies. Each supercluster, hundreds of millions of light-years across, contains smaller clusters of galaxies. These clusters vary in size. Some may contain thousands of galaxies; ours, the Local Group, contains about two dozen, spread out over a region about 3 million light-years in diameter.

Our galaxy, the Milky Way, is about 100,000 light-years in diameter—just 3 percent that of the Local Cluster. The Milky Way is a flat rotating disk of stars, gas and dust, with a bulging nucleus and two spiral arms. The central bulge is about 10,000 light-years thick; the disk is about 5,000 light-years thick. The galaxy is lit by the radiation of more than 100 billion stars, spaced an average distance of 5 light-years apart. Our sun is a medium-sized star on a minor spur of one of the galaxy's spiral arms. Located about 30,000 light-years from the galaxy's center—more than halfway, but not quite on the outer edge—it and its system of planets revolve around that center once every 200 million years.

Gas and Dust

Interstellar space is not completely empty. Atoms of gas and tiny solid particles of dust are spread throughout the wide reaches between stars, though not uniformly. The gas and dust are thicker in the spiral arms than in the regions between the arms. In places, the gas and dust clump into clouds or nebulae, some of which are several light-years across. Interstellar gas and dust, even in the spiral arms, is very thin by Earth standards—on average, about one atom of gas per cubic centimeter, and between twenty-five and fifty microscopic "grains" of dust per cubic kilometer. The nebulae may be as much as a thousand times denser. But this is still more of a vacuum than scientists are able to achieve in the laboratory.

Viewed from afar, nebulae might look either like dark blotches that dim or block out the stars behind them (dark nebulae) or beautiful luminous clouds (bright nebulae). If you were to fly your ship through a nebula, however, chances are that it would be far too thin to look like anything. However, it would somewhat obscure your ability to see outside the nebula, and the bright nebulae would be hotter than the rest of interstellar space.

Inside and outside nebulae, interstellar gas is about 75 percent hydrogen; another 20 percent or so is helium. It is many times more abundant than solid dust, but it is also transparent and does not significantly dim the stars. Accumulations of dust, on the other hand, do obscure the stars. The dust consists of tiny particles (less than a thousandth of a millimeter in size) of water ice, silicates, graphite and other elements.

Dark nebulae obscure the stars because of relatively high concentrations of dust. Bright nebulae are mostly hydrogen gas. They glow because of the presence of nearby stars. Sometimes these stars are within the nebula itself. A hot star inside or nearby a nebula will ionize the hydrogen gas, which will radiate visible light. These nebulae are known as emission nebulae. If the nearby star is too cool to ionize the hydrogen, the dust particles within the nebula might still reflect light. These nebulae are called reflection nebulae.

Planetary nebulae aren't really planets or even protoplanets, although they do resemble them when viewed through a small telescope. They are the expanding shells of aging stars, swelling at a rate of more than 10 kilometers a second. Once the "wall" of the planetary nebula is too far away from its aging, cooling star, it will gradually diffuse into interstellar space. The *visible* life expectancy of a planetary nebula is only about 10,000 years. Some nebulae are remnants of large stars that met with sudden violent deaths. A catastrophic explosion (see "Supernovae" in this chapter) hurls most of the star's mass into space at thousands of kilometers per second.

Why would space travelers purposely visit a nebula? It is unlikely that a spacecraft with a living crew would venture into a nebula for detailed study — the distances are too great, the time frame too long and the work could easily be done with a computerized unmanned ship. A ramscoop ship might plot a path through the wisping clouds of a nebula to capture raw materials from a source far richer than the relative emptiness of interstellar space.

Stars

Star Formation. Stars originate as clumps of dust within the cold dusty nebulae. Because the temperature in these nebulae is within 30 degrees K of absolute zero, there is not enough heat to disperse the dust and gases. They can accumulate, and the weak gravitational pull of a dust clump can attract material from the surrounding region. Eventually the mass of the accumulating dust and gas becomes so great that the gravitational collapse heats up the interior but still manages to attract more and more of the surrounding matter. It has become a protostar.

A protostar will continue to contract for millions of years. Once the density is great enough and the temperature has risen to 6 million °F, hydrogen will start fusing to helium. Four hydrogen nuclei will fuse into one helium nucleus, giving off a single gamma ray photon. That photon will spend the next million years working its way toward the surface of the star, where it will be radiated into space as visible light. Once nuclear fusion has begun, the gravitational collapse of the star will be counteracted by the pressures and high temperatures radiated by the nuclear reactions in the star's interior.

The shock waves of a nearby supernova can trigger the collapse of the interstellar clouds and the formation of new stars. It can also send an influx of heavier materials such as carbon and oxygen into the condensing clouds of dust and gas.

Upon entering one of these gigantic stellar nurseries, space travelers would find that the dark and gloomy exterior had masked the light of hundreds or even thousands of newborn stars on the inside. These stars would be much closer together than they would be later in their lives.

Stars that are very close together exert a strong gravitational pull on each other. A group of stars held together by mutual gravitation is called a star cluster. The stars in a cluster may range in number from many thousands to only a few. Since each star in a cluster moves under the gravitational influence of all the other stars, their individual motions are hard to calculate and predict.

Some stars are even more closely associated. A binary star consists of two stars revolving around a common center of mass. Multiple-star systems consist of two, three or more stars revolving around each other. It is now thought that most stars are members of such systems.

Strange things can happen in a binary star system. When a star is expanding into a red giant (see below), its outer layers may begin to flow toward its companion star in a process called mass exchange. A river of matter may flow through space between the stars. Such a spectacle is one of the favorite sights of galactic SF.

Exploiting the Riches of a Protostar

Space travelers wouldn't be likely to find life on the asteroids and tiny planets—planetesimals—orbiting a protostar. The visitors wouldn't find inhabitable planets or even a planet large enough to be worth terraforming. Because the protostar wouldn't have reached high enough internal pressure and temperature for fusion to begin, it would not be emitting solar energy.

But there would be minerals. While the protostar is collapsing in the center of the once-nebulous cloud of dust and gas, planetesimals are orbiting the protostar in much the same way as the asteroid belt orbits the sun. There are distinct advantages to settling near and upon asteroids rather than planets. Not only are there rich mineral resources available, they are far more accessible because spaceships can be launched without having to fight the gravity well of a planet.

While the asteroids between Mars and Jupiter have never been able to clump together to form a planet because of the gravitational effects of Jupiter, there would be no such disruptions in this newly forming solar system. The rocks and chunks of ice would continue collecting into larger and larger clumps. In the meantime, an entire solar system's worth of mineral riches could be exploited. At its center would be a dull hazy orange mass, the infant sun whose gravitational pressure had not yet raised the temperature high enough to begin hydrogen-helium fusion. Around it an entire civilization might de-velop—beings living within space colonies with little knowledge of or need for gravitational liabilities like planets.

Eventually, however, the pieces of rock and ice will clump together into planets and will exert gravitational pull. The critical temperature in the protostar will be reached and nuclear fusion will begin. What kind of transformations would this civilization of miners have undergone in the meantime? How might they adjust—or fail to adjust?

Attributes of Stars. Stars differ in size, brightness, and many other characteristics. The most important attribute is mass: the total amount of material in its body. The amount of material that collapses into the original protostar will determine its size, temperature, brightness, life span, and even the way in which it dies. Stellar masses are often described in terms of our sun's mass $(2 \times 10^{33}$ grams): The red dwarf star Ross 614B is about one-twelfth of a solar mass; the red giant Plaskett's Star is about fifty solar masses.

Astronomers use a scale called stellar magnitude to describe the brightness of stars. Apparent magnitude is the brightness a star has as seen from Earth. Absolute magnitude is the brightness a star would have if it were observed from a distance of 10 parsecs. Ascending numbers of the magnitude scale indicate a decrease in brightness; each step on the scale is about two and a half times dimmer than the step below it. Thus a second-magnitude star emits two and a half times *less* light than a first-magnitude star. Our sun's absolute magnitude is +5. Most stars have absolute magnitudes in the range 0 (very bright) to +15 (very dim).

A star's spectral class describes the characteristics of its spectrum: the way that its light is dispersed when it passes through the grating or prism of a spectroscope. The star's spectrum is related to its temperature and color. The hottest stars are blue stars: From warmest to coolest, these are spectral classes O, B, A, and F. White or yellow G stars are cooler than blue stars; K stars, cooler still, are orange to red; M stars, the coolest, are red. (For temperatures of each spectral class, see "How Hot Is a Star?" page 95.)

Spectral classes are each divided into ten gradations. The hottest class-F stars are F0, followed by the cooler F1 stars, then F2, F3, and so on to F9 and G0. Our sun is spectral class G2 — pretty hot for a yellow star.

Together, the spectral classes make up the spectral sequence into which most stars fit. The sequence, from hottest to coolest, can be remembered with this mnemonic: "Oh, Be A Fine Girl, Kiss Me!"

The Main Sequence. Another way of classifying stars is to state whether they are "on" or "off" the main sequence. The main sequence is a band of points on a graph (called the Hertzsprung-Russell diagram) that compares a star's temperature, or spectral class, to its luminosity, or absolute magnitude. The narrow band of the main sequence ranges from hot bright stars (which are large and blue) to cool dim stars (which are small and red); most stars fall in this band. Some stars, however, are small and yet hot (white dwarfs); others are large and yet cool (red giants and supergiants).

The "main sequence" is where most stars — blue, yellow and red — spend most of their lives. "Red giants" and "white dwarfs"

How Hot Is a Star?

A stars temperature determines its color and its spectral class. Below are the seven spectral classes, with their color, temperatures and examples:

Class	Color	Temperature (in °K)	Sample Star
O	Blue	More than 25,000	10 Lacertae
B	Blue	11,000-25,000	Rigel
A	Blue	7,500-11,000	Sirius
F	Blue to White	6,000-7,500	Canopus
G	White to Yellow	5,000-6,000	Sun
K	Orange to Red	3,500-5,000	Aldebaran
M	Red	Less than 3,500	Betelgeuse

actually represent late stages in the evolution of certain stars, after they have "fallen off" the main sequence. The particular course of a star's history depends on its mass at the time of its formation.

Types of Stars. Protostars without enough mass (brown dwarfs) never become stars; those with too much mass (blue giants) burn themselves out relatively quickly; others fall somewhere in between. Here are some of the possible paths protostars may take.

Brown Dwarf. If the protostar possesses less than 0.1 solar masses (less than one-tenth the size of the sun), its internal temperature will never reach the critical threshold and so hydrogen will never fuse into helium. Without the heat given off by hydrogen-helium fusion, a brown dwarf will never really become a star at all. Instead, it will cool and shrink down to about the size of Earth, but with a mass greater than Jupiter's. In fact, a brown dwarf would be so cold, dark and small that it would resemble a planet more than a dwarf star.

Red Dwarf. A red dwarf has about one-third of the mass of the sun, massive enough to raise temperatures in the interior to the point where fusion begins. The internal pressures and temperature will be low enough so that it will take a long time to fuse all its hydrogen fuel — about 30 billion years. There will not be enough pressure for helium to begin fusing into heavier elements, so it will then begin to cool and contract. Like the brown dwarf, it will eventually fade from view entirely, becoming an inert ball, a black dwarf.

Sun-Class Stars. While stars of about the same mass as our sun are still quite small compared to giant stars, they are large enough to continue nuclear fusion after the core has been fused from hydrogen to helium — after a period of about 10 billion years. The helium at the star's core will begin to compress under its own weight, igniting a shell of hydrogen surrounding it and causing the star to swell to twice its original size. It is leaving the main sequence and becoming a red giant. Once the core has heated to 100 million degrees F, helium will begin to fuse to carbon. The surface of the star will become a shell of hydrogen. It takes about 100 million years for the core to fuse entirely to carbon. Stars this size don't have sufficient gravity for the carbon to fuse to heavier elements. The shell will drift away. After the star has shed most of its material, it will cool and shrink, becoming a white dwarf, a small bright star only a few thousand miles in diameter. Occasionally a white dwarf will flare briefly, during which it will glow a hundred to a million times more brightly. These events are known as novae. A white dwarf may burn like this for billions of years, cooling gradually. The novae become less and less frequent, until the white dwarf dims and finally flickers out.

Blue Giant. The greater the mass of a star, the greater its internal pressures and temperatures and the shorter its life span. It will exhaust its hydrogen fuel far more quickly (even though it contains more hydrogen than a sun-sized star), moving on to helium-carbon fusion. Unlike smaller stars, however, a blue giant will continue nuclear fusion even after the core has been fused to carbon.

Few stars of greater than three solar masses survive for more than 100 million years. Most of them don't even last that long. Because of their short life expectancy, giant stars are very rare and are usually found in close company with other stars in the nebula in which they formed.

While they are rare and short-lived, giant stars are important to the evolution of a galaxy, not only because they are responsible for the creation of the heavier elements, but they also redistribute these heavy elements through cataclysmic events.

Variable Stars

Not all stars are as constant as our sun. Many stars pulse or vary in size and brightness, as a result of an imbalance between the weight of the outer layers and the pressures at the core. As gravitation causes the star to contract and dim, its internal pressures build up, eventually causing it to expand and brighten; as it expands, the pressures are relieved, and the outer layers begin to collapse inward again. The result is a pulsating variable star.

The period of a variable star is the time it takes to go from bright to dim to bright again. The amplitude is the difference in the star's magnitude from its brightest point to its dimmest point. Variable stars change in size during their periods. The yellow giant δ Cephei gets 7 to 8 percent bigger at its maximum; the red giant Mira gets 20 percent bigger.

Here are some of the more important kinds of variable stars.

Cepheid Variables. These are relatively rare yellow giants (F-G) with periods of three to fifty days. Their amplitudes (changes in brightness) range from .1 to 2 magnitudes. The star rapidly reaches maximum light, then falls more slowly to minimum light. Polaris and δ Cephei are examples.

Long-period ("Red") Variables. The most common kind of variable stars, these are red giants and supergiants (M). Their periods are somewhat irregular, and average months or years. Their amplitudes range from 2.5 to 7 magnitudes and up. Mira is an example.

Irregular and Semiregular Variables. These are red variables with little or no regularity in their pulsations. An irregular variable shows no pattern at all; a semiregular variable (like Betelgeuse) sometimes pulsates according to a period, and at other times becomes disturbed. The amplitudes of both kinds of stars are usually less than 2 magnitudes.

Supernovae

A supernova — the explosive death of a star — is an event of spectacular proportions. The initial blast may briefly shine billions of times more brightly than before, possibly outshining the entire galaxy. Maximum brightness will be reached in a few days or less; within a few months or years the star will fade from sight.

The explosion will unleash enough cosmic, gamma and ultraviolet rays to pose a threat to life on any planet within ten to fifteen light-years. And yet, the destructive power of a supernova can also stimulate the formation of new solar systems, as the shock waves it sends out stimulate the condensation and collapse of vast clouds of interstellar gas. And it is within large dying stars that elements such as carbon, oxygen, sulphur, silicon and iron are formed. The supernova unleashes these chemical elements, seeding the newly forming solar systems with the building blocks of organic compounds necessary for life.

What kind of a star can become a supernova? It can happen to a star only twice the mass of the sun, but many candidates are far larger — sometimes 60 or more solar masses. A star that large is under far greater internal pressure than the sun, with temperatures many times hotter. It burns brighter and more quickly, fusing hydrogen atoms to form helium, helium to form carbon, carbon to form neon, neon to form oxygen, and oxygen to form silicon. At 3 billion °C, silicon reacts to produce iron. Up until this point, the fusion process will have exerted enough outward pressure to counteract the enormous gravitational pull. But since iron will not fuse no matter how high the temperature, the gravitational pressure exerted on the iron core will cause the iron atoms to break apart, resulting in a mighty implosion, a rapid collapse releasing enormous energy. The resulting shock wave will tear the star apart.

It would be wrong science to have our own Sun go supernova. The Sun is too small and too stable. It is also only halfway through its life span of about 10 billion years. The life span of a star massive enough to go supernova would only be 10 to 100 million years. It is doubtful that this would be enough time for an intelligent race to evolve on a planet orbiting such a star. It took the Earth 4 billion years to produce a species advanced enough to even conceive the idea of a supernova.

Space travelers could colonize the planets orbiting a massive star. If it is a binary star system consisting of a giant and a smaller companion, the small star might have hospitable worlds orbiting it. Would a race intelligent enough to travel through space and either terraform a world or build sealed cities also recognize the potential disaster building within their new star system?

Would a colonizing race worry about the possibility of a supernova 1 or 5 million years in their future? Is it a problem they would even consider? And when the disaster finally became

Supernovae: The View From Earth

It is estimated that in the Milky Way galaxy there are one or two supernovae every century. Clouds of dust and gas often prevent their light from reaching the Earth. Several supernovae have been recorded in the last thousand years, the most recent of which was witnessed by astronomers throughout the southern hemisphere in 1987.

Perhaps the most famous supernova remnant is the Crab Nebula. When the light from this supernova first struck the Earth in 1054, it lit up the night sky and was visible in daylight for weeks afterward. And yet this supernova occurred more than 6,000 light-years away. It is possible that more ancient supernovae, occurring far closer to our own solar system, may have triggered waves of extinctions on Earth.

The cloud of interstellar gas from the supernova of a nearby star would outshine every object in the sky except for the Sun and Moon. In its first few weeks it could leave the world in perpetual daylight, a glowing scar stretched across the sky. Animals, including humans, would succumb to radiation sickness, cancer and widespread mutation. If the supernova were close enough, the escaping gases could cloak the Earth, cutting down sunlight and plunging the planet into an ice age. Alternatively, the gases might trigger a runaway greenhouse effect, melting the polar ice caps and flooding world coastlines.

imminent, how would this species try to escape the cataclysmic end of their solar system? They would have to travel a considerable distance to escape the destructive energies released by the supernova — perhaps as far as 20 light-years.

In the aftermath of a supernova, patches or rings of gas would remain to mark the violence of the explosion. But not all of the star's mass would have escaped.

Neutron Stars and Pulsars

When a star of three or more solar masses goes supernova, the core collapses under its own gravity, crushing in on itself and smashing electrons and protons together to form neutrons. All that remains in the aftermath of the explosion is a small sphere. This is a neutron star, so-called because it is made up almost entirely of neutrons, electrically neutral subatomic particles.

A neutron star is usually no more than five to ten miles in

diameter, though it still contains two or three times the mass of the Sun. The neutron star matter (also known as neutronium) is so dense that a teaspoon of it would weigh 100 billion tons. It also spins very fast. The neutron star at the center of the Crab Nebula, for example, spins at 30 revolutions per second. We know this because we can detect it as a pulsing radio source. But why would a neutron star seem to pulse?

The two magnetic poles of neutron stars give off beams of radio waves. If the axis of the neutron star's rotation is *not* the same as the axis of its magnetic poles, the conical beams of radio waves will rotate with the star. As each of the beams passes the observer, it will be detectable as a brief flash of visible light and radio waves. Most of the neutron stars astronomers have detected in our galaxy give off these pulses, and so they are known as pulsars.

The gravitational attraction of a neutron star would be tremendous and would increase dramatically as one drew closer to the surface. A ship approaching the star too closely would be subject to severe tidal forces. The part of the ship closest to the neutron star would experience a gravitational pull many times more powerful than the rest of the ship — and those tidal forces could tear the ship apart. The exact "safe distance" would depend on the mass of the star.

What would a solar system be like in the wake of a supernova, with only a tiny, relatively dim neutron star spinning furiously at its center? There is evidence that some neutron stars might have planets orbiting them. Could a planet actually survive a supernova explosion? It isn't likely, and even if a planet does survive, it's even less likely that any living thing will survive with it.

One possibility is that the planets orbiting neutron stars could have been captured after the supernova. Either way, these planets could be colonized by a spacefaring race. Their "sun" would be a small dim star. Unless the star is very old, there could be clouds of supernova debris surrounding a neutron star. This cloud could contain many of the same elements the supernova had spewed into space (carbon, hydrogen, oxygen, iron, etc.), and there is a possibility that, because of their presence, life could somehow exist within the clouds themselves.

In Larry Niven's novels *The Integral Trees* and *The Smoke Ring*, human beings actually seed the ring of cloud surrounding a neutron star, terraforming it into a free-fall environment, full of spherical lakes and gigantic floating trees. Their smoke ring orbits the tiny neutron star once every five hours.

In the Robert Forward novels *Dragon's Egg* and *Starquake*, a tiny pulsar appears in the vicinity of our solar system, spinning at a rate of five revolutions per second. Scientists studying this star discover life upon its surface. These tiny creatures — no bigger than sesame seeds but with about the same mass as humans — live their lives at an accelerated pace, literally millions of times faster than we live our own.

It is also possible that an intelligent species living on an orbiting planet conceived some way to survive the destruction of their sun. This is a tall order to imagine, but you may be able to do it. Could they somehow shield their planet from a supernova explosion, or move it out of range? Perhaps they abandoned their home planet in space arks just before the supernova, then returned to orbit the neutron star, perhaps hundreds or thousands of years later. What would be their motivation? Why their attachment to an exploded star?

Black Holes

The gravity on the surface of a neutron star would be so great that for something to actually escape its gravitational pull, it would require an escape velocity of more than half the speed of light. What would happen to a massive star whose gravitational contraction was so great that the escape velocity actually exceeded the speed of light? If light itself couldn't escape the star's surface, nothing could, because nothing travels faster than light. The force of gravity would crush the entire mass of the star, along with all radiation, to a single mathematical point of infinite density — a singularity. Once called collapsars, they are now popularly known as black holes.

A black hole consists of the singularity and a spherical boundary that surrounds it — the event horizon. Nothing that reaches the event horizon can escape it. The diameter of the event horizon can be determined by an equation known as the Schwarzschild Radius. The event horizon of an object containing the mass of Earth would be about the size of a marble. For an object as massive as the Sun it would be 1.75 miles. But the event horizon of a black hole containing ten solar masses would be roughly 36 miles in diameter.

A Visit to a Black Hole

Astronomers hunt for potential black holes within X-ray binary systems, as the pulses of strong X rays are the most obvious clue a black hole would send out. Cygnus X-1 is an X-ray source near a blue giant star. It is believed that these X rays could emanate from an accretion disk 2.5 million miles in diameter, as matter is pulled from the star toward the black hole that was once its companion star.

Astronauts searching for black holes would initially be hunting for these powerful X-ray sources. But as they drew closer they would see a ragged stream of luminous gas emerging from the star and stretching toward the black hole. The stream would coalesce into a vast rotating disk around the event horizon, growing brighter the closer it swirled around the black inner core.

Drawing close to a black hole would cause enormous tidal stress on a spaceship and the crew inside it. Just as our oceanic tides are caused by the fact that part of the ocean is always closer to the Moon (and to a lesser degree, the Sun) than another part, the end of the ship closer to the event horizon will experience more gravitational pull than the rest of the ship. The closer the ship draws to the event horizon the bigger the difference there will be from one end of the ship to the other. This will cause intense tidal stress on the ship and also on everything inside the ship, including the people. Tidal stress could eventually tear the ship apart.

A black hole would not be completely invisible, however. It would be visible because of the massive influx of matter toward the event horizon. In a binary star system, matter would pour off the black hole's companion star, drawn toward the spinning black hole, which would cause these gases to form an accretion disk surrounding the event horizon. The outer edges of the accretion disk wouldn't be orbiting the event horizon as fast as the gases closer to the inner edge. This would cause friction, heating the inner edge of the accretion disk to 3 million degrees F and sending out powerful X rays.

Harnessing Black Holes. Could a singularity be captured, or perhaps even created in the laboratory? If so, it could be kept in a safe orbit around Earth and the energy of its enormous gravitational pull could be harnessed to generate electricity. It would also make an extremely efficient trash compactor. The creation, capture and safe maintenance of a mini-black hole depend on imaginary science, but for a highly advanced civilization, they could be an effective solution to the problems of energy resources and garbage disposal.

A mini-black hole will lose energy over time. The smaller its mass, the shorter its life expectancy. How much good or damage it could do would depend on its size. In Greg Bear's novel *The Forge of God*, two singularities orbiting each other at the Earth's core destroy the planet at novel's end. In David Brin's *Earth*, the singularities inside the Earth are harnessed, their orbits brought under control and used for a number of purposes, good and bad — including the destruction of cities and the carefully controlled generation of gravity waves, which are then used to launch or even levitate ships.

Were a massive enough singularity to fall into the Earth's core, the planet could be destroyed in as little time as a year. During that period, natural geologic forces — earthquakes and volcanic eruptions — would increase dramatically as the crust was put under enormous gravitational stress. The final annihilation of the Earth's crust would be a very sudden event of short duration. The surface of the planet — ravaged but still intact — would be sucked into the singularity in the final minutes.

But it is a black hole's effect on space and time itself that has entranced SF writers and readers the most. According to the General Theory of Relativity, gravity causes time to slow down. If you were to watch a spaceship approaching a black hole, you would not see it falling at a faster and faster rate; rather, the ship would seem to slow down, so that when it reached the event horizon it would stop altogether. And yet, to those inside the ship, time would pass normally; they would feel that they were indeed falling faster and faster. Observation of distant space from inside the ship would show events taking place outside at a greatly accelerated pace.

Physicists have also theorized that a black hole could have not one, but two event horizons. If the black hole is spinning rapidly enough, the singularity will be a ring rather than a point, and will connect the two event horizons, so that the black hole will have, in a sense, punched through the fabric of space and time. Physicists refer to these hypothetical tunnels as wormholes.

If a ship were able to enter a rotating black hole, passing within the ring-shaped singularity without being torn apart by tidal forces and crushed out of existence, where would it end up? Some physicists believe it would end up in another part of the universe — and in another time. Others believe these wormholes might be gateways to other universes altogether. In either case, black holes in this theory might actually serve as a basis for the hyperspace tunnels beloved by SF writers.

For black holes to serve as practical shortcuts through space, travelers would have to learn precisely where (and when) the entrance and exit points of black holes would lead them. They could then create a map of the universe riddled with wormhole "highways," and allow for instantaneous travel across vast distances. But even if they could accurately gauge the location of a black hole's exit, could they gauge the time? Would they appear in the past or the future? The physics of black holes suggests that it could be either. Or would they be in a different universe altogether? Even among scientists, these are all speculations. Some believe, for example, that if a spaceship could dip through the event horizon and reemerge without even approaching the singularity, it would *still* end up in another time or another universe.

The Hee-Chees of Frederik Pohl's novels *Gateway, Beyond the Blue Event Horizon, Hee-Chee Rendezvous* and *Hee-Chee Chronicles* were an advanced spacefaring race that became so frightened after an encounter with a hostile alien race that they hid their civilization *within* a black hole. In Jeffrey Carver's *From a Changeling Star*, human beings are able to provoke the star Betelgeuse into a premature supernova. Their technology is so advanced that they will be able to control the route through space-time created by the resulting black hole. Some of the most outlandish imaginary science ever found in SF deals with the possible effects and uses of black holes.

The Center of the Galaxy

The core of the Milky Way galaxy is obscured by interstellar dust, so that optical telescopes can tell us very little about conditions there. But infrared and radio telescopes focused on these central regions (about 30,000 light-years from Earth) have revealed several amazing things. There may be up to a thousand stars per cubic light-year packed into the galactic core, which is a million times more crowded than it is in our part of the galaxy. There is also evidence that a vast whirlpool of rotating hot gas is being expelled from the core at high velocity. Astronomers estimate that there is enough matter in this ring to make up 100 million stars the size of our sun. The ring may be the result of a tremendous explosion at the galactic core about 10 million years ago. What would cause such an incredible explosion?

A supermassive black hole at the center of the galaxy could cause occasional explosions of this sort. The disk of dust and gas spiraling in toward the black hole might cause gravitational instabilities of the infalling matter, leading to an occasional explosion on a scale that would account for the expanding ring hurling outward from the core. There is also some evidence of other rings, larger and more diffuse, moving out from the core. Maybe these explosions are a regular occurrence.

The center of the galaxy rotates faster than the outer regions, so fast that astronomers wonder how the matter can keep from hurtling outward from centrifugal force. It would take a powerful gravitational force to keep this furiously spinning matter from coming completely apart. It would require the mass of 5 million suns packed into an area no larger than our own solar system, at the center of which is a massive object that occupies only a mathematical point, a singularity.

In Gregory Benford's novels *Big Sky River* and *Tides of Light*, human beings in the far future inhabit planets near the galactic center. The matter spiraling into the supermassive black hole at the galaxy's center is visible as a "river" of bright light in the sky. Also in these novels is a machine civilization hostile to all living organisms, harnessing some of the vast energy from the supermassive black hole.

Taking Benford's analogy, it is possible that advanced civilizations could cluster around black holes for the same reason early civilizations clustered near the banks of great rivers, as the Egyptians did along the Nile to take advantage of abundant resources. However, it is doubtful that life could be sustained for any long periods on a planet so near the galactic center. The gravitational effects of neighboring suns would pull planets out of their orbits and destroy them.

Maybe your characters live on a planet near the center of the galaxy, just far enough away that their home world has been able to sustain a few million or billion years of life. Their skies would be filled with a much denser cluster of stars than ours, but they may or may not see them all because of the movements of dust inward, toward the galactic core. What dangers would these characters face because of their proximity to so many other stars?

Whether at the galaxy's center or among the stars closer to us, no planet has yet been detected with certainty outside the solar system. It is likely, however, that many stars have planets orbiting them, and some may have life. For information on designing a planet, see chapter 6.

Leaving the Galaxy

The oldest stars in the Milky Way form a spherical halo about 100,000 light-years in diameter. Known as globular clusters, these tight-knit groups of stars were once thought to mark the outer edges of the galaxy. Recently, however, radio astronomers have discovered a thin cold halo of matter — a corona — that extends far out from the globular clusters. While this medium is very thin (like interstellar space, it might contain as little as one atom per cubic centimeter) it isn't nearly as empty as true intergalactic space. While many astronomers believe that there isn't enough matter in this corona to form into clouds, others believe that it could be populated with dead burned-out stars.

The Magellanic Clouds orbit our galaxy, the larger one at a distance of about 150,000 light-years. These have been called dwarf galaxies. But given the fact that the galactic corona stretches well into the reaches of both the Large and Small Magellanic Clouds, some astronomers feel that rather than galaxies or even dwarf galaxies, they should be thought of as remote areas of star formation in our own galaxy.

As your starship leaves the globular clusters for the relative emptiness of the corona, the Milky Way will begin to assume a definite shape, similar to other spiral galaxies. Depending on the direction your ship is headed, the galaxy might be seen edge on, assuming the shape of a saucer, or from above, as a vast winding spiral. Ahead lies the emptiness of intergalactic space.

Intergalactic Space and Other Galaxies

How empty is intergalactic space? It's estimated that the average concentration of matter in intergalactic space is only about one atom per cubic meter. The stars and gases that make up the galaxies account for less than .01 percent of the space in the universe.

The galaxies aren't scattered randomly through the universe. Galaxies and groups of galaxies are drawn together by their gravitational attraction. The Milky Way is part of a cluster of about two dozen galaxies, known as the Local Group. As galactic clusters go, the Local Group is rather small. Some clusters contain thousands of individual galaxies. Just as the Moon orbits the Earth, and Earth orbits the Sun and the Sun orbits the center of the galaxy, the galaxies within a cluster all orbit around a common center of gravity.

The clusters aren't scattered randomly, either. Our own Local Group is one of about fifty clusters of galaxies that make up the Local supercluster. This is sometimes called the Virgo supercluster because of the preeminence in it of the large Virgo cluster of galaxies. The Virgo Cluster, 50 million light-years away, exerts a gravitational pull on the galaxies in our local group. Our galaxy, in fact, is traveling toward the Virgo Cluster at a speed of about 150 miles per second.

Even the superclusters aren't randomly scattered across the universe. They appear to be concentrated in thin roughly spherical shells. Astronomers have likened the universe to a bubble bath, with the film of the bubbles representing superclusters of galaxies surrounding a cosmic void.

While the concentration of gases in intergalactic space — whether between galaxies, clusters or superclusters — seems to us to be very thin, there appears to be a large amount of hot gas spread throughout it, some of it left over from the formation of the galaxies, some of it ejected from the galaxies after their formation. The temperature of this hot gas is estimated to be somewhere between 10 million and 100 million degrees F. The amount of hot gas within a cluster of galaxies may equal the amount of matter in all the stars within the galaxies of that cluster.

In addition, there is the possibility that intergalactic space is filled with dark matter — a form of matter that has never been observed, but is believed to exist because of its gravitational effects on detectable forms of matter. The presence of this dark matter would explain why there is enough gravitational attraction within clusters of galaxies to keep the hot gases from dispersing into an even more rarified form.

Cosmic Voids and Cosmic Strings

Going back to the bubble bath analogy, if the film on the bubble represents the matter contained in the galaxies, clusters, superclusters, hot gases and the hypothetical dark matter, what is *inside* the bubble?

Cosmic voids may occupy 90 percent of the space in the universe. Astronomers speculate that the voids are vaguely spherical in shape and about 100 million light-years in diameter. The wall of the cosmic voids are the superclusters and the intergalactic space between them. The largest superclusters are located where two "bubbles" meet. But the voids themselves might be almost entirely devoid of matter. The matter within the voids would have to be especially cold and dark to avoid detection by X-ray telescopes. But since cold matter clumps together efficiently, one would predict this matter to have formed galaxies, and no galaxies have been detected within the voids.

No one really knows what lies within the cosmic voids, or why they even exist. But the superclusters surrounding the voids are moving at speeds of 1 million kilometers per hour, and without the existence of any matter within the voids, there is no way to account for this motion.

A cosmic string is a hypothetical form of matter, designed in part to explain the movement of the superclusters. A cosmic string would be millions of light-years in length and very, very thin — .000000000000000000000000000001 centimeter in diameter. A linear version of a black hole (a line instead of a point), the cosmic string would be nested inside the voids, massive enough to pull all of the matter in the universe into the shape of the surrounding superclusters. The vast energies surging along the tangled loops of the cosmic string would create too much turbulence within the void to allow the cold dark matter to coalesce into galaxies.

There is no direct evidence for the existence of cosmic strings, but they do help to explain the arrangement of matter within the universe, and their movements would help explain the motion of the superclusters. SF writers have used (relatively) small superstrings to move matter in large-scale construction projects. The arthropodal cyborgs in Gregory Benford's *Tides of Light* have harnessed a cosmic string to pull precious metals from the interior of an Earthlike planet. A cosmic string is used in an attempt to provoke Betelgeuse into going supernova in Jeffrey Carver's *From a Changeling Star*.

Quasars and the Limits of the Universe

Quasars (short for "quasi-stellar object") are luminous cosmic objects (many of which are also sources of powerful radio emissions) located at the center of distant galaxies. Scientists believe that there are supermassive black holes at the center of every quasar, and that the tremendous amount of energy sent out by quasars is caused by the high velocity of the gas spiraling into the black holes. No more than a light-year or two in size, quasars are a thousand times more luminous than galaxies with diameters of 100,000 light-years and are believed to be the most energetic objects in the universe. Because of this, they can be clearly observed from great distances. The most luminous of these, called BR 1202-07, is 12 billion light-years away from Earth.

When observing BR 1202-07, scientists are actually looking 12 billion years into the past, when the light originally left the quasar. This is before the formation of the Milky Way galaxy. It is also very close to what is believed to be the birth of the universe itself. Because of their brilliance, quasars allow astronomers a detailed glimpse into the most remote periods of the universe's history.

According to the Big Bang Theory, the universe emerged from a highly compressed state about 15 billion years ago and has been expanding ever since. While gravitational attraction pulls nearby stars and galaxies together, the continuing expansion of the universe is pulling every part of space farther apart from every other. Imagine drawing a diagram of all the matter in the universe on a deflated balloon and then blowing up the balloon. As the skin of the balloon stretches, every point on the surface pulls away from the others.

Will the universe continue to expand? Or is there enough matter in the universe to slow down and stop the expansion and then, because of gravitational attraction, pull all the matter back into the primordial ball from which the universe originally came? Is there another, more plausible explanation for the formation and evolution of the universe? If your human or alien characters are products of a sophisticated spacefaring civilization, these may be important questions. Most SF writers base their vision of the universe according to the latest findings of physics, astronomy and cosmology. But how might our current models agree or disagree with those of human beings a million years from now, living on worlds in far-flung sectors of the galaxy?

For many writers, the universe is just a canvas to be filled with exotic creatures that can interact — peacefully or violently — with human beings. For others, it is a frontier that human beings, perhaps the only technological beings in the galaxy, can colonize with terraformed planets and space colonies. A single species of intelligent creatures could spend thousands of years spreading throughout the galaxy, and millions of more years evolving into completely separate types of creatures, with no memory of their common ancestry. How wide that canvas is depends on the amount of time they've been spreading their influence and whether or not they've mastered faster-than-light travel.

O

The current understanding of planet formation (see chapter 3) suggests that planets may be almost as common as stars. But the most popular planets in SF are not just any planets; they are "habitable" or "Earthlike" worlds. Such a planet has a comfortable and fairly steady temperature, tolerable air pressure, gravity that doesn't crush humans, free oxygen to breathe, water to drink and indigenous life-forms. How common planets like these are is a matter of hot debate. There is simply not enough data to be sure.

There is enough data, however, to speculate intelligently about what conditions could give rise to such planets, and to rule out some that probably could not. Many parameters are known to affect the habitability of a planet: stellar mass, distance from star, planet mass, rotation. Other parameters, such as chemical composition, tectonics, and the interaction between the planet and its life-forms, are less well understood, but worth considering. Grounding your speculation in the best available knowledge will improve the plausibility of your story—and perhaps suggest ideas you hadn't thought of before.

CHAPTER SIX
DESIGNING A
PLANET

Of course, your planet does not have to be "Earthlike." Following the principles outlined in chapter 3, your characters can terraform Marslike or Venuslike worlds orbiting distant stars. You can set up enclosed self-sustaining bases on moons vaguely like our own or Jupiter's. You can put space stations in orbit around worlds as uninhabitable as Pluto. You can also imagine organisms very different from ours evolving on planets that are very hot, very massive or lacking in oxygen. From what we know of biochemistry, such life-forms are unlikely, but they have a valid place in SF speculation. Chapter 8, "Aliens," will offer some ideas on "non-Earthlike" life.

Still, if you're like many SF writers, what you really want is a planet that humans can call home. You want a planet that is already habitable when humans get there, and that has evolved its own life-forms—possibly even sentient ones. You want it to

---

Help for Planet Builders

Designing planets is a favorite topic of SF writers and readers, along with scientists of a speculative frame of mind. Basic print sources consulted for this chapter include Stephen Dole's *Habitable Planets for Man*, Poul Anderson's article "The Creation of Imaginary Worlds" in *Writing Science Fiction and Fantasy*, and Stephen Gillett's article "On Building an Earth-like Planet" in *Analog*, July 1989.

Several software programs may also be of interest. *SimEarth: The Living Planet* (Maxis) is an Earth simulation in which you control the evolution of continents, life and civilization. It also allows you to terraform Mars and Venus. For CompuServe users with a knowledge of BASIC, a downloadable program called *Kepler* (Don Sakers, © 1988) generates habitable planets based on your inputs. It is available in Library 4 of the Model 100 Forum (GO M100SIG).

---

be different from Earth — but not so different that humans cannot stay a while. This chapter will help you build such a planet.

Hazard Warning: Common Mistakes

Before starting out to design a planet, be advised of some common pitfalls among planet-builders.

Oversimplifying. One of the most overused motifs in SF is the planet that is all jungle, or all ice, or all desert, or all one thing or another. When enough creative thought is put into it, this sort of thing can work: The desert world in Frank Herbert's *Dune* and the ocean world in Stanislaw Lem's *Solaris* are examples. But too often, such a planet design stems from lazy imagination. Jerry Pournelle describes the syndrome as "It was raining on Mongo that morning." Planets are big places; Earth includes mountains, deserts, meadows, rain forests. Why should your planet be less complex?

Picking the Wrong Star. Novice SF writers often set their stories on planets circling famous stars, such as Betelgeuse, Sirius, Vega and Rigel. The trouble is these stars are among the least likely to have Earthlike planets. What makes them famous is that they are bright — and the reason they are bright is that they are big. They are old red giants that have expanded to enormous size. During their expansion, they burned or consumed all of their inner planets. The outer planets may have warmed up, but these stars will probably die before life can evolve.

Before choosing a star for your planet, make sure it is the right kind of star to support the kind of planet you are describing. When in doubt, make up a star. With 100 billion stars in the galaxy, there is no reason to restrict yourself to the top ten.

Constellations. Beware of describing constellations as if they would look the same from any point in the galaxy. Constellations are simply the arrangements stars have when viewed from Earth. For example, from a planet orbiting our nearest stellar neighbor, Proxima Centauri (4.5 light-years away), the constellation Cassiopeia would have six bright stars instead of the five we see. The brightest star would be our own — Sol.

Incidentally, if your planet is more than about 55 light-years from Earth, don't have your characters look up in the sky at faraway Sol. From this distance, Earth's Sun would not be visible without instruments.

Multiple-Star Systems

For the sake of simplicity, this chapter will mainly concern single stars (the favorite of most SF writers). However, it is worth mentioning that some 75 percent of all stars are estimated to be part of binary or multiple-star systems. These are systems in which two or more stars orbit around a common center of mass. Opinions differ on how likely these stars are to have habitable planets. If the stars are close together, a planet could orbit both of them as though they were a single star. If the stars are widely separated, each may have its own planets. To a greater or lesser degree, the gravitation of multiple stars will complicate the orbits of any planets that do exist.

Brian Aldiss's Helliconia trilogy (*Helliconia Spring, Helliconia Summer* and *Helliconia Winter*) deals with a planet in a binary star system. The planet's orbit around its two stars takes 2,592 Earth years, during which the planet undergoes severe extremes in temperature. In reality, these extremes might make life impossible.

Much depends on the relative size of the multiple stars. If Jupiter had had fifty times more mass than it does, it would have grown hot enough to begin nuclear fusion. It would have become a red dwarf in a binary system with our Sun. Even if this had happened, it might not have affected the evolution of life on

Earth. Robert Harrington of the U.S. Naval Observatory in Washington, D.C., created a computer model that replaced Jupiter with a star the same mass as the Sun. The orbits of Mercury, Venus and Earth remained as they are, but the orbit of Mars became very unstable.

Stellar Parameters

The first thing to determine about your planet is what kind of sun it has. The sun has to be bright and hot enough to sustain life, but also stable and old enough for life to evolve. On Earth, 3.5 billion years went by before multicellular life appeared. The hottest and brightest stars, type O, burn stably for only a few million years—too brief by several orders of magnitude. After that, these blue giants explode in supernovae. You can put a planet around a blue giant, but it will either be barren or inhabited only by simple one-celled organisms, prokaryotes like algae and bacteria.

(We assume throughout this chapter that the pace of evolu-

The Centauri System

Our nearest stellar neighbors are part of a triple-star system called the *Centauri System*. Centauri A and B are medium-sized stars that revolve around each other every eighty years. Their mean separation is about 3.4 billion km, less than the separation between Neptune and the Sun. This distance represents 23 astronomical units (AU)—that is, 23 times the distance between the Earth and the Sun. The smaller third star, Centauri C (or Proxima), is separated from A and B by another 10,000 AU (1.5 trillion km). It revolves around A and B once every million years.

Centauri A is a type G2 star, about as massive, bright and yellow as our Sun. Centauri B is somewhat cooler, type K0, an orange star. Either or both A and B are massive enough to sustain a habitable planet, but Centauri C is not: it is only type M5, a red dwarf. This is too bad, because Proxima is slightly closer to us than the other two stars.

Centauri A and B, from a distance, look to the naked eye like a single star, which we traditionally call *Alpha Centauri*. As a spaceship approached, Alpha Centauri would gradually resolve into two distinct stars.

tion on other planets roughly follows that of Earth. That is the most conservative position to take, though it may be wrong. If you decide that evolution can go faster, bigger stars are open to you.)

As it turns out, the only likely candidates for Earthlike worlds are main sequence stars of spectral classes F, G and K. (For a review of spectral classes and the main sequence, see chapter 5.) Within this group, F stars will be more massive and hot, G stars medium (like our Sun), K stars smaller and cooler. The exact optimal range for life is uncertain; Stephen Dole has suggested that the limits are F2 to K1, while Poul Anderson has speculated it might be F5 to K5. (Remember that the spectral classes are a continuum in which stars decrease in temperature in a series like this: F8, F9, G0, G1.)

For main sequence stars, knowing the spectral type gives you a rough idea of the star's mass. For example, an F2 star is about 1.4 solar masses. A K1 is about 0.72 solar masses. The chart on page 117 gives estimated masses for several stars in the range F-G-K.

A star's mass ultimately determines its total energy output, or luminosity. Luminosity tells you at what distance a planet has to be to receive enough energy to sustain life. That distance, in turn, partially determines how long the planet's year will be.

It is up to you to decide how precise you want to be in figuring out your star's parameters. It may be that, for story purposes, all you want to know is whether the star is hotter than the Sun, or whether the year is longer. Or, for your own satisfaction, you may want to work out exact figures. This section will offer mathematical formulas for those with a taste for numbers. It will also state things in English for those who are content with a rough idea.

Luminosity. The star's total output of energy depends on its mass. The chart on page 117 estimates luminosities for several stellar masses in the F-G-K range.

If you want to work out the luminosity for a given star yourself, realize that for main sequence stars, luminosity (L) is roughly proportional to the star's mass (M) raised to the 3.5 power:

$$L = M^{3.5}$$

The main thing to note is that the dependence of luminosity on mass is highly sensitive. If the star is just a little heavier, its energy output goes up a lot. If the star is just a little less massive, the energy output falls rapidly. If your star is only one and a half times as massive as the Sun, it will be nearly five times as bright.

Insolation. Also called illuminance or irradiation, this is the total energy that reaches the planet. This figure depends on the star's luminosity and the planet's distance. The closer the planet is, the more energy reaches it. The farther out it is, the less energy gets there.

The chart on page 117 calculates approximate distances for planets of different stars in order for them to get exactly the insolation Earth gets. The main thing to note: If your star is bright, the planet has to be farther away. If the star is dim, the planet has to be closer.

For those who want more precision, here is how the math works. Insolation (N) is proportional to luminosity (L) and inversely proportional to the square of the distance (D):

$$N = \frac{L}{D^2}$$

This formula will tell you how far away your planet must be from its star to receive a given insolation. Let's say you want your planet to get *exactly* the insolation Earth gets. Earth's distance from its Sun is 1 astronomical unit (AU). (A common unit for measuring planetary distances, 1 AU equals about 93 million miles or 150 million km.) Its insolation (N) can also be considered 1. In that case, if you're using solar luminosities to measure luminosity:

$$N \times D^2 = L$$
$$1 \times D^2 = L$$
$$D = \sqrt{L}$$

In this case, then, *the distance of your Earthlike planet in AU will be equal to the square root of the star's luminosity.* If your planet gets 30 percent more or less insolation than Earth, then N will be respectively, 1.3 or 0.7. The planet's distance (D) will be respectively smaller or greater.

Habitable Zone. For every star, there is a region in space within which Earthlike life can evolve. This region is called the habitable zone or biozone. Within the habitable zone, surface water can

Sample Stars

To aid you in designing planets, the following chart records approximate values for several hypothetical F, G and K stars. Mass and luminosity are recorded in terms of the Sun. The Sun, a G2 star, has mass 1 and luminosity 1. The "Earth twin distance" is how far a planet would have to be from the star to receive the same insolation that Earth receives from the Sun. For a G2 star, the distance is 1 AU.

You can use this chart to determine roughly what kind of parameters any star in this range would have. For example, an F7 star would be somewhere between 1 and 1.3 solar masses, closer to 1.3.

Spectral Class	Color	Mass	Luminosity	Earth Twin Distance (AU)
F0	Blue to white (Hot)	1.5	4.8	2.19
F5	Blue to white (Hot)	1.3	2.3	1.5
G2	White to yellow (Medium)	1.0	1.0	1.0
G5	White to yellow (Medium)	0.91	0.7	0.84
K0	Orange to red (Cool)	0.74	0.3	0.55
K5	Orange to red (Cool)	0.54	0.1	0.32

exist in a liquid state and temperatures will not become too extreme. On planets too close to the star, water vapor will never condense into oceans. On planets too far away, ice will never melt into liquid water. The presence of surface water is believed to be critical to the evolution of life.

No one knows exactly how big the habitable zone might be. Temperatures on a planet's surface are not easy things to predict. They are generally warmer at the equator and colder at the poles. Temperatures are moderated by such factors as atmosphere, length of day and year, and axial tilt. (These topics are discussed below.)

Taking everything into consideration, Dole suggests that a

star system's habitable zone is the region within which insolation (N) gets no lower than 0.65 Earth-normal, and no higher than 1.9 Earth-normal. In the case of our solar system, the outer limit would be 1.24 AU (about halfway between Earth and Mars), and the inner limit 0.725 AU (a little farther from the Sun than Venus). You may decide that the insolation limits are wider, but, realistically, you cannot make them much wider.

Planets on the outer edge of the zone will generally be glacial places, with habitable areas restricted to the equator. Planets on the inner edge will be hot places, with habitable areas in the middle latitudes only. For example, on an Earth-sized planet getting 30 percent more sunlight than Earth, the equatorial regions would be unbearably hot, barren deserts most of the year. But life could evolve in two narrow bands occupying latitudes 51°-66° N. and S. In each of these cooler bands, creatures would evolve separately from the other band, becoming very different from each other in the process.

If you are so inclined, you can calculate exactly what the habitable zone is for a given star. For example, to get the outer limit (D) for a star of 2 solar luminosities (L), let insolation (N) equal Dole's suggested limit of 0.65 Earth-normal. Then:

$$D^2 = \frac{L}{N}$$

$$D^2 = \frac{2}{0.65}$$

$$D^2 = 3.077$$

$$D = \sqrt{3.077}$$

$$D = 1.754$$

This star's habitable zone stretches 1.75 AU into space — well past the orbit of Mars.

Stellar Appearance. How big will the sun look in your alien planet's sky? About as big as our Sun, if you follow the lead proposed so far. True, F stars are somewhat more massive than G and K stars, but a main sequence star's radius tends to vary only slightly in relation to its mass. An F star is much brighter than a K star, but not much bigger.

Of course, your habitable planet orbiting an F star may be as much as six times as far away as a habitable planet orbiting a K star. That means the distant, bright F star will be somewhat smaller in the sky than the nearby, dim K star. The difference is subtle, and when the star is high in the sky, you won't notice it much — who looks straight at the sun anyway? But at sunset, the F star would look strangely tiny and white on the horizon, the K star bloated and red.

Sunsets and sunrises would be subtly altered in color. Our yellow sun sets the tone for the reds and oranges of dusk and dawn. How would a white sun look at sunset? Or an orange sun? During the day, how would each sun quietly affect the hues of mornings and afternoons? Shadows on an F planet would tend to be sharp-edged and bluish. Shadows on a K planet would tend to be soft-edged and reddish.

Incidentally, F stars are more active in the UV range than smaller stars, and have more solar flares. Colonists on an F planet would have to guard more against sunburn and skin cancer, and might have more trouble with radio interference from violent solar flares.

Life Span. Generally, the more massive stars will burn themselves out faster than the less massive ones. An F5 star might last only 5.4 billion years, while a G8 will last 20 billion (our G2 sun is expected to last 10 billion). In any case, there is plenty of time for life to evolve. But F star inhabitants are more likely to face the death of their sun relatively soon after evolving to sentience. And F stars will be relatively rarer than G and K stars, since they last a shorter time.

Year. A planet's year is its orbital period — that is, its period of revolution around its sun. The length of the year is determined by two things: the mass of the star and the planet's distance from the star. A more massive star exerts more gravity, and therefore its planets have faster orbits and shorter years. But a more distant planet has a bigger orbit to travel, and therefore takes longer to make its rounds.

Of the two, the more significant factor is the distance. A planet faraway from an F star, for example, will have a longer year than Earth's by roughly the same factor as it is more distant than Earth. Figure then, that if your planet is 1.3 AU from its F sun, its year might be about 1.3 Earth years. A planet 0.3 AU from its K sun might have a period of about 4 Earth months.

These figures are only approximations. If you want to do the math, this is the formula you need, where Y = planet's year in Earth years, D = distance in AU, and M = star's mass in solar masses:

$$Y = \frac{\sqrt{D^3}}{\sqrt{M}}$$

This formula assumes that your planet's orbit is nearly circular, as Earth's is. If you want to have a planet with a very eccentric orbit — where it swings way out half the year, then veers close to the sun on its return — you will have trouble making it habitable. Such a planet would be scorched half the year and frozen the rest. On planets with a nearly circular orbit, the axial tilt is much more important than the orbital eccentricity in determining seasons. That takes us to the next subject: the parameters of the planet itself, as opposed to its sun.

Planetary Parameters

So far, this chapter has concentrated on defining your planet's sun, and the planet's orbit around the sun. Now we turn to the planet itself. How big is it? How dense? What is its gravity? How fast does it rotate? What are the seasons like, the atmosphere, the temperatures?

These questions lead easily to speculations about native inhabitants: for example, what would be the sleep cycle and metabolic rate of a native of a planet with a 100-hour rotation? For the most part, these questions will be reserved for chapter 8, "Aliens." This chapter deals mainly with the planet itself.

Gravity. The first thing you will want to know about your planet is its gravity in relation to Earth. How high can g forces get without crushing any life-forms that evolve? How low can they get and still allow the planet to retain oceans and an atmosphere?

Once again, the exact figures are open to speculation. Dole has suggested the range for habitable planets might be 0.68 g (g = 1 Earth gravity) at the "light" end to 1.5 g at the "heavy" end. On the heaviest planet, a person who weighed 150 pounds on Earth would weigh 225 pounds. On the lightest, the same person would weigh only 102 pounds.

Either of these conditions would present inconveniences. On

Stars to Call Home

Here is a list of known stars in the F-G-K range that are within 20 light-years of Earth and could have habitable planets. In your future world, Terran starship planners may well target them for visits.

Star	Distance From Earth (Light-years)	Spectral Type
Alpha Centauri A	4.3	G4
Alpha Centauri B	4.3	K1
Epsilon Eridani	10.8	K2
Tau Ceti	12.2	G8
70 Ophiuchi A	17.3	K1
Eta Cassiopeiae A	18.0	F9
Sigma Draconis	18.2	G9
36 Ophiuchi A	18.2	K2
36 Ophiuchi B	18.2	K1
HR 7703 A	18.6	K2
Delta Pavonis	19.2	G7

the low-g world, the atmosphere would be thin, and human colonists would have to adapt to breathing it. They would jump higher, fall more gently, and be subject to less muscular stress than on Earth. They would look younger longer. But they might also face a planet with a weaker magnetic field (see below), and therefore more radiation from cosmic rays and solar flares.

On a high-g world, colonists would have to develop thick, strong muscles. Fat would be even more of a burden than it is on Earth. The air would be denser, and might even seem "soupy" at first. Sagging faces would make people look older faster. Accidents would multiply, because falling, or getting hit by a falling object, would happen faster and harder.

The two planets would look different. On the high-gravity world, mountains would be shorter. Rain and rivers would erode the land more quickly, smoothing out rough edges. The oceans would be calmer and more extensive, with lower wave heights. The atmosphere would be drier, because evaporation would happen more slowly. Water would take longer to boil. Clouds would hang lower in the sky.

Reverse these characteristics for a low-gravity world. There would be higher mountains, rougher land features, bigger continents, smaller oceans. Water would evaporate and boil quickly; the air would tend to be humid. Air pressure would tend to drop more slowly in relation to altitude (you might be able to breathe even on the tops of high mountains). Planes could fly higher with smaller wings, while planes on a high-g world would need larger wings.

Mass and Radius. Assuming the planet is roughly spherical, its gravity is determined by two things: its mass and its radius. The more massive the planet, the stronger its gravitational pull. The smaller its radius, the more strongly it will pull the objects at the surface. (For information on how to calculate gravity from mass and radius, see "Gravity From a Mathematical Perspective," page 123.)

Dole's suggested limits for an Earthlike world are 0.4 Earth masses to 2.35 Earth masses. These limits may be adjustable if you vary the planet's radius, taking the surface closer or farther from the center, and thus altering the gravity. This amounts to changing the planet's density: its mass per unit of volume.

Density. Density for habitable planets is largely determined by chemical composition: the ratio of heavy elements (such as nickel, iron, uranium) to lighter elements (aluminum, calcium, silicon and carbon, as well as gaseous elements like oxygen). This, in turn, is largely determined by interstellar abundances: whatever elements were around in the cloud of gas and dust that formed the star system. These abundances may vary a great deal, so you can feel free to design a planet that is very rich (or poor) in heavy metals, carbon, whatever.

Density gives you one more parameter to play with. You can design an enormous but loosely packed world, poor in heavy metals — and it may have the same gravity as a small dense world rich in heavy metals. Your less dense world will have bigger, taller continents. Natives might never leave the stone age, since metals will be rare. Jack Vance's *Big Planet* is about a large world poor in metals.

On a small dense planet, there will be more radioactive material fueling the engines of tectonics, the planet-building processes that result in earthquakes, volcanoes and high mountains. Radioactivity will lead to a higher mutation rate, which will speed evolution, and natives might come sooner to an understanding

---

Gravity From a Mathematical Perspective

Mass, radius, gravity and density are all interrelated. You can calculate gravity and density if you know mass and radius. You can also calculate gravity if you know only density and radius. (Note: All of the following formulas depend on using Earth values as units of measurement: Earth gravity, mass, density and radius.)

A planet's surface gravity (G) is proportional to its mass (M) and inversely proportional to the square of its radius (r^2). In other words, $G = M/r^2$. A planet with a mass 2.7 times Earth's, and a radius one and a half times that of Earth, will have a gravity 1.2 times that of Earth.

A planet's density (d) is proportional to its mass (M) and inversely proportional to the cube of its radius (r^3). Hence, if you know only mass and radius and want to know the density, use this formula: $d = M/r^3$. The planet mentioned above would have a density 0.8 that of Earth.

A planet's surface gravity (G) is proportional to the product of its density (d) and its radius (r). In other words, $G = dr$. A planet 0.8 times as dense as Earth, with a radius 1.5 times that of Earth, has a gravity of 1.2.

---

of nuclear science. Your less dense world, by contrast, will have less tectonic activity—an outcome that can be hazardous to its ability to sustain life (see "The Interior" later in this chapter).

Rotation. Any planet rotates on its axis, and the period of rotation is its day. As far as we know, period of rotation is not related to year (period of revolution). It is related somewhat weakly to the planet's mass: The massive gas giants Jupiter and Saturn have ten-hour days, while Earth's is twenty-four hours. But among terrestrial planets (small, rocky worlds like Earth, Mars and Venus), there is no clear relation between mass and rotation. Feel free, then, to make up a day for your planet independent of other attributes.

One thing to note: If your planet has an Earthlike atmosphere, a very slow day will result in sharp extremes of temperature from day to night. During a night that lasts 100 Earth days, the night-side of the planet will become unbearably cold, while on the day-side, the high temperatures will cook away any organisms that try to evolve. As night turns to day, the two sides will each experience the opposite horrors. Wind speeds will also be affected by very slow or fast rotation; see "Climate and Weather."

Dole suggests 96 hours as an outer limit: four times as long as an Earth day. Things will get unpleasant at high noon and in the middle of the night, but not unbearable. On an average day in the habitable regions, the temperature might drop to the teens (°F) at night, and rise above 100° F during the day.

Oblation. If your planet's day is shorter than Earth's, temperature variation from day to night will be less pronounced than on Earth. But a very short day means a high rotation, which will tend to flatten the planet — that is, make it more oblate. If a planet with the mass of Earth has a day only three hours long, it will be considerably thicker at the equator than at the poles. Gravity will alter noticeably with latitude; it would be lowest at the equator (where the radius is longest), and grow higher as one journeyed toward the poles. Hal Clement's planet Mesklin in *Mission of Gravity* has been crushed by its high period of rotation (eighteen minutes) into a lozenge shape, with wildly varying gravity from equator to poles.

Magnetic Field. A planet's magnetic field appears to be generated both by its rotation and by the presence of a molten iron core. (The core is made hot by compression, and so is related both to mass and density.) It is possible that a light planet, or one with slow rotation, would have a weak or nonexistent magnetic field. A dense fast-spinning planet would have a strong magnetic field. The magnetic field on Earth helps to keep out dangerous solar-wind particles and cosmic rays. What would life be like on a planet wihout this protection?

Axial Tilt. The tilt of a planet on its axis is what mainly produces its seasons. Earth's equator is tilted about 23.5 degrees from the plane of the planet's orbit around the Sun. Winter comes to the northern or southern hemisphere when it is slanted farther from the sun; as the planet proceeds in its orbit, that hemisphere comes to be slanted closer to the sun, resulting in summer.

Axial tilt is up to you. Slant your planet more than Earth, and the seasons will be more extreme. Slant it less, and seasons will be milder. Other factors will also play a part. For example, a very long year means a longer winter and summer, which gives each hemisphere more time, respectively, to freeze and cook. On a planet with extreme seasons, one might expect annual floods from melting snow, followed by drought, forest fires and rapid cooling. Extreme seasons would also lead to more violent storms and hurricanes (see "Climate and Weather").

The most extreme case would be a planet with a 90 degree axial tilt, where the northern hemisphere is completely in shadow during the winter, then constantly in sunlight during the summer. The equator would receive the same weak, constant illumination year-round. Such a planet could probably not support life, but would be interesting to visit. At the other extreme is a planet with no axial tilt, and therefore no seasons. Oddly, such a planet might be more arid than Earth, since there would be no annual snow melt, which is crucial in providing fresh water during the summer in Earth's temperate zones.

If the planet has no axial tilt, seasons could still be provided by an eccentric orbit. The planet would be hotter when it was closer to the sun, colder when it was farther. Then the entire planet would undergo the same season at the same time — though, as on Earth, it would always be warmer at the equator than at the poles.

Moons, Rings and Tides. You decide whether to give your planet satellites or not. Earth has one fair-sized moon; Mars has two tiny ones; Venus has none. If you are describing a terrestrial planet, however, beware of peppering its sky with lots of moons. Their gravitational effects on each other, and effects from the sun and other planets, will eventually pull such moons away. Very massive planets far from the Sun, like Jupiter, can keep a large number of moons.

How far from the planet surface will the satellite be? It can't be too far out, or the planet's gravitation will not be able to hold it. It can't be too close, or the satellite will break up because of tidal forces (unequal gravitational pull between the near and far sides of an object).

This inner boundary is called Roche's limit. For Earthlike worlds, the limit is about 2.5 radii from the planet center, or about 1.5 radii from the surface. Your planet, like Saturn, may have a ring of dust and rock within Roche's limit — the remnants of a moon that got too close, or one that never formed.

The satellite will exert tidal forces on the planet, resulting in ocean tides. If the satellite is nearer or bigger than our Moon, the tides will be higher. (The sun will also raise tides to a greater or lesser degree depending on the planet's distance and the sun's mass.) Tidal braking will probably force your moon to present only one side to the planet at all times, just as our Moon does. Tides will also slow your planet's rotation.

The moon's apparent path in the sky is a complicated issue, involving the moon's actual period of revolution (determined largely by the planet's mass and the moon's distance) and how that period relates to the planet's daily rotation. Unless you want to work it out exactly (starting with a good astronomy text on our Moon), keep this matter vague. Your moon will have phases, waxing as it circles to the side of the planet farther from the sun, waning as it circles to the side nearer the sun.

Most likely, your moon, like Earth's, will orbit near the plane of the planet's equator, in the same direction as the planet's rotation. However, varying these parameters may result in some interesting effects.

How big will your satellite look in the sky? The apparent diameter will be roughly equal to its actual diameter compared to our Moon, divided by its distance from the planet surface compared to our Moon.

Advanced Planetology

You now know the basic astronomical parameters for designing a habitable planet. But planets are complicated systems. A great many factors go into determining actual conditions on the surface — perhaps more factors than anyone can ever know. These involve the air (atmosphere), the oceans (hydrosphere), the rocky interior (lithosphere), and the action of living things (biosphere). These four systems are interrelated, all contributing to a planet's climate, history and habitability.

The rest of this chapter will touch on some important aspects of these topics for planet designers. The treatment is far from exhaustive; further reading in Earth science and planetary science is advised if you are serious about planet designing. But this chapter will suggest possible ways to begin fine-tuning your planet.

Atmosphere

If you want humans to breathe freely, you will need an air composition something like Earth's: 78 percent nitrogen, 21 percent oxygen, 1 percent argon, carbon dioxide and other gases. Water vapor, sulfur compounds and dust particles will also be present to varying degrees.

The air pressure has to be in some such range as 0.8 to 1.2 Earth normal to be easily breathable; if you push the limits, some humans may need respirators at least part of the time to breathe. Air pressure will vary with altitude, especially on high-gravity worlds. On some worlds, bearable air pressure might be found only in deep canyons or high mountains.

Primitive atmospheres for Earthlike worlds will be largely the result of outgassing from the planet's interior. The traditional view is that these atmospheres will consist of compounds like methane, ammonia, carbon dioxide and water vapor. Some scientists, however, now think that nitrogen and carbon dioxide are more likely to be the main components. The issue is not yet resolved, but in either case, these are not atmospheres your human travelers will be able to breathe. If algae evolve, and use the sun's energy to make food through photosynthesis, they will extract the carbon dioxide and produce the oxygen you need after several billion years.

There are several subtleties here. If the oxygen content is too high — say, more than 30 percent — the air will be highly flammable and corrosive. Even damp vegetation will tend to catch fire. (The native life-forms might evolve a flame retardant skin, perhaps including halogen compounds.) If the carbon dioxide level is too high, your planet will experience a marked greenhouse effect — with the atmosphere growing warmer as carbon dioxide, water vapor and sulfur compounds act to trap heat. The planet may get too hot for oceans to survive or life to evolve — and will finally be as hot and uninhabitable as Venus. A runaway greenhouse effect is more likely if, like Venus, the planet is close to the sun and has enough gravity to keep a sizable atmosphere.

Note that the greenhouse effect does not have to be a bad thing. A planet far from its sun will benefit by being massive enough to have a greenhouse effect to help keep it warm. Some have suggested that if Mars and Venus had swapped orbits, both might be habitable.

Oceans

Oceans of water, with dissolved gases and minerals, are important for many reasons. Earthlike life requires this environment to evolve. Oceans moderate the climate by storing heat and circulating it through currents. Ocean water may keep the upper layer of the Earth's mantle lubricated, allowing plate tectonics (see below).

Oceans are also involved in the carbonate-silicate cycle, which helps keep carbon dioxide levels in equilibrium. In this process, carbon dioxide dissolves in water, then reacts with calcium from silicate rocks to make calcium carbonate — limestone. The limestone locks up the carbon dioxide, keeping it from building up in the atmosphere and preventing a runaway greenhouse effect. Aquatic life-forms contribute to the same process, using dissolved carbon dioxide and calcium to form shells and reefs.

Oceans, then, are good things to have. Your planet will get the necessary water as a result of volcanic outgassing, and perhaps also from impacts of ice-bearing comets. Water vapor will collect in the atmosphere until the planet cools enough for the vapor to condense into clouds. Rain from those clouds will form the oceans.

Whether your planet keeps its water depends partly on its gravity, and partly on whether the atmosphere ever gets cold enough for the water vapor to condense. If so, the atmosphere is said to act as a cold trap. If the air remains too hot, look for a runaway greenhouse effect and no oceans.

The salinity of your oceans will depend on how much chlorine is in the neighborhood when the star system forms. Very salty water evaporates more slowly, and might be easier for a low-gravity world to hold onto. Fresh water will come as seawater evaporates, clouds form, and rain pours onto continents, forming rivers and lakes (the evaporation-condensation-precipitation cycle). Just as on Earth, some aquatic organisms on your planet will require saltwater bodies, some freshwater.

Your planet's sea level is for you to decide. On Earth, it has varied widely throughout the planet's history. You may decide to have large continental landmasses like those on Earth — or chains of small islands peppering a world ocean. In any case, the oceans will probably dominate, as they do on Earth, where they cover two-thirds of the surface. Continents and islands are bodies of land that manage to rise higher than the sea. Just how high they can rise depends on the planet's internal forces.

The Interior

Like Earth, your habitable planet's interior will probably include a molten core of heavy metals, a mantle of silicate rocks, and a relatively thin crust of lighter materials. The crust may support continents — large structures of light rocks, such as granite, that manage to rise above sea level.

The land surface will tend to be rocky or sandy, until generations of living things produce a layer of topsoil in some areas. The peculiar richness of topsoil results from its combination of organic matter with moisture, air and inorganic nutrients.

The planet's interior layers will have been differentiated early in its history, when much of the planet was in a molten state and lighter materials floated to the top. But it will not be perfectly differentiated. Small quantities of heavy metals like iron, gold and uranium will be found even near the surface.

The most important thing to know about the interior is that it radiates heat. Much of the heat near the surface comes from the decay of radioactive rocks in the mantle. The heat will rise to the surface by a process called convection — the transfer of heat by the movement of hot materials into colder areas. Convection is influenced by gravity: The hotter materials are less dense, and therefore rise to the top. Inside the mantle, molten rock (magma) will tend to rise toward the surface, where it will produce new crust.

These forces are tectonic: They build and destroy crust. On Earth, and perhaps on your planet, the forces will take the form of plate tectonics. On such a planet, the crust is broken into structures called plates, which float on the molten layer below. Some of the plates support parts of the ocean floor; some (continental plates) support continents. Tectonic forces operate at the boundaries between plates, pushing them apart, driving them together, grating them against each other.

A diverging boundary occurs where crust is created, pushing plates apart. Here undersea ridges will form; if the boundary is under a continent, rift valleys will be created and continents may split into pieces. A converging boundary (or subduction zone) occurs where one plate is pushed underneath another. Here undersea trenches form, or (on land) mountain chains like the Andes and the Himalayas. At a neutral boundary, one plate slides along another. Here (as at the San Andreas fault) earthquakes will occur.

On a planet with high tectonic activity (a dense, massive one with high radioactivity), expect volcanoes, earthquakes, high mountains, and over long ages, the movement of continents. On a less active planet, continents will flatten and seas will be shallower. Tectonics may be vital to the evolution of life, because it keeps the crust stirred up, raising nutrient minerals, water vapor and other valuable substances.

Younger planets will generally have more tectonics than older ones, because there are more radioactive materials that have not yet decayed. On any Earthlike planet, the forces building up mountains will be balanced by wind and water forces eroding them.

Climate and Weather

Weather refers to day-to-day atmospheric conditions; climate to long-term patterns. Both of these topics are among the least predictable of planetary attributes and the most open to speculation. You will have to decide your planet's average temperatures, humidity, cloud cover, winds, precipitation (rain, snow, hail) — as well as the extremes these conditions can reach in particular regions. All we can do here is sketch a few factors to consider.

Unequal Heating. Different regions of your planet will have different climates because they get more or less of the sun's heat. Given a small to moderate axial tilt, the tropics, or equatorial zone, will receive more insolation per unit of area, and therefore be warmer. The poles will receive the least insolation, and the middle latitudes (on Earth called the temperate zones) a middle range. Wind and ocean currents will moderate the surface variations in climate.

It is important to note that insolation and axial tilt vary over time. A given region of your planet may be habitable during some eras, and inhospitably hot, cold, wet or dry during others. Likewise, the habitable zone for each planet will differ depending on factors like total insolation and axial tilt. On a planet with high insolation, the equator will be too hot for life; on a world with low insolation, *only* the equator will be warm enough for life. Altitude can also affect climate. Perhaps life will be concentrated on mountain peaks (where it is cooler) or around seacoasts (where it is warmer).

Winds. Winds arise principally because the air in the tropics is warmer than the poles. Because of convection, warm equatorial air rises and moves toward the poles, while cool polar air sinks and moves toward the equator. Thus, winds help moderate temperatures across the surface of the planet.

Why don't winds blow directly north and south? Because the planet's rotation generates a Coriolis effect. The tropics of any planet rotate faster than higher latitudes, because a spot on the equator has farther to travel in a given day than a spot near one of the poles. That means the air near the equator is traveling eastward at a faster rate than does air near the poles. As currents move north and south, this unequal eastward velocity results in winds that appear to be deflected either eastward or westward (hence "easterly" and "westerly" winds). The Coriolis effect also leads to the spiraling rotation of winds around a low pressure area, which results in the destructive power of hurricanes and tornadoes.

On a planet with high rotation, the Coriolis effect will whip winds to higher speeds and generate more violent hurricanes. Other factors may also lead to more violent weather on your planet. A planet with very slow rotation, or with extreme seasons, will experience high winds and fierce hurricanes as warm air moves from the hot side of the planet to the cold side.

Ocean Currents. Even as winds carry warm air into colder areas, surface ocean currents carry warm water from the equator toward the poles. Meanwhile, cold polar water, which is denser, sinks under the warm surface water and flows toward the tropics. Ocean currents, like winds, will be stronger depending on rotation and temperature extremes.

The ocean and the atmosphere interact to affect weather. Ocean currents carry warmth from the equator toward the poles, warming the air above them as they travel. The wind blowing over the ocean removes water vapor from the surface, which condenses to form clouds, then precipitates to form snow and rain. Rivers and groundwater eventually return the water to the sea.

The most dramatic rainstorms, thunderstorms, occur when convection causes warm, moist air to rise, leading to instability at higher altitudes and the development of a very tall cloud called a cumulonimbus. Thunder and lightning occur when ionization causes electrical charges to build up in the cloud. If some regions of your planet get very hot (and have enough moisture), violent thunderstorms will arise. Your planet may also have taller thunderclouds, and more powerful lightning, if the gravity is low, allowing the troposphere — the region where weather occurs — to rise to higher levels.

Suspended Particles. Clouds are essentially masses of water droplets or ice crystals. They form in the presence of condensation nuclei — particles of volcanic ash, dust, smoke or salt. If your planet is heavy with such particles, your skies will be cloudier. If the particles are heavy in compounds like sulfuric acid (whether natural or industrial in origin), your lakes will suffer from acid rain, which inhibits life.

Clouds of water or ice affect climate by changing the planet's albedo. Albedo is how much light the planet reflects, compared to how much light it receives. White clouds have a high albedo and tend to reflect sunlight; they therefore cool the planet. This is balanced by the fact that water vapor is a greenhouse gas and traps heat.

Suspended particles of soot, dust, ash — whether from volcanic eruptions, natural fires, industry or war — can cut down the amount of sunlight a planet receives, also cooling the planet. This may be harmful to a planet that needs all the heat it can get — but it can help a planet that is too close to a hot star and needs to be cooler.

Ice Caps and Ice Ages. A planet's ice caps form because the poles do not receive enough heat to melt the ice that accumulates in winter. The ice caps can recede (and even vanish) during periods of global warming. They can advance when the planet cools, even covering most of the planet's surface with ice. Such ice ages may last for long eras; their precise causes will have to do with long-term variations in the planet's orbit and axial tilt, leading to changes in insolation patterns. On Earth, past ice ages lasted for tens of thousands of years, and occurred every few hundred million years.

All other things being equal, a planet with ice caps will be cooler than one without, because ice raises a planet's total albedo. If the glaciers advance to cover the entire planet, the total albedo may be so high that the ice will never melt. Such a planet has experienced runaway glaciation.

This chapter gives you an idea of the many factors that go into designing a planet. Bear in mind that a planet is not a loose collection of such "factors," but a complex entity in which all of the factors interrelate to produce a more or less stable picture called "equilibrium." The planet's state of equilibrium varies over time, and conditions vary from region to region. Feel free to draw maps of continents and islands, imagine weather patterns, invent a natural history. The more thoroughly you imagine your planet, the more credible it will be — and the more story ideas it will suggest.

◯

As the last chapter shows, planets are complex entities. Designers of planets and their life-forms need all the help they can get. Fortunately, an example of a lifebearing planet already exists: Earth. Investigating the history of Earth's biosphere is the best preparation for imagining alternate life-forms.

This chapter begins by explaining the basic workings of evolution and ecology. It goes on to trace the history of organic life as it has interacted with earth, water and air over the course of several billion years. Your alien planet will not evolve in exactly the same way, but many of the factors that influenced Earth's life story will be acting on your planet also.

Two facts about natural history are especially helpful to the SF writer. First, Earth has looked different at various stages in its existence. If alien astronauts had arrived on Earth during its first 2.5 billion years, they would have found only barren continents and oceans scummy with algae. At other times, they would have found a planet mostly covered with glaciers, a planet with a single supercontinent in the middle of a world ocean, a planet with a sooty atmosphere left over from an asteroid impact.

CHAPTER SEVEN
A CASE STUDY OF A LIFEBEARING PLANET

Knowing the history of our planet gives you access to many alternate Earths — Earths that can be the basis for alien worlds. It may also inspire you to write stories of time travel to previous eras of Earth's existence. (See the section on time travel in chapter 11.)

The second fact to remember, as Stephen Jay Gould has argued, is that the history of life depends heavily on contingency. A planet's organisms evolve not randomly (for no reason at all) or deterministically (by the operation of unchangeable laws), but in response to prior conditions. Change the conditions slightly, and life will develop in different directions. Since the conditions can never be completely known or predicted, it is impossible to predict exactly how life will turn out.

This means that you can start imagining extraterrestrial life by asking *what if?* What if sexual reproduction had never evolved. What if the ancestor of vertebrates had become extinct in the

Precambrian waters, leaving only insects to inherit the land? What if the path of an asteroid had been different by a few degrees, and the dinosaurs had never died out? What if giant birds had been more successful than large mammals? What if abstract reasoning had not been tied in its origin to the emotional makeup of a primate, but to the nervous system of a very different organism?

Knowing the turns that life on this planet took can help you identify and explore the roads not taken. For more speculation on life on other planets, see chapter 8, "Aliens."

Evolution: The Basics

The particular changes that make up the history of life are governed by contingency. But the underlying mechanism of change is governed by rules. That mechanism is evolution. To write about the history of life on Earth or elsewhere, you need a firm grasp of what evolution can and cannot do.

Descent With Modification. Evolution is in some ways an unfortunate term. It suggests a vaguely mystical process toward a glorious goal; it is often used that way by writers explaining how the spirit of mankind is "evolving" or how your marriage can "evolve." A more exact term for the mechanism of change in the history of life — a term favored by Charles Darwin in *The Origin of Species* (1859) — is "descent with modification."

All living things die, but before they die, they leave descendants. Their descendants share the parents' genes: units of inheritance that determine how the organism will develop. These are carried in molecules of a substance called DNA in the organism's cells. (For more on the biochemistry of genes, see chapter 13, "Remodeling Humans.") In species that reproduce from a single parent, such as bacteria, most descendants will have the same DNA as the parent. But random mutations, or copying errors in the DNA, will cause some to be slightly different. Mutations happen naturally at a slow pace; they can be increased by factors like radiation and some chemicals. Whatever their cause, mutations introduce variation.

In species that reproduce sexually, the pace of variation is stepped up. Half of each organism's genes come from one parent and half from the other, allowing for a virtually infinite number of distinct individuals. These variations would tend to cancel each other out, except for pressure from natural selection — environmental conditions that favor individuals with certain traits but not others. As a result, individuals with favored traits survive and reproduce, while others die out. Thus species are said to undergo modification. Over time, as a result of natural selection, whole species are modified and new species arise. A species is a group of organisms that has become so different from other groups that it cannot interbreed with them.

Natural Selection. Natural selection begins from the premise that life is tough. Creatures have to compete with each other for food and mates, do battle with (or run away from) predators, defend themselves from disease, survive during famine and drought, and make sure that their young survive childhood. The individuals that survive this process of natural selection are those best adapted, or fitted, to the conditions in the region in which they live.

Here evolutionary science meets ecology, the study of the interactions between organisms and their environment.

Basic Ecology. When all of the life-forms and physical aspects of a given area are considered as a whole, they are called an ecosystem. Every creature draws nourishment from its ecosystem, faces dangers, and interacts with other creatures. The particular place of an organism in its environment is called its ecological niche.

There are only a limited number of niches in a given ecosystem. Some creatures will be producers of energy (the green plants); some will eat the plants (the herbivores or primary consumers); some will eat the eaters (the secondary consumers, including predators, parasites and scavengers). Finally, some creatures, the decomposers (such as bacteria and fungi), take apart organisms that have died. These levels of the food chain are called trophic levels. (The entire set of interrelated food chains in an ecosystem is called a food web.)

The number of creatures that can survive at each trophic level is limited by how much energy is available at lower levels. Generally, the higher up you go, the fewer organisms can be supported. That is because a lot of energy (up to 90 percent) is wasted at each step in the process of converting sunlight to plants, plants to beef, and beef to carnivore flesh.

The Struggle for Survival. Individuals struggle to fill the niches in the ecosystem. Individuals of the same species compete hardest with each other, but migration may bring two species into competition for the same niche. Competition of any kind is a powerful spur to evolve or exploit adaptations. So is any change in the ecosystem — such as a drop in the temperature or rainfall — that alters the delicate balance by which local populations of a given species are maintained.

Individuals of a species also compete for the right to reproduce. They may compete by bullying other suitors out of the way; they may also undergo sexual selection. In this process, creatures choose their mates on the basis of physical characteristics that seem attractive to them (bright feathers, long tails, loud calls, big biceps). As individuals with attractive traits are selected, the whole species tends to be modified in that direction.

As a population becomes too large for a region to support, it tends to spread out in search of greener pastures. As a species evolves into many different forms to exploit new food sources and habitats, it is said to undergo adaptive radiation. Mammals have had a spectacular adaptive radiation, making the most of diverse niches as they evolved into moles, rats, bats, whales, lions, antelopes and humans.

These principles of evolution and ecology will be useful to you when designing alien life-forms. What environmental changes spurred your alien species to evolve the way they did? Are all of the available niches in the food web being exploited? How do all of the species together manage to stay in equilibrium? How do all your scary predators survive when their only prey organisms seem to be visiting astronauts?

Common Mistakes

Stories about evolution are subject to a number of errors that are easy to avoid. First, it is wrong science to suppose that the ancestor of giraffes stretched its neck trying to reach a tree, then passed the stretched neck on to its children. If this were so, men who are circumcised would father sons without foreskins — a situation clearly in the realm of fantasy, not science fiction. Natural selection favors only characteristics that already exist in the genes — not acquired characteristics.

It is also wrong science to suppose that giraffes evolved long necks because long necks represent the ultimate goal of evolution. By the same principle, it is wrong to suggest that evolution tends toward the emergence of intelligence. Natural selection is a process of nature, with neither mind nor intent. It favors individuals better adapted to their present time and place, not necessarily those more complex or intelligent. Cockroaches are well suited to their environment; eagles to theirs. Intelligence evolved in humans not so that they could one day produce Aristotle and Mozart, but so their ancestors could survive more efficiently on the African savannah.

As a corollary, it is wrong science to think that evolution must represent progress. From a scientific perspective, it is only the history of life-forms adapting to (and altering) their environments. Humanity represents a step forward only in the context of human belief. To the organisms that decompose our bodies after death, humanity represents food.

An Evolution Toolkit

To aid you in designing evolutionary pathways for your alien creatures, here are some of the basic tools used by evolution on our planet. The trick is to speculate about how they would apply on your world.

Time. Evolutionary change requires many generations. The time scale for the evolution of new species is in the hundreds-of-thousands to millions of years. The exact pace of evolution is disputed. According to gradualism, evolution happens at a more or less constant, gradual pace. According to the theory of punctuated equilibrium, a planet's species spend most of their existence in relative stasis, punctuated by short bursts of rapid evolution. These bursts typically follow decimations, catastrophic changes in environment that wipe out many species, leaving the survivors to diversify and fill the available niches.

Changing Environment. Whether catastrophic or gradual, global or regional, environmental change is what will spell extinction for some species on your planet, adaptation and success for others. The factors that can change include sunlight, rainfall, ocean salinity, soil content, invading species and much more.

Geographic Separation and Union. As populations of a species get separated (because of migration or the movement of continental plates), they will tend to diverge over time into different species. If a new land bridge or the creation of a super continent brings long separated species together on your planet, expect extinctions and rapid change as they try to adjust to one another's company.

Isolation. Some ecosystems on your planet will develop odd communities because of their isolation from other regions. Because Australia has been long disconnected from the Eurasian land mass, its marsupials managed to fill most of the niches filled by placental mammals elsewhere. Isolated island chains like the Galapagos, formed late in the planet's history by volcanic activity, will be populated only by creatures who can fly, swim or float there.

Convergence. Species on your planet will resemble Earth species insofar as they fill similar niches. When land mammals on Earth started to exploit the sea, they came to evolve some of the same streamlined features as fish. However, the convergence is only superficial. It is impossible for species long separated (like whales and fish) or never linked (like extraterrestrials and humans) to ever become genetically identical.

Imperfection. Don't imagine that every species is perfectly suited to be what it is. The only way evolution can take place is if every species is more or less imperfect. You could probably design better means of walking erect than the lower back and knee of a human. But these shaky structures evolved from what our ancestors had to work with — ancestors who did not know that their children would one day be asked to walk on two feet. Your alien creatures will be more authentic if they too have jury-rigged parts that point to the ad hoc nature of evolution.

Vestiges. As organisms evolve new structures, some old body parts will become useless. Evolution tends to reduce or eliminate these. Vestigial structures like our appendix and coccyx (or tailbone) are remnants of parts that were useful to our ancestors, though no longer to us.

Common Ancestry. However much creatures evolve, they will show signs of their descent from earlier species. The genes of each species will be more or less shared with those of related species, depending on how long it has been since their ancestors diverged. The human skeleton betrays family ties to all other vertebrates — fish, frogs, chickens, mice. The mitochondria in our cells links us even further back, to Precambrian bacteria. Your alien creatures will show a similar family tree — one that has different roots and branches from ours.

Adaptability and Redundancy. For evolution to happen,

creatures must have adaptable parts (structures that can be adapted to serve different functions) and redundant parts (different structures that can serve the same function). Nostrils evolved originally as smelling devices to help fish detect food; only later were they adapted for use in breathing air. Lungs evolved from outcroppings of the digestive tract. While lungs and nostrils were evolving, fish continued to get oxygen from water through gills. Thus, they had redundant respiratory systems to get them through the transition from water to land.

Modularity. An organism's traits are not parts of an inseparable whole, but distinct modules that can be dissociated. Each module or unit can evolve separately from the others, at a different pace. The ancestors of humans started walking on two legs long before the brain had evolved to larger size.

Specialization. Evolution often proceeds by starting with cells or tissues that are more or less the same and specializing them to serve different functions. Neurons, muscle cells, and red blood cells are all variations on a single cell structure. Primitive organisms tend to have more generalized structures than their descendants. How different would humans be if our fingers had been specialized to serve different functions — say, the index finger as a knife, and the other fingers as sifters of fine food particles?

Segmentation and Fusion. The tissues of many creatures tend to repeat themselves in more or less identical segments — the segments of earthworms, the exoskeletal parts of insects, the bones of vertebrates. Individual segments can evolve separately as specialized modules, and segments may fuse together to form new structures. The head of a crustacean, for example, is formed from fusion of at least five ancestral segments, the "legs" of which have evolved to serve as two pairs of sensory organs and three pairs of mouth parts. The body plans of your creatures may show similar variations on a few simple structures.

Altered Developmental Timetables. Every creature's development is determined by its genes. In humans, the gene for brain cell production turns off later than in apes. Juvenile characteristics (such as playfulness and curiosity) extend late into our lives. The result is an organism that can think more and learn more. One way to imagine extraterrestrial creatures is to ask what would happen if a certain trait (a nose, emotional swings, perfect pitch, hairiness) was exaggerated in its development, or another inhibited. How could such a change help the creature to exploit its environment?

Having discussed the basic principles behind life's history, it is time to examine one case study of a lifebearing planet. Necessarily, the pace from the origin of life to the birth of humanity will be breakneck. But it may help you to speculate how your planet's life-forms can evolve in their own distinct directions.

Origins

As chapter 3 indicated, Earth was created about 4.6 BYA (billion years ago) from the accretion of planetesimals in the disk surrounding our infant sun. For several hundred million years, the force of the colliding particles kept the planet in a molten state, but by about 4 BYA the planet was cool enough for water vapor to condense into rain and oceans to begin forming. Volcanoes from internal heat were still highly active, and orbiting debris still regularly gouged craters into its surface.

Chapter 6 noted that there is controversy about the composition of Earth's early atmosphere. The traditional view is that the atmosphere was heavy in methane, ammonia, carbon dioxide and water vapor. These compounds, subjected to energy from solar UV radiation, lightning and volcanic heat, spontaneously formed molecules called amino acids, the building blocks of protein and of organic life. The amino acids rained into the ocean, forming a warm smelly soup under a cloudy sky and torrential storms.

An alternative view, now held by many scientists, is that the early atmosphere was rich in nitrogen and carbon dioxide. In such an atmosphere, production rates of amino acids and other organic compounds would have been quite low. But, according to this view, a large share of the organic compounds necessary for life could have been transported to Earth by such external sources as meteorites, comets and interplanetary dust.

However they arose, the complex molecules of amino acids gradually evolved into the proteins of living cells, perhaps in shallow tidal pools where they could concentrate underwater, protected from harmful UV radiation. By 3.5 BYA, prokaryotes had formed: simple single-celled creatures, lacking organelles or internal structures. They reproduced by dividing, making copies of the cell-building instructions coded in the chains of nucleic

The Dawn of Life

A space traveler approaching a planet like Earth during its earliest stages of life (on our world, about 3.5 BYA) would not have seen our familiar blue and white sphere. Such a planet would be a hazy brownish-red world, too cloudy to allow a good look at its surface from orbit. It is the abundance of oxygen in our modern atmosphere that bleaches the air clear and blue.

Having landed on the planet, the visitor would see a dull orange sun (similar to our modern sunset) in a pink sky. The ocean would reflect the sky in varying shades of brown.

At low tide, the visitor might find evidence of life in the form of rocky mushroom-shaped structures called stromatolites—formed from calcium carbonate secreted by colonies of cyanobacteria. In stagnant ponds the visitor might also discover matted patches of black and green bacteria.

acid called DNA. Among their number were the cyanobacteria— the blue-green algae—and the bacteria that fed on them.

The cyanobacteria lived on photosynthesis, using sunlight to convert carbon dioxide and water to oxygen. Long ages of their activity created an oxygen-rich atmosphere by about 2 BYA. Finally, by about 1.4 BYA, a new type of organism evolved: eukaryotes, single-celled creatures with organelles such as nucleus and mitochondria (amoebas and paramecia are present-day examples). The eukaryotes may have evolved from colonies of prokaryotes; mitochondria even look like whole prokaryotic organisms.

The Birth of Sex

Why does it matter that eukaryotes evolved? Because only eukaryotic cells have pairs of chromosomes (structures in the nucleus carrying DNA), and pairs of chromosomes are essential to sexual reproduction. In sexual reproduction, each of the two parents contributes one half of a complete set of chromosomes; the fusion of the two halves creates a new and unique organism. As explained earlier, sexual reproduction vastly increases variation, which allows evolution to proceed at a faster pace. It is possible that without the invention of sex, multicellular life as we know it would never have evolved.

It is all the more chilling, then, that there appears to be no reason why eukaryotes have to evolve. Three billion years — two-thirds of Earth's existence to date — went by without them. Why not five billion — in which case we would not be here? Why not ten billion — long enough for the Sun to explode before eukaryotes could evolve?

It is quite possible, then, that your space travelers will come across planets where the continents are barren of life, and only blue-green algae populate oceans, ponds and damp rock. Even if eukaryotes do evolve, the evidence is that it took another 800 million years before colonies of eukaryotes evolved into multicellular organisms.

The earliest multicellular life appeared about 600 MYA (million years ago). These organisms were soft-bodied, like seaweed and jellyfish, and were already differentiating into plants (which make their food from sunlight) and animals (which feed on other organisms). The Ediacara fauna were animals in the form of quilted mats, shaped like pancakes, ribbons and sheets. Eventually, creatures with hard mineral parts — like shells and skeletons — evolved. The rapid profusion of such creatures during the Cambrian period (570-470 MYA) is called the Cambrian explosion.

Life Abounding

Multicellular structure allows for rich diversity, as living things evolve complex organ systems to better find and process food, improve the chances of reproduction, and do all the things organisms do. On Earth, the evolution of multicellular organisms in past ages has yielded creatures utterly unlike any species now walking, flying, swimming or crawling. In fact, Stephen Jay Gould has argued, somewhat controversially, that the age of maximal disparity, or difference, in animal body plans occurred soon after multicellular life appeared — during the Cambrian period. (The Cambrian period was the first stage in the Paleozoic Era. See the "Geologic Time Scale" on page 146 for details.)

All modern phyla, or basic body plans, were represented in the waters of the Cambrian period: mollusks, jellyfish, sponges, chordates. Gould has argued that many of the creatures belonged to phyla now extinct, though other paleontologists disagree. In any case, the fauna of the Cambrian explosion as detailed by

Gould in *Wonderful Life* may provide you with inspiration for speculating about life on other worlds.

The Precambrian fauna included arthropods, a phylum that today includes crustaceans, arachnids and insects, and then included trilobites. The arthropod design of segmented body and exoskeleton has proven durable and successful: 80 percent of all known animal species today are arthropods. Also represented were primitive chordates — creatures with stiffened rods (notochords) running along their backs, joined to zigzagging bands of muscle. These wormlike creatures, the ancestors of modern vertebrates, appear to have been minor players in the Cambrian waters. They might easily have become extinct, in which case fish, amphibians, reptiles, birds, mammals and humans would never have arisen. What might have arisen in place of vertebrates would make a good starting point for designing an alien biosphere.

The End of a Period

A mass extinction occurred at the end of the Cambrian period, wiping out most of the species then living. Such extinctions appear to happen with some frequency on Earth — about every 26 million years. (They may be related to periodic bombardment by meteorites.) These decimations leave their imprint in extreme disruptions in the fossil record: layers of rock where some kinds of fossilized remains stop appearing and new ones start appearing. These disruptions are used by geologists to demarcate periods of Earth's prehistory, such as the Cambrian, Ordovician, Silurian and so on.

Your alien planet may well suffer similar decimations, and have similar geologic eras. The survivors would not be those best suited to the conditions that preceded the cataclysm, but those that, by chance, were able to endure the catastrophic change — the drop in temperature, the drop in rainfall, whatever. Those that survived would multiply and diversify in the new emptier world that followed. Survival, then, goes not only to the fittest (those best adapted to their environment) but to the luckiest (those who happen to have what is needed in times of change). Chance is a key element in Earth's evolution and will be on your planet also.

Since decimations are followed by periods of rapid evolution,

Geologic Time Scale

This chart gives the traditional sequence of geologic time intervals. Like years, months and days, these intervals are arranged in a hierarchy from largest to smallest: eras, periods and epochs. More than 85 percent of Earth's history to date took place during the Precambrian era (4.6 BYA to 0.57 BYA), largely before the advent of multicellular life.

Era	Period	Epoch	MYA (Millions of years ago)
Cenozoic	Quaternary	Holocene	
		Pleistocene	1.8
	Tertiary	Pliocene	
		Miocene	
		Oligocene	
		Eocene	
		Paleocene	65
Mesozoic	Cretaceous		136
	Jurassic		190
	Triassic		225
Paleozoic	Permian		280
	Carboniferous		345
	Devonian		395
	Silurian		440
	Ordovician		500
	Cambrian		570
Precambrian			4600

how would a planet's evolutionary pace be affected by much more frequent mass extinctions — say, every million years?

From Sea to Land

The organisms that survived the Cambrian mass extinction diversified over the last 500 million years into a variety of classes, genera and species. Among other things, they spread for the first time from the water to the land.

In the Ordovician period (500 to 430 MYA), primitive jawless fish appeared — the first known vertebrates, or animals with backbones. They flourished and evolved during the next two periods, the Silurian and Devonian (430 to 345 MYA). Some were huge armored fish with soft cartilaginous skeletons, like sharks; some, the bony fish, developed internal skeletons.

During the Silurian, plants began to move onto dry land, followed soon by arthropods — the ancestors of modern spiders, scorpions and insects. So did some bony fish known as lobe-fin fish, which had evolved to exploit shallow waters. They had primitive lungs that enabled them to breathe air for short intervals, and fins with an unusual structure of central axis and branches, which enabled them to crawl on dry land. By the late Devonian, about 350 MYA, some lobe-fins had evolved into amphibians; the fins evolved into the limbs of all the reptiles, birds and mammals that followed. On your planet, the precise skeletal structure of amphibians might be different — leading to a different body plan for all the planet's vertebrates.

Even on land, no creature escapes its aquatic origins. Land creatures, then and now, still need to bathe their cells in water for the chemical reactions of life to take place. Your blood is a system that reproduces the fluid conditions living cells have needed since the beginning of time. Alien organisms will probably resemble ours in at least that respect — or can you imagine organisms that are much drier than we are?

Mastering the Land

During the Carboniferous and Permian periods (345 to 225 MYA), both plants and animals completed their adaptations to life on dry land. Amphibians have never been fully terrestrial. Their eggs, like fish eggs, have to develop in water; their moist skin is in danger of drying out. But some of them evolved about 345 MYA into reptiles. Their eggs contained an amniotic sac that provided a portable fluid environment; their dry scaly skin kept the fluids inside from evaporating. The reptilian features — inherited by us mammals — constituted a kind of spacesuit to allow aquatic creatures to live in a hostile environment. Reptile limbs

---

Colonists of the Land

What did Earth look like in the late Devonian, when living things had just begun to make a habitat of dry land? Plant life on land consisted mostly of liverworts, flat or leafy plants with leafless capped stalks, growing close to water. There were also primitive branching plants lacking leaves and true roots, but with a vascular system to transport fluids internally. The first amphibians dwelt in moist areas: the ancestors of modern frogs and salamanders, as well as many other lines that have entirely died out. Insects were around, including some that could fly. Away from the mostly barren continents, the planet's oceans teemed with fish.

---

were also better adapted to fast locomotion on land, and reptile heart and lungs better adapted to breathing air.

At the same time, the first forests began to spread across the Earth, containing many species of trees now extinct: lycopsids with the first true roots and leaves; sphenopsids with jointed stems and whorls of leaves at each joint. Ferns and conifers also evolved. The lushness of Carboniferous forests is the source of much of today's coal. Insects also began their first great adaptive radiation during the Carboniferous.

About 225 MYA, the Permian period (and the Paleozoic era) was brought to an end by the greatest mass extinction Earth has ever endured. More than 80 percent of all of the species then living were wiped out. Those few that survived were the ancestors of all creatures now living.

Dinosaurs

Among the creatures that survived into the Mesozoic era (225 to 65 MYA) was a group of large active reptiles called therapsids. These died out by about 190 MYA, but they left behind descendants called mammals — warm-blooded creatures that feed their young with milk from mammary glands. Most of the early mammals were tiny and nocturnal, living in well-hidden niches. They had to lie low because another group had taken over the role of large land animals. The actors in this role were descended from thecodonts, a separate reptile lineage. They remain the most well-known of all prehistoric creatures: dinosaurs.

Incidentally, the role of "large land animal" is only of special significance in life's story because mammals (including humans) currently occupy that role, and we like to know who was there before us. Whoever gets this role is popularly thought of as "winning" the evolution game. Scientists, however, know that this role is insignificant in terms of the Earth's total biosphere — where the winners, in terms of number of individuals and species, are things like microorganisms, plants, insects and aquatic life. As an SF writer, you are writing for humans, who will want to know who the "large land animal" is on your planet. But you will be more true to science if you recognize how small a place these creatures will have in the planet's total biosphere.

Whatever the reasons, dinosaurs remain of endless interest to humans. The age of the dinosaurs spanned 160 MYA — more than 50 times longer than hominids have been around. They evolved in the Triassic period, flourished in the Jurassic, and reached their apex in the Cretaceous (all periods of the Mesozoic era). They radiated into many niches (plant-eaters, carnivores, scavengers); their many species ranged in size from that of a chicken to more than 100 feet long. New species are still being discovered in the fossil record, and scholarly speculation about dinosaur physiques and habits rivals anything found in science fiction.

The fact that dinosaurs are extinct has never stopped SF writers from writing about them. Countless stories, including L. Sprague de Camp's "A Gun for Dinosaur," have taken time travelers back to the Mesozoic. Arthur Conan Doyle and Edgar Rice Burroughs both had remnant populations of dinosaurs surviving in unexplored areas to the present day (an unlikely prospect better suited for fantasy than SF). Harry Harrison wrote an alternate history called *West of Eden* in which humans live side by side with dinosaurs that have never become extinct. In Michael Crichton's *Jurassic Park*, genetic engineers clone living dinosaurs from fossilized cells in the hope of exhibiting them in a theme park.

In short, there are several ways to get dinosaurs into your story, if that is what you want to do. Paleontology is a fast-changing field; to avoid outdated ideas, make sure you read up on recent research. Scientists used to imagine that sauropods — the huge, long-necked, vegetarian creatures most popularly represented by apatosaurs (brontosaurs) — were too heavy to move freely on land, and had to confine themselves to swamps. Many paleontologists now believe they were as mobile as elephants, walking on long legs with tails held high. They appear to have been herd animals, protective of their young. The herds may have migrated annually to follow the cycles of rainfall and plant regeneration. Some scientists believe that dinosaurs, unlike modern reptiles, were warm-blooded: able to maintain a constant body temperature. That issue is still debated, but you can decide one way or another in your story.

Similar reevaluations have happened for the carnivores, including everyone's favorite, Tyrannosaurus Rex, now believed to have been nimbler, faster and smarter than previously thought. But scientists have also uncovered numerous species that may be of more interest to you as an SF writer than the traditional war-horses. Starting with a little-known human-sized carnivore called velociraptor, Crichton in *Jurassic Park* created a terrifying picture of fierce, agile, pack-hunting predators as intelligent as chimpanzees. The hints that fossils drop may provide the material for wonderful science fiction—whether you are writing about dinosaurs or speculating about alien species.

After the Dinosaurs

The dinosaurs vanished about 65 million years ago in the extinction that ended the Mesozoic era and began the Cenozoic. More than two-thirds of Earth's species died with them. There is evidence that the primary cause of this decimation was Earth's collision with an asteroid several miles across. Dust from the impact would have blocked sunlight across the planet for months, killing most plants, along with most of the animal species that ultimately depended on the plants for food.

After the dinosaurs were gone, the role of "large land animal" was disputed for a time between mammals (previously insignificant in size and domain) and the winged feathered descendants of the dinosaurs known as birds. The crown could have gone to the large flightless birds of the early Tertiary period (65 MYA to 1.8 MYA), but it went instead to mammals. Mammals radiated across the planet, filling many of the niches that dinosaurs had previously filled. Their stories are many and fascinating, but the most interesting to humans—and the most important to the SF writer—is that of the mammal that became intelligent. If you

---

Pangaea

The Mesozoic era provides a textbook example of how the Earth's lithosphere (its rocky interior) can interact with its biosphere (its life-forms). Because of the movement of continental plates, driven by internal heat (see chapter 6), the landmasses of Earth were pushed into one supercontinent about 225 MYA. We call that supercontinent Pangaea. Its violent formation, accompanied by the disappearance of many thriving coastal waters, may have been a major cause of the great Permian extinction that took place at that time.

Once the dust had settled, Pangaea allowed many species to roam freely, and compete freely in ecosystems that had long been separate. It allowed the dinosaurs to spread throughout the world's land area and push the therapsids out of business. Near the end of the Triassic, however (about 200 MYA), Pangaea began to separate into smaller masses. In time, the movement of these masses formed the continents we know today. By the end of the Mesozoic era, creatures on distant continents had evolved into very different forms. As a result, there was much greater diversity among plant and animal species in the late Mesozoic than in the early Mesozoic.

Plate tectonics will continue to push the continents around in the future, perhaps long after humans are extinct. It may also operate on alien planets. How will it affect the evolution of species on the planet in your story?

---

want to speculate about how higher intelligence could take root in some alien species, begin by trying to understand how it took root in us.

Human Evolution

The first arboreal primates appeared early in the Cenozoic era, about 60 MYA. These mammals were adapted to a life in the trees, and their adaptations became part of our inheritance. Their limbs, paws and tails were designed for maximum freedom of movement in grasping and swinging from branch to branch. Their eyes were close together in the front of a flattened face, to provide the stereoscopic vision needed to localize nearby branches accurately. Their brains were relatively large to coordinate eye and hand action.

By about 18 MYA, the ancestor of both apes and humans had evolved in the African forests. Some scientists identify it as a chimpanzee-sized primate called Proconsul. This genus was distinguished from earlier primates by its larger brain, lack of tail, and a tendency to walk semi-erect when on the ground. Some of its descendants stayed in the trees; some took to the grasslands.

All primates might have stayed in the trees, except for a change in climate that happened about this time: a global cooling trend that began about 40 MYA and culminated in the ice ages of the Pleistocene epoch (1.8 MYA to 10,000 years ago). Ice ages appear to happen every few hundred million years, in response to periodic variations in the Earth's orbit and axial tilt. During these periods, Earth's surface cools, polar ice caps form, and glaciers or ice sheets advance and retreat in alternating stages. It is uncertain whether we are now out of the last ice age, or only in an interglacial period in the midst of it. (See chapter 14 for more details.)

Glaciation locked some of the Earth's water into ice sheets, lowering sea levels and rainfall. Gradually, the tropical forests receded, giving way to grasslands. Some primate groups adapted to the loss of their habitat by becoming specialized for a life of foraging and hunting on the savannah plains. One lineage that did so was the family *Hominidae*: a family that includes humans and their humanlike ancestors.

The first known hominids were the genus *Australopithecus* about 4 to 1.5 MYA: animals less than four feet high, probably covered with hair. Their brains were no larger than apes of similar size, but they stood erect and walked more or less as we do. Their bipedal stance and grasping hands were adaptations for foraging on the plain — makeshift alterations of features originally designed for life in the trees. The most famous australopithecine is Lucy, a young female of the species *Australopithecus afarensis*. She lived about 3.5 MYA in what is now Ethiopia. Her fossil skeleton is the most complete one yet found of any human ancestor.

About 2 MYA, the first humans had evolved — that is, the first representatives of the genus *Homo*. *Homo habilis* had a brain twice the size of the australopithecines — a brain that enabled this species to make and use tools. Like their ancestors and like modern apes, *Homo habilis* lived in groups with complex social relations. They lived by foraging, scavenging and perhaps hunting, with all members of a group sharing the food collected.

Homo habilis was followed by Homo erectus (about 1.6 MYA), bigger brained, smaller jawed, with more sophisticated tools and more of a bent for big game hunting. Homo erectus was the first to spread out of Africa to Europe and Asia, where some populations got the name "Java Man" and "Peking Man." About 500,000 years ago, Homo erectus populations living in cold northern climates became the first hominids to use fire for cooking and warmth.

Having branched into several areas, the separate populations of Homo erectus seem to have taken different evolutionary paths. The exact sequence of events is still debated. The Asian populations appear to have died out. European hominids evolved into Homo sapiens neanderthalis, the Neanderthals of popular lore. Some scientists think the Neanderthals were ancestors of modern humans, while others think they were a separate line that became extinct. According to the latter theory, African Homo erectus evolved into our own subspecies, Homo sapiens sapiens, about 200,000 years ago. About 100,000 years ago, they migrated out of Africa. Among the places where they settled as they migrated out of Africa was Cro-Magnon, France — whence the name "Cro-Magnon Man."

Neanderthals and Cro-Magnons apparently lived side by side for some time. Jean Auel's prehistoric epics, beginning with The Clan of the Cave Bear, speculate about their interactions. The two subspecies of Homo sapiens were not that different in intelligence. Neanderthals made advanced tools, took care of their aged and sick, and buried their dead ritualistically — indicating some kind of religious beliefs.

Only Cro-Magnons, however, show signs of the kind of abstract reasoning we consider particularly human. Their counting blades attest to the ability to reason mathematically; their cave paintings and figurines display, for the first time in Earth's long history, the ability to represent nature artistically. Had the Cro-Magnons died out in Africa and the Neanderthals survived, art, mathematics, logic and science might never have arisen.

The Cro-Magnons did not die out. By displacement, extermination or absorption — no one knows for sure — Neanderthals disappeared about 35,000 years ago while Homo sapiens sapiens multiplied. Out of the latter's unusually developed primate brains, their genes for social behavior, their gift for language (evolved no one knows when), came all that we know as culture and civilization. All living humans today are members of a single species, the only species in their genus; all human races are superficial variations of that one entity. It did not have to be so. In theory, several intelligent species — perhaps of varying levels or kinds of intelligence — might have survived to modern times. On the planet of your SF stories, such a scenario may be the case.

The important thing for the SF writer to realize, in Gould's words, is that "*Homo sapiens* is an entity, not a tendency." Nothing in natural history suggests that higher intelligence is the goal toward which evolution tends. Nothing in natural history suggests that intelligence must take the form of a primate who dreams, talks, reasons and feels just the way we do. Had the ratlike ancestor of primates died with many other species in the late Cretaceous, there would have been no human species — but there might someday have been some other organism that awoke to discover its own existence.

Every living species, including ours, is a unique product of contingency. No fact of natural history is more important as you set out to imagine the kinds of species that may populate other worlds.

O

Aliens are what first draw many readers to science fiction. Literary descendants of monsters and demigods, the intelligent nonhumans of SF can haunt, delight, terrify and provoke thought. What makes them different from their ancestors in myth and fantasy is that aliens are grounded in the scientific possibility that life may exist on worlds other than our own. Whatever blow science may have struck to the world's mythologies, the discovery of this possibility may be one of the luckiest breaks the human imagination ever got.

Of course, you don't need to invent extraterrestrial intelligence if you don't want to. The galactic empires in Asimov's *Foundation* series and Herbert's *Dune* series are made of the descendants of humans from Earth who have colonized the galaxy unopposed. Whether such a scenario is more or less likely than a galaxy full of thinking aliens is still a matter for debate (see below). But probability aside, interactions between humans and aliens make for fascinating fiction. Grounding your creatures in what is known about biology, planetology, mechanics and so on will make your story all the more satisfying for SF readers.

CHAPTER EIGHT

ALIENS

Are your aliens physically possible? Could their attributes have developed through natural selection? Do their ecology and society make sense? If they are supposed to be bizarre and exotic, are you sure they are even as strange as living things on your own planet? In writing about aliens, you are walking a tightrope of credibility. This chapter will help you walk that tightrope successfully.

The Odds for Aliens

No one knows how many alien civilizations there may be in the galaxy. It depends on many variables for which there is no agreement: how many stars have planets; how many of those planets are habitable for Earthlike life-forms; how likely it is that life, let alone multicellular and intelligent life, will evolve on a habitable planet. Astronomers Frank Drake and Carl Sagan devised an equation that takes many of these variables into account. It is used to estimate the possible number of civilizations in the galaxy with which we might be able to communicate.

$$N = R^* \times f_p \times n_e \times f_l \times f_i \times f_c \times L$$

The equation seeks to find N, the number of communicative civilizations. R^* represents the number of stars in the galaxy; f_p the fraction of stars with planetary systems; n_e the average number of Earthlike planets per solar system; f_l the fraction of Earthlike planets where life develops; f_i the fraction of planets where life evolves intelligence; f_c the fraction of intelligent species that release detectable signs of their existence (like radio signals) into outer space; and L the length of time during which the civilizations release detectable signs.

The figures that should stand in for these symbols are all unknown. There is still even dispute over N, the number of stars in the galaxy. Depending on what values they assign to the variables, different scientists have attained results ranging from 10 billion to 100 million to 100,000 to one — our own.

Thus, it is up to you to determine the approximate number of civilizations in your galaxy. It may be, as in Asimov's *Foundation* galaxy, that human civilization is alone. Or, as in Larry Niven and Jerry Pournelle's *The Mote in God's Eye*, civilizations may be exceedingly rare: Humans may colonize the stars for many years before stumbling one alien intelligence. A galaxy where every halfway-suitable star has an Earthlike civilization is unlikely — but there are many plausible gradations between this extreme and the other. If aliens do exist, it may be that we will learn of them by radio long before we encounter them in person.

Alien Biochemistry

To qualify as life, organisms have to meet a few basic criteria. They have to have structure (to keep them from dissolving into the environment); they have to take in energy and use it (i.e., feed and metabolize); they have to reproduce. If they are intelligent, they need to be able to store, manipulate and communicate information, and perhaps display some of the less tangible characteristics we associate with intelligence: abstract reasoning; self-awareness. On Earth, life and intelligence were made possible because of carbon-based molecules reacting chemically in a water

Searching the Skies

For more than thirty years, scientists have periodically turned radio telescopes to the skies in search of radio signals from extraterrestrials. This kind of undertaking, known as SETI (Search for Extraterrestrial Intelligence), has often been dismissed as flaky, and has so far yielded no positive results. But at least one $100 million NASA project is currently (as of this writing) dedicated to scanning billions of channels of radio waves for signs of extraterrestrial intelligence over the next ten years.

SETI projects can make for compelling SF without the need for starships or alien visitations. James Gunn's *The Listeners* is the most famous novel to deal with radio telescopes receiving alien communications. The novel describes the momentous changes this brings about in human civilization. Jack McDevitt's story "Cryptic" tells of a very different alien communication. Radio telescopes pick up signs of hostilities between the civilizations within the Sirius and the Procyon system. The information is kept secret by the head of the SETI project to keep humanity from learning that the first extraterrestrial contact is an eavesdropping on two civilizations at war.

environment. As far as we know, life and intelligence on other planets are likely to adopt the same basic biochemistry.

Carbon Molecules. Because of its atomic structure, carbon has the ability to form long molecular chains of varying shapes and composition. In living things, carbon molecules bond primarily with hydrogen, nitrogen, oxygen, phosphorus and sulphur (a useful mnemonic is CHNOPS). In living systems, these elements combine to form four kinds of organic compounds: carbohydrates, proteins, lipids and nucleic acids. The first three of these are important in providing structural tissue for cells. In addition, carbohydrates (such as the simple sugar called glucose) carry energy, proteins act as catalysts (they speed the rate of the chemical reactions that make use of energy), and nucleic acids (especially DNA and RNA) store and transmit the information that allows living things to reproduce.

All organic activities depend on the suspension of chemicals in a bath of water. Such a suspension medium has to be directly available to every living cell, or, at most, a few cells away. The chemicals necessary for life are transported into and out of this medium across the cell membrane.

To obtain energy, green plants use sunlight to convert carbon dioxide and water into energy-rich sugars — the process called photosynthesis. In the process called respiration, they take in oxygen to oxidize the sugars — that is liberate energy for use by the cells. Most other organisms, directly or indirectly, live off the sugars synthesized by the plants. They too use oxygen to obtain energy from the sugars.

For all of these processes to work, a habitable planet like those described in chapter 6 is needed — one with free oxygen, liquid water, carbon and hydrogen, temperatures that won't freeze or cook the cells, and so on. Most likely, organic life on other planets will share the basic biochemistry of Earth organisms. But it is possible that some will not, and you may choose to write about these.

If you want to describe such life-forms in any great detail, you had better know your chemistry: the specific ways that atoms bond to form molecules is a highly technical matter. The safer bet is to base your aliens on hydrocarbon molecules and put them on Earthlike worlds. Such a scenario makes scientific sense, protects you from having to get into too many chemical details, and still allows for tremendous diversity of life-forms. With that warning, here are some of the alternate paths you can take.

Substitutes for Carbon. In SF, the most popular substitute for carbon as the basic structural element of life is silicon. Like carbon, silicon atoms can form long chains, but they also tend to form hard crystalline structures that lack the flexibility of organic compounds. This may be why carbon is used by Terran life-forms even though silicon is much more abundant. Still, carbon-based life-forms may evolve some silicon-bearing structures: On Earth, the one-celled *foraminifera* grow shells containing silicon. Chains of silicon atoms alternating with oxygen atoms can form silicones, compounds that include oils, waxes and rubbers. It is at least theoretically possible that an organism could grow a computerlike silicon chip as a brain.

Joseph Green's *Conscience Interplanetary* depicts a planetwide silicon-based plant intelligence. It generates electricity from sunlight; its individual, specialized, bushlike units are connected by a nervous system of silver wire.

Substitutes for Oxygen. Not all living things require oxygen for the release of energy. Anaerobic organisms such as yeast and some bacteria can metabolize sugars in the absence of oxygen through a process called fermentation, which results in waste products such as alcohol or lactic acid. This process, however, is more inefficient than aerobic (oxygen-based) respiration, leaving a lot of energy unused.

Hal Clement, in an article in *Writing Science Fiction and Fantasy*, points out that other compounds besides oxygen could be used to release energy from sugar, including gaseous fluorine and chlorine and liquid nitric acid. These substances, like oxygen, would have to be drawn from the environment; usable percentages might be built up by organic processes the way oxygen was on Earth. To breathe nitric acid, of course, an organism's tissues would have to be heavily lined with mucus or some other protection.

Substitutes for Photosynthesis. Green plants rely on water as a raw material and sunlight as their energy source. But some bacteria on Earth use hydrogen sulfide rather than water as a raw material for photosynthesis (they give off sulphur instead of oxygen as a by-product). Such bacteria, living near undersea volcanic vents, rely on volcanic heat rather than sunlight for energy. They can become the base for a food chain of other animals — tube worms, clams, mussels. Such environments may also occur on other worlds: Arthur C. Clarke described one on the Jovian satellite Europa in *2010*. Volcanic vents are fairly transient; they work better if you treat them as one part of a larger ecosystem.

Substitutes for Suspension Media. On Earth, organic chemical reactions must take place in water. On gas planets like Jupiter, it may be taking place in ammonia and methane. On Earth, these compounds will only become liquid (and so suitable as suspension media) at temperatures too low to sustain life. But under the pressure of Jupiter's dense atmosphere, methane and ammonia may exist as liquids at temperatures that are relatively high. Arthur C. Clarke's story "A Meeting With Medusa" describes enormous jellyfish-like medusas in Jupiter's atmosphere, preyed on by smaller mantas.

Energy Beings. One of the favorite entities of science fiction is the being of pure energy. How such a creature would be any more complex than a rain of photons is hard to explain. To qualify as life, an organism needs structure. It is possible that electric and magnetic fields could supply the structure — perhaps maintained by charged particles. Fred Hoyle's novel *The Black Cloud* imagines that a cloud of interstellar dust could evolve life and intelligence, sustaining its processes by drawing energy from a star.

Designing an Alien

Whatever biochemistry you use for your aliens, two forces will be operating in their design. The first one is scientific plausibility; the other is narrative interest. You want to design a plausible alien, but you also want to design one that will work in your story—one that is human enough to serve as a character, or at least bizarre enough to pique the reader's curiosity, wonder or fear. If you want the creature to communicate with humans, it will have to be enough like us so that each species can recognize the other's intelligence.

You may decide your creature does not have to be intelligent. If all you want is a raging monster, or background fauna for your story (like the herd of cattle in a Western), then you can stick with nonsentient life, which has a better chance anyway of being abundant in the universe. However, if you want creatures who can interact with humans as characters, then some degree of intelligence will be needed.

You can start in several ways. You can imagine a story you want to tell, and design aliens to fit the roles. You can start by designing a habitable planet, as in chapter 6, then imagine the life-forms that might fit there. Or you can start with a *what if*— what if we had eyes in the back of our heads; what if squids became intelligent—and design a planet to fit them. Such speculation may lead to story ideas you would never otherwise have thought of.

Don't forget to explain (at least to yourself) what evolutionary advantages your organism obtained by developing the way it did. Why would hands be useful to a tree? Why would a clam need intelligence? From what preexisting parts did the new structures develop? The heat is off if some of your creature's weirder aspects are the result of genetic engineering or cybernetic additions. But much of the fun of designing aliens is trying to figure out what nature can come up with on its own.

For an invaluable compendium of aliens designed by other authors, see *Barlow's Guide to Extraterrestrials* by Wayne Douglas

Barlowe and Ian Summers. In text and pictures, the book details dozens of strange but plausible aliens from SF literature that can help get you thinking about creatures of your own.

Common Mistakes

Humans With Warts. In TV series and movies, aliens are often depicted as basically human, but with some distorting characteristic — a big brow ridge, webbed hands, a fright mask. Sometimes they are even identical to humans. This is all right for TV and movies, where the realities of having to work with human actors on a limited makeup budget may override everything else. But in literature, more creativity is possible — and expected. As the previous chapter explains, the human form is a highly contingent product of evolution. It is unlikely that evolution on other planets will come up with just our size, skeletal structure and facial features. Slapping a few warts on a human will not help.

Interbreeding. Mr. Spock notwithstanding, it is wrong science for a human to interbreed with an alien and produce a viable offspring. The definition of a species is a group whose members can breed only with each other. Humans and chimpanzees are close relatives sharing 99 percent of their genetic material, but they cannot produce offspring together. Humans and aliens would be unlikely to share any genes at all.

Very Large Creatures. Insects the size of elephants tramping around worlds with Earthlike gravity are wrong science. The reason comes down to a hard physical fact: Surface area increases as the square of an organism's linear size, but mass as the cube. Supporting structures like bone are related to surface area; weight is related to mass. That means that an ant thirty times its normal size would be 900 times as strong — but would weigh 27,000 times as much. Its legs and exoskeleton could not support that burden.

The same goes for any other Earth organism expanded beyond its normal dimensions. Our leg bones are adapted to supporting our typical weight; an elephant's to supporting its weight. If you want to create a creature as big as an apatosaurus, it will need thick leg bones like an apatosaurus.

If your planet has low gravity, some of the parameters are relaxed — a bigger creature can get along with a more fragile skeleton. But insect-like creatures are unlikely to get very big on any planet without modifications that resemble those of vertebrates. On a large scale, exoskeletons do not provide as much support as internal skeletons. And insects do not possess lungs — only tracheae, tubes that distribute oxygen directly to all the insect's tissues. This works fast enough on a small scale, but would suffocate the insect on a bigger scale.

Apatosaurus-sized animals might be intelligent, but they couldn't have a brain localized at the top of the body like ours. The brain and braincase for such a behemoth would be too big for the neck and spine to support. Brain tissue, however, might be distributed in other parts of the animal's body. Or the creatures could be aquatic, like whales — able to support a large brain and body mass because buoyancy in water keeps them from collapsing.

Very Small Creatures. Intelligent creatures the size of a mouse are about as unlikely as giant insects. Because mice have a much larger surface area in relation to their volume than do humans, they lose heat more easily, and must spend more time obtaining food to maintain their body temperature. Those exigencies do not leave much room for the evolution of higher intelligence. In addition, brains require an abundance of units that can store and exchange information — in Earth's case, cells. A very small creature, evolving from Earthlike biochemistry, will not have enough of these units to possess higher intelligence.

There are some ways around this problem. Your tiny creatures could have evolved something like a silicon chip in which information processing occurs on a much smaller scale. Could they be naturally occurring nanomachines, in which atoms or subatomic particles act as information carriers? (See chapter 10.) Or each tiny creature could be one unit of a communal intelligence. The "brain" would be a network of all of the brains, coordinating the group's activities.

One-Celled Giants. The ravenous blob that consists of a single house-sized cell is wrong science. Cells vary in dimensions, but most do not get beyond microscopic size. The surface area-to-volume ratio keeps them small: Cells need exchange surfaces to obtain and eject chemicals. If the cell is too big, it will die from the inability to exchange materials quickly. Also, the cell's control center, the nucleus, cannot control the cell's activities if the parts are too far away. If you want size and complexity, you will need multicellular organisms.

What Kingdom Is It?

Once you have decided to go with multicellular life, the most basic decision about your alien is its kingdom — whether it is a plant, a fungus or an animal. Plants alone manufacture their food through photosynthesis. Fungi (like molds, ringworm and mushrooms) absorb nutrients directly from their environment, either from dead organic matter or parasitically, from living hosts. Animals get nutrients by eating plants, fungi or other animals.

If you want your alien to be a plant, you will run into physical limitations. Plants are sessile (attached to one spot) and relatively simple in structure because photosynthesis does not supply enough power for an active life — and because there is no need to catch food or evolve intelligence. Your grasslike creature will be about as boring as grass, unless it can make better use of sunlight and find some reason to move and think. The low-energy diets and simple structure of fungi make them even worse candidates, though here too you may be able to make modifications.

The best choice is to let your creature be an animal. However, it can have some plantlike or funguslike characteristics: Perhaps it uses photosynthesis as a backup system in times of famine. Perhaps organisms on your planet have evolved other ways of acquiring energy. The plant/animal/fungus distinction might be meaningless when applied to your world.

What Phylum Is It?

On Earth, there are at present about 30 phyla, or basic body plans. The phyla are further subdivided into class, order, family, genus and species. All of the divisions are ultimately meant to indicate closeness of descent. Two members of the same genus shared a common ancestor more recently than two members of different genera but the same family.

Our phylum is that of the chordates. This includes the subphylum of vertebrates (animals with a backbone, such as fish, birds and mammals), along with invertebrates that possess a notochord, or flexible rod along the back. Other major phyla include the arthropods (insects, spiders, crustaceans), mollusks (clams, snails, squid), echinoderms (starfish, sea urchins), sponges, coelenterates (jellyfish, hydras, corals), flatworms (tapeworms, planaria), and annelids (earthworms, leeches). As the last chapter suggested, there may have been other phyla that are now extinct.

Getting to know Earth's phyla — present and past — is a good way to see what kind of diversity life-forms can take. The phyla on your planet will be different, but they may share some similarities with the creatures of Earth — thus allowing for "birdlike" or "jellyfishlike" aliens.

The Alien-Builder's Workshop

What will your creature's basic design be? How will it carry out its life functions?

The traditional favorite is the humanoid. These aliens are like humans in that they are warm-blooded vertebrates, with an internal skeleton and central nervous system. They are bipedal, with at least one set of "hands" free to use tools, and a head containing the brain and major sense organs. There is some scientific basis for thinking that such a design is a prerequisite for higher intelligence and civilization as we know it. It is what nature came up with here; maybe it is essential. But there is plenty of room for variations on this basic body plan. And since no one knows for sure, you can choose to start with a different design altogether.

Here are some ideas to get you thinking.

Symmetry. Most animals show some kind of symmetry — a tendency to grow similar parts on opposite sides of a dividing line. Vertebrates (like humans) and some invertebrates (like arthropods) have bilateral or two-sided symmetry. Some animals, like starfish, have radial or wheel-like symmetry: These animals are usually slow-moving or sessile. You can also imagine creatures that have spherical or cylindrical symmetry, or that are partly asymmetrical (e.g., one arm specialized for grasping, the other for cutting). Damon Knight's novel *Rule Golden* describes a creature with trilateral (three-sided) symmetry — three legs, three arms and six eyes.

Cephalization. This is the tendency among many Earth animals to have the major sense organs, mouth and brain grouped in a head at the anterior (front) end of the body. However, not all animals exhibit this tendency. Starfish and jellyfish, for example, have their mouths on their underside. Sense organs can appear wherever they are useful. Scorpions detect ground disturbances with slitlike organs on their eight legs.

In cephalized animals, the anus is usually at the animal's posterior (rear) end. But starfish have their anus on their topside, and jellyfish combine mouth and anus in one orifice. Does the animal have to have only one head? How would two or more heads interact?

Body Cavity. Most animals have a body cavity in which the major organs are contained, protected from the outside by some kind of covering (skin, hide, hair, scales, feathers, etc.). The organs can be more or less specialized: A sponge's body cavity shows little differentiation of tissue. Very simple animals, like the extinct *Ediacara* fauna of Precambrian times, have no body cavity at all. The *Ediacara* were quilted creatures consisting of layers of cells in long ribbons, pancakes or sheets. Could such a creature ever become complex enough to attain intelligence?

Structural Support. What holds up your creature? What allows it to move? On Earth, animals have evolved three basic solutions to these problems: soft tissue with no hard parts at all, but that can move by contracting and extending; hard outer coverings; and internal skeletons.

The hard outer covering may resemble a mollusk's limestone shell or the reefs secreted by sedentary colonies of tubelike coral. Or it may be the chitin exoskeleton of arthropods (insects and crustaceans). Exoskeletons work all right for small animals, but on a larger scale creatures need internal support, an endoskeleton. This can be as simple as a sponge's endoskeleton of needlelike crystals called spicules (made of lime or silica) or as complex as the cartilage or bone skeletons of vertebrates.

Perhaps your organism has both an exo- and an endoskeleton? Perhaps it relies on other metals besides calcium?

Locomotion. Not all animals move around in search of food. Filter-feeders like sponges, clams and corals may stay rooted in one place, straining small particles of organic matter from the water. Most animals, however, rely on locomotion to take them to the food. They also have to grip the food—either with their mouth parts or with prehensile structures like hands and tentacles.

Animals with skeletons rely for movement on muscles that contract, pulling on the bone or chitin like a lever. In internal skeletons, the bones are articulated with movable joints; different groups of muscles work on the same bones, extending it, lowering it, and so on. Wings require especially large chest muscles (along with an animal light enough to be kept aloft).

Animals with tentacles, like squids, use muscles without bones as prehensile organs. These appendages are generally not as efficient as bony ones, but they are often used in SF for their strangeness value.

If you really want strangeness, tinker with the vertebrate design of axial skeleton (skull and spine) crossed with two sets of appendicular structures (shoulders, hips, limbs). Why only two sets? Could shoulders, hips and knees be better designed? Could one set of arms reach forward, the other set backward?

Keep an eye out for mechanical sense. A few long limbs (like a giraffe) make for more efficient running than many short ones (like a millipede). But why couldn't creatures evolve wheels like a car? Piers Anthony in *Cluster* postulates a creature that rides on a single wheel in a muscular socket.

Hands. Does your alien have at least one set of appendages free to manipulate objects? If it needs all its limbs for walking, could it evolve intelligence, tools and culture? Could the "hands" have evolved from mouth parts or head tentacles? How many digits does it have? What kind of opposable "thumb" or "thumbs" does it have to grip things with? Are all the fingers opposable, as with Robert Heinlein's Vegans in *Have Spacesuit, Will Travel*?

Nervous System. A central nervous system — encased in a spine and culminating in a brain — is only one of the ways Earth creatures have developed to coordinate their functions. Other creatures make use of a nerve net in the body wall, nerve rings, or a collection of nerve cords. Higher intelligence may not be able to function with these simpler structures — or maybe it could, if the whole population of a species functioned as parts of one communal intelligence.

Senses. How do your aliens see? With retinal eyes like ours; with compound eyes like an insect; with simple light detectors like many marine creatures? How well developed are their senses of smell and hearing — well enough to substitute for sight? Be careful here: Echolocation like a bat's would not be able to resolve the different letters on this page, nor could smell detect the phases of the Moon. Such aliens would be blind to much that we see, and we would be blind to much that they "see."

What other senses do they have? A highly developed magnetic sense? There is evidence that some creatures on Earth use tiny magnetite crystals in their brain cells to navigate using Earth's magnetic field. Could your aliens have evolved UV or infrared detectors? Perhaps radio receivers and transmitters? You may choose to give your creature telepathic or empathic powers — though, for now, these rely on imaginary science and will be suspect to some of your readers.

Other Bodily Functions. In your zeal to explore alien intelligence, don't neglect the more mundane things animals do — eat, breathe, reproduce, digest food, excrete wastes, circulate fluids, produce hormones, maintain body temperature, camouflage, defend, attack, communicate, sleep. As you study Earth organisms and speculate about your own, you may find that one of these processes becomes central to your story.

Ecology

Aliens don't just appear out of the sky in spaceships. Like humans, they are beings that have evolved within coherent ecosystems. No adaptation — whether it's intelligence, manual dexterity, great strength, or the ability to fly — develops without a reason or within an unsuitable ecosystem. You will never be able to develop a worldwide ecology with the variety and complexity of Earth's — you'd spend the rest of your life just designing life-forms and food chains. But you can give your reader a taste of the web of life that lies behind your alien character.

Food. One of the biggest flaws in designing aliens is not giving them a natural easy-to-acquire source of food. Even though most humans are divorced from nature, we must eat and occupy the same part of the food web as we have for hundreds of thousands of years. Like other omnivores, we still eat both plants and animals; we just acquire and prepare them differently.

A stable ecosystem has to be able to exploit various sources of energy. Plants exploit sunlight. Herbivores exploit plants. Predators and scavengers exploit herbivores. Insects, worms and microorganisms devour what's left over, enriching the soil and helping the plants. An ecosystem might degenerate to the point where there were only ravenous carnivores remaining, but they would have nothing left to eat but each other. Such a situation is too unstable to last for long.

A Sample Alien

If you want to make sure that your extraterrestrial is truly "other-worldly," you might test it by comparing it to some of the stranger life-forms that exist on Earth.

A touchstone for this purpose is the starfish.

The starfish is an echinoderm—a spiny-skinned aquatic inverte-brate that is pentaradially symmetrical (shaped like a wheel with five spokes). Its five arms are connected to a central disc; each arm is studded with hollow tube feet. The tube feet are capable of extending and contracting, and clinging to objects by suction. Using its tube feet, the starfish can move slowly along the sea floor, or pull open the shell of a clam for dinner.

The starfish is spiny because of an internal skeleton composed of plates of calcite. The plates are perforated by tiny holes through which soft tissue grows—giving the starfish its bumpy appearance. The mouth is in the lower surface of the central disc, the anus in the upper surface. When the starfish feeds, the lower part of its stomach pushes out through the mouth, secreting digestive enzymes onto its prey. The partly digested food is then swallowed into the upper stomach.

The starfish has no brain—only nerve cords that run along the axis of each arm. The cords are linked together by a ringlike nerve cord in the animal's central section. For sensory impressions, the starfish relies on receptor cells that respond to touch, smell and light.

Starfish breathe through numerous tiny gills scattered over their skin. They come in two sexes, but they don't copulate. Instead they shed eggs and sperm separately into the surrounding water, where fertilization takes place. Starfish can regenerate parts. If an arm is cut off, not only does the starfish regenerate a new arm: The detached arm itself may regenerate a new starfish.

This would be a prizewinning alien in any SF story—except that it actually exists on Earth. In fact, it inspired Naomi Mitchison to create the Radiates in her novel *Memoirs of a Spacewoman*. The intelligent Radiates have evolved from starfish-like creatures, but with modifica-tions like retractable arms and a ring of blue eyes. As might be expected of pentaradial creatures, the Radiates do not think in dualistic terms, but according to a five-valued system of logic.

Enemies and Competitors. An animal's natural enemies are generally either those animals that hunt it for food or those who compete with it for the same food. Animals will kill for food, or to protect themselves or their young, or to keep trespassers out of their territory.

As chapter 7 indicates, it is possible that two intelligent species could evolve on the same planet — perhaps in different regions or from different stocks. When they made contact, they might cooperate or compete. Whatever they did, it would shape the planet's history.

Parasites. Aliens in SF are often parasitic, feeding off the human mind, as in Jack Finney's *The Body Snatchers* or Robert Heinlein's *The Puppet Masters*, or using the human body as a protective, nourishing part of the reproductive cycle, as in the *Alien* films. The creature in *Alien* has an interesting analog on Earth: The larva of the ichneumon fly are embedded in a caterpillar, from which they eventually eat their way out. On Earth, however, parasites are usually highly specialized, feeding off a few select species. It is unlikely that an alien could roam the stars, feeding off whatever life-forms it found on individual planets.

Nevertheless, parasites are still potent in SF. The frightening thing about them is the way they steal the will and substance of another living being without immediately killing it. Parasites may exploit several different organisms during their life cycle. The larvae of the liver fluke *Dicrocoelium dentricum* are contained in snail slime eaten by ants. Some of the larvae travel to the ant's brain, driving it crazy and causing it to climb up a blade of grass. A sheep eats the grass, ant and parasite. The liver fluke's eggs are excreted by the sheep and eaten by snails, and the cycle begins anew.

Symbiotes. Sometimes organisms depend so much on each other that they aren't parasitic so much as symbiotic. A fish cleaning a shark's teeth or a bird picking parasites from a rhino's back performs a service to its host, while acquiring food for itself. Protozoans in the intestines of termites and cockroaches digest cellulose for those insects.

It is unlikely that humans could enter into a symbiotic relationship with aliens, unless the symbiosis developed over many, many generations. But you could design aliens living in fascinating symbiotic relations with other creatures. Bruce Sterling's story

"Swarm" is about a symbiotic society made up of many different parts, all living in intricate harmony within a hollowed asteroid.

Planetary Parameters

The specific features of your habitable planet will greatly affect the creatures that arise. Here are just a few aspects worth considering.

Gravity. Organisms on a low-gravity planet could grow far larger and be more delicately constructed than they could on Earth. Flying creatures might proliferate, perhaps even resulting in airborne ecologies of plankton (minute plant and animal organisms) drifting on air currents, with food chains dependent on them. Your planet, however, would need an unusual combination of low gravity and relatively dense atmosphere if winged creatures are to manipulate air currents and remain aloft. A gas-giant planet's methane and ammonia atmosphere might just fit the bill (see above, "Alien Biochemistry").

Creatures on a high-gravity world would tend to be thicker and shorter than those on Earth. They would need more muscle and bone, and their reaction times would be faster to respond to quicker rates of falling.

Rotation. The length of day and night could affect your aliens. If a planet takes 100 or more hours to rotate on its axis, the sleep cycles, the hunting or grazing cycles, and breeding cycles would be influenced by the long periods of sunlight and darkness. The creatures might not be as tied to day and night as we are, but adapted to sleeping in short bursts and hunting, grazing and socializing in both day and night. Or they might have long binge periods during their preferred awake time (day or night) and then sleep away the alternating period.

If the day-to-night change was slow enough, animals might even be able to follow the light or darkness from one end of the continent to the other and beyond. Flying creatures could circumnavigate the planet as it turns, remaining in perpetual day or night.

The rotation of the planet might exactly equal its orbit around the sun, so that one side of the planet always faces the Sun, while the other is in perpetual darkness. Life on opposite sides of the planet would differ radically. Daylight animals wandering onto the night side might die from the cold or from lack of a vitamin that they can only get from sunlight. Creatures from the darkness might be unable to cope with sunlight, and unable to digest green plants — so unlike the moldlike forms that might prevail on the nocturnal side.

High rotation can also produce unusual adaptations. The small ground-hugging Mesklinites in Hal Clement's *Mission of Gravity* have adapted both to the planet's high gravity and its 18-minute rotation period. The fast rotation has flattened the planet into a lozenge shape, with gravity varying by a factor of several hundred from poles to equator.

Climate. The climate (or climates) in which your creature evolves will affect its adaptations. Earth's warm lush equatorial regions can support a wide variety of cold-blooded animals (animals unable to maintain a constant body temperature). Such regions are more intensely competitive than other parts of the Earth. In colder regions there are fewer large cold-blooded animals, and fewer plant and animal species generally. The animals are well insulated and, especially in the case of plant-eaters such as reindeer, able to withstand long winters with little or no food.

In temperate regions the ecology seems to change with the seasons. Plants appear dead in the winter but blossom to life again come spring. Some birds migrate to warmer climates. Lung-fishes and various frogs and salamanders can dig their way into the mud and hibernate through long dry spells. Clearly, organisms can adapt to a wide range of seasonal variation. Some desert plants will bloom only on those rare occasions when it rains in the desert.

What about a planet where the climatic extremes are not only severe but very long? Brian Aldiss's Helliconia trilogy tells of a planet whose seasons last for thousands of years at a stretch. The dominant plant and animal forms on Helliconia have long dormant periods or else go through drastic transformations when the seasons finally change. The heavyset cold-dwellers are hit with a deadly disease at the beginning of spring, which leaves the survivors thinner and better adapted for warm weather.

Beyond Dry Land

Conventional wisdom states that an advanced technological civilization can only develop on dry land, where sunlight and building resources are readily available. But SF is largely about questioning conventional wisdom. Could an airborne ecology and intelligence develop on a low-gravity world? What about an arboreal civilization, restricted to the high branches of trees? Or a "vertical" civilization, clinging to mountain slopes where the air is purer, less dense or cooler? Here are ideas for two other possible settings: undersea and underground.

Undersea Civilizations. Dolphins and whales have the largest brain-to-body mass ratios of any mammals other than humans. They appear to be highly intelligent, and their complex vocalizations may turn out to be true languages after all. But are whales self-aware? Are they civilized? Lacking manipulative appendages, they show no signs of toolmaking, one of the foundations of what we call civilization, and a probable spur to the evolution of the higher brain. Could an intelligent toolmaking life-form evolve in a completely aquatic environment?

Perhaps your aliens are not fully aquatic, but retain close ties to the sea. They may be semiaquatic mammals like seals or amphibians like frogs. Do they even have to be vertebrates? A group of mollusks known as cephalopods (the octopus, squid and their relatives) have a central nervous system that evolved independently from vertebrates, but functions in much the same way. One can imagine an intelligent cephalopod using its tentacles for sign language and toolmaking.

Of what materials would aquatic civilizations build their artifacts? Mollusks secrete their shells; coral secrete the vast colorful reefs in which they live. Could an aquatic intelligence *secrete* complicated structures and machines able to withstand the corrosion of water?

Underground Civilizations. Most animals living underground have little or no eyesight. But minerals for construction are plentiful, and other senses might substitute for sight. Sensitive whiskers, appendages or flagellae might delineate enclosed spaces. Pressure receptors in the skin, or infrared and sonar faculties, might gauge surroundings. Plant roots, decomposing matter or organic matter retrieved from the surface could supply the food base.

Wayne Douglas Barlowe, through his own artwork and text, designed an entire planet of creatures, none of whom possess eyes, in his book *Expedition*. If such creatures were to evolve in the darkness underground, and if their sensory organs were advanced enough, there might be no pressure for them to evolve eyes once they came to the surface. Such creatures could have evolved intelligence in their underground lairs, along with a society like that of ants. Maybe the spaciousness of the open surface, once conquered, would spur evolutionary or cultural changes in the former tunnel-dwellers, weakening their interdependence and fostering individuality as they spread across an uncolonized surface.

Intelligence and Consciousness

What is higher intelligence? How would you know a sentient alien if you met one? Does intelligence require the ability to make and use tools? Does it require awareness of one's self as a coherent ego? How could one species demonstrate to another that it is self-aware — and not merely behaving like an automaton?

These questions are hotly debated among scientists and philosophers. Here is one example of the questions that might affect your alien design. Computer scientist Marvin Minsky in *The Society of Mind* theorized that intelligence emerges from a network of simpler processes. The impression of one's "self" as a free willed discrete entity, dwelling inside our brains like a dwarf, is an illusion. It masks the reality of many simpler competing neural agencies, each adapted to perform a particular task. The interplay among them, evolved over many ages, is what we call intelligence. If this is so, why couldn't aliens on other worlds have evolved intelligence without the illusion of the "self" — without conscious egos?

The whole point of your SF story might be to ask such questions or try out hypotheses about the topic. There are, however, some practical questions you must answer to have a story. In what concrete ways does the alien's intelligence manifest itself? What clues show how the alien's intelligence is different from ours? How will your human characters recognize that the alien is intelligent? If they fail to recognize it, why?

The Utods of Brian Aldiss's *The Dark Light Years* are aliens whom most humans refuse to accept as intelligent because they can't believe that an intelligent creature could have such repulsive personal habits (Utods literally wallow in their own excrement). They hold to this belief in spite of evidence that the Utods have a complex language and are philosophical beings with a long cultural heritage.

In designing an alien intelligence, consider all the aspects of human consciousness — thinking, feeling, imagining, dreaming. Does the alien experience what we call pain? Can it get obsessed? Here are a few more questions to think about.

Emotion. Sometimes aliens are depicted as highly logical beings with little or no emotion; the Vulcans of "Star Trek" are examples. In such scenarios, humans are portrayed as balanced combinations of logic and emotion. But why wouldn't aliens also rely on a balance of emotion and abstract reasoning — though perhaps a balance with different elements or proportions?

Whatever the emotions are, they have to make sense in terms of the creature's evolution. Anger, sexual desire, fear, parental affection were all useful neural mechanisms to motivate humans in the environments in which we evolved. Some — such as suspicion of strangers — are perhaps not as useful on our modern global and national scales as they were in the Ice Age. What emotions motivate your aliens? Which have become liabilities to them?

Memory. Human culture is based on our talent for recording information and passing it from generation to generation. However, we cannot directly transmit learned experience from one brain to another: Learning must be mediated by books, talk, magnetic tape and so on. What if a species was able to access the memories of every single ancestor? The memories might be stored in chemicals (perhaps in the air or water) that every creature could emit or absorb. Or perhaps it is stored in the creatures' DNA. On Earth, it is impossible for learned experience to alter DNA, but perhaps DNA on your planet is subject to mutation by the individual's nervous system.

In such a culture, many things would not need to be learned. The distant past, stretching back many generations, could be reconstructed by inherited memory. Pain and trauma contained in ancestral memories would be transmitted as well — and might make the aliens highly sensitive to injuries committed long ago. It might be difficult for such a culture to change because of the weight of past heritage. Individuality would be affected. Where would your own memories end and those of your ancestors begin?

In Michael Swanwick's story "Midwinter's Tale," an alien carnivore feeds off the brains of its prey and absorbs their intelligence and experience. In this way it has a wide understanding of the habits of its prey. Whenever an individual in the pack dies, the rest eat its brain to absorb a bit of the departed's mind. When humans arrive on this planet, one falls prey to a carnivore that suddenly inherits human intelligence. It sacrifices itself to the rest, and these predators are on their way to becoming an intelligent species.

Behavior and Culture. Few things are more unsatisfying than an alien that looks utterly unworldly but acts like a suburban American. Why go to all the trouble of designing a bizarre physiology, when the creature's behavior is not even as distinctive as that of an eccentric you might meet in a twenty-four-hour diner? Nor is it enough simply to model your aliens on remote human cultures like those of Amazon tribes. Human culture is ultimately based on human physiology; alien culture will have a fundamentally different base.

Taking the time to think through your creature's behavior and culture can pay off handsomely. Some of the most poignant stories of alien-human contact in recent years, such as Kathe Koja's "True Colors" or Pat Cadigan's "Angel," deal with aliens whose strange behavioral and physiological traits only bond them more closely to their alienated human companions.

Alien culture might be so different as to be almost incomprehensible. Few SF stories have captured the mystery of alien society as well as Michael Bishop's "Death and Designation Among the Asadi," the novella on which his novel *Transfigurations* was based. In this story, a researcher tries to conduct a field study among the Asadi, an apelike creature that seems at first glance to be no more intelligent than a baboon. The scientist sees behaviors that he believes to be ritualistic. As the novella progresses, he makes more and more educated guesses, but is thwarted at every turn by revelations that perhaps the Asadi are too alien to ever be comprehensible. The central conflict of the story is understanding the alien society, the significance of their rituals, the history and evolution that molded these rituals.

You can get ideas about how alien civilizations might develop by reading SF authors, as well as nonfiction sources on animal behavior, anthropology, and political and social history. Here are a few issues to consider.

Language. It is a convention of SF that aliens and humans are able to learn each other's languages and speak in normal conversation. But the English-speaking alien might be an impossibility. Human speech is the product of precisely formed vocal

---

The Small Details

It is important to understand the "macro" level of your alien culture—government, economics, arts, fashion, religion, science and technology, war and peace. But it is just as important to think about the "micro" level—the small details of behavior that define a character. With humans, these things are easy to spot; with aliens, it takes a great deal of imagination. Just to inspire you, here are some of the many behaviors in which humans in our culture engage. What analogs might your alien culture have developed?

Smoking. Scratching. Building with blocks. Telling jokes. Laughing at something funny. Laughing nervously at something unpleasant. Stiffening the upper lip in anger. Wanting to see how a story turns out. Stopping to see the site of a car crash. Picking lint off a jacket. Dancing. Being shy about dancing. Bobbing on one's heels. Doodling. Being proud of one's work. Talking in superior tones to a secretary. Talking respectfully to a boss. Checking one's appearance in the mirror. Skipping. Hugging a loved one. Sizing up a stranger. Fistfighting. Stealing. Running away from danger. Finishing someone's sentences. Being lazy at work. Being too wired to sleep. Holding the door open for someone. Slamming a door. Praying. Eyeing someone attractive. Necking. Delivering a put-down. Dozing on a warm afternoon. Trying to sell something. Blushing. Folding one's arms. Crossing one's legs. Using pet names for lovers. Cursing.

---

parts—palate, tongue, lips, teeth, larynx. The precise timbre of human speech might be impossible for alien mouth parts to reproduce, and vice versa. Furthermore, human syntax (verbs, nouns, and so on) may have deep roots in human neural design; alien sentences may differ in construction from those of any known human language. What about linguistic creations like metaphors, puns, lies, arguments and stories? What variations or alternatives can you imagine?

Does your alien have to speak with its mouth? Blind underground dwellers might have a completely tactile language. They might "speak" by touch and read by touching raised or engraved letters. Underwater aliens might have a complicated sonar language—one that could somehow transmit pictures as well as words. Aliens might communicate visually, by altering their skin pigmentation or transmitting colored light signals. The latter method is used by the Asadi in Michael Bishop's *Transfigurations*.

If humans and aliens can't understand each other's native languages, they might use some kind of translating device, or they might invent a third language — like the sign language humans have trained chimps and gorillas to use. In *Transfigurations*, a chimp/baboon hybrid with raised intelligence serves as an interpreter between humans and the Asadi.

Mating. Your aliens will probably reproduce sexually, since that seems to be a spur for the evolution of complex organisms. But sexual reproduction does not require sex. On Earth, many aquatic creatures reproduce by expelling sperm and egg cells into the water and letting the currents fertilize what they may. Other creatures may reproduce sexually sometimes, but be able in a pinch to reproduce asexually, either by budding or by parthenogenesis (the development of an embryo from a cell containing only the mother's genes).

If your aliens do reproduce by mating, are there only two sexes or more? (There are three in Isaac Asimov's *The Gods Themselves*.) Can all individuals mate, or are some sterile siblings, like worker bees? How does the physiology of sex among your aliens affect territoriality, gender relations, and other cultural questions?

What if your aliens are very solitary and aggressive, like most scorpions? The mating rituals between male and female scorpions are complicated and risky. They clasp claws and dance violently for a long time, with the male repeatedly stinging the female. After mating, the female may eat her partner. There are many other arthropods (including black widow spiders and praying mantises) whose mating ritual is fatal to the male.

Sometimes males of a species will be much smaller than the females. They seem to serve no other purpose than to fertilize her eggs. A female angler fish will sometimes be seen with several similar, but much smaller, fish attached to it. These aren't babies, but attendant males. In Frigyes Karinthy's *Capillaria*, the females of an intelligent aquatic species are humanoid, but the males are monstrous little creatures kept as pets.

Your aliens may be hermaphrodites, possessing both male and female sex organs. In Ursula LeGuin's *The Left Hand of Darkness*, individuals at certain points in their biological cycle alter to become one sex or the other — and not necessarily the same sex every time. In this way a single individual might be mother to one child and father to another.

Childhood and Child Rearing. What kind of life cycle do your aliens have? Does it involve metamorphosis, like the larval and pupal stages that turn tadpoles into frogs and caterpillars into butterflies? These stages might last a long time; the alien might not even remember its earlier stage, or recognize pictures of itself. In Asimov's *The Gods Themselves*, the stage when aliens become parents is a kind of adolescence. Later, the three parents merge into a single adult form. This stage of their life cycle is kept secret from the adolescents.

Do children hatch from hard-shelled eggs, like birds? Are they born live? In their early childhood, do they go through a period when they are carried in a pouch, like marsupial young? Females, by definition, produce egg cells (larger and more energy-rich than the mobile sperm cells of males). But do females have to carry the fertilized egg cell to term? Among the fish called seahorses, the female deposits egg cells in the male's abdominal pouch. The eggs are fertilized there, and the pregnant male carries and gives birth to the embryos. If your aliens evolved from such creatures, how would this process affect the relative status of males and females throughout history — and all the related issues?

Don't assume that the parent who gives birth will be the primary caretaker of the young. In birds, both parents usually take care of offspring. In fish species where any childcare is given, males usually do all or some of the work. On Earth, female mammals nurse their young — but what if the males in your alien species are the ones with the mammary glands? What if the young are nourished through regurgitation of food partially digested by a parent?

Do the parents raise the young at all, or are they raised by a distinct infertile subspecies specialized for that task? Do the parents give birth to one, two, twelve or a hundred individuals at a time? How much care and education is needed before the young can be independent? How long does it take before the child is sexually mature?

Social Organization. How social are your aliens? Many animals lead fairly solitary lives. Your creatures may never get together except to mate, raise young, or fight over mates. Humans, however, developed from a very social order of mammals — the primates. Our intelligence evolved in the context of communicating,

ALIENS

working in groups, using tools, sharing food, and supporting offspring through long periods of helplessness. Without that context of social interdependence, it is possible that intelligence would never have evolved.

To develop advanced culture, your aliens will almost certainly require a society that can store information and differentiate tasks. How much that society will resemble primate societies is open to question. Perhaps individual aliens go through phases when they are extremely solitary; perhaps they are only social during brief mating stages in their lives.

A favorite model in SF for alien societies is that of the social insects — wasps, ants, bees and so on. As suggested earlier, individuals in this society would be specialized for particular tasks, and would not need a great deal of intelligence or freedom. The society's "intelligence" would lie in the community as a whole. Could such a society evolve and adapt with the speed of human cultural institutions? Would individuals be valued at all, or would independent action be considered damaging, like a cancer?

Perhaps your aliens evolved from pack hunters, like dogs. Perhaps, like hominids, they began as foragers, but later added pack-hunting to their repertoire. What about a species that never hunted at all? A vegetarian society would not necessarily be free of violence, but its culture might differ from ours in a number of ways. How would its religions evolve without totemic animals, animal sacrifice and hunting rituals?

Which is more important in your society — dominance or consensus? Are human concepts of dominance related to the mammalian tendency for males to compete aggressively for mates? Be careful about rooting alien cultures too strongly in biology. Think of the diversity of cultures on Earth, arising within broad biological constraints. Why wouldn't your aliens develop a similar diversity? In fact, one characteristic of higher intelligence may be the freedom to develop behaviors that are not rigidly determined by instinct.

Alien societies are often used as metaphors or test cases for human political questions. This is not a bad thing, as long as you remember to be scientifically plausible and entertaining as well. However interesting your aliens are as speculations, they are ultimately there to serve a human story.

○

One of the most durable settings for science fiction is the galactic civilization. Sometimes a democratic federation, sometimes a military empire, this kind of imaginary locale can be the stage for a whole series of short stories or novels. It can offer opportunities for adventure, character study, satire, and meditation on human societies.

Many young writers want nothing more than to invent their own galactic civilization, with its own history, aliens, weapons, etc. But if you want to avoid clichés that date back to the 1930s, you'd better put a little more thought into it. How do people get around this empire? How do they pay for it? Why do they bother? Who holds power—and how do they keep it?

This chapter will consider the problems, advantages and mechanics of building a galactic civilization.

The Problem of Scale

CHAPTER NINE
GALACTIC
CIVILIZATIONS

Whether humanity or some other species colonizes the galaxy, they will have to start small. They will start with exploration and experiment and proceed to some kind of commercial use or colonization. They will reach out first to a moon, neighboring planets or mineral-rich asteroid belts. At the farthest limits of their solar system they will be able to exploit and divert the orbital paths of water-rich comets. Beyond that is interstellar space, and the stars.

Here your colonizers will come face to face with the problem of scale. Let us assume that they want to do in distant space what they have already done in nearby space: build a network of outposts that can communicate and exchange goods. This basic goal of civilization becomes increasingly difficult with interstellar distance.

Our sun's closest stellar neighbors are a little over four light-years away. Within a range of about 13 light-years from the sun there are thirty stars. This accounts for just a small portion of the stars in a single spiral arm of the Milky Way galaxy. Even using the most sophisticated imaginary science, such as faster-than-light travel and wormhole shortcuts, it would take a civilization a long time to extend its range of influence over a sizable portion of the galaxy.

In our modern world, communication can operate worldwide at the speed of light, so that information can travel far faster than people can. Across interstellar distances, even speed-of-light communication would be achingly slow. Without a form of "instantaneous" communication — or at least a form of faster-than-light travel that can transmit messages faster than it can objects — communication within the galactic civilization will be limited in the same way that it was before the invention of the telegraph. You may want to introduce an instantaneous form of communication. You might also consider that the slow cumbersome job of maintaining adequate communication throughout a far-flung empire can create all sorts of interesting conflicts.

Another alternative is to restrict your characters to sublight speeds. Messages traveling at the speed of light will be faster than the ships traveling the same route but would still take years to reach their destinations. Time dilation will have an effect on all inhabitants of this civilization. In a civilization where people regularly travel great distances without aging but reach their destinations in the far future, how would people's outlooks on time and travel, emotional attachment and long-term political stability be different from our own?

In Isaac Asimov's original *Foundation* series, the galactic empire was so ancient and dispersed that they had forgotten the location of the Earth. Earth had become the mythological birthplace of the human race. An SF story taking place far enough in the future could scatter the human race throughout the galaxy, where they would diversify and, if the civilization collapses, be reduced to an isolated and perhaps even primitive state. It is true that a civilization without the means for galactic travel might become no more primitive than we are (since we, too, lack the means). But some citizens might consider this a shameful state of savagery, and might try to do something about it.

Why Connect?

Let us assume that your colonizers have solved the technical problems of travel and communication over galactic distances. There is still the question: Why bother?

On Earth, distant societies form connections for good reasons. International trade allows us to sell goods abroad at a profit and import goods that we need at home or in industry. But the cost of space travel might make interstellar trade unfeasible. Why pay ten million galactic dollars for a ton of iron from Betelgeuse that you can just as easily mine in your own asteroid belt for a lot less? The cost of space travel must be very cheap, or else your home world must have eaten up most of its own resources (in which case it must be very old and very populous).

Another possibility is that your distant worlds have commodities that are desirable and scarce. Alien arts and technologies may serve as such commodities; so may rare chemical compounds. Frank Herbert's *Dune* series posited a spice called melange that was crucial to interstellar navigation and only available on the planet Arrakis. Such a device can seem creaky, however, unless you explain why the compound cannot be synthesized or the technology reproduced. If they can put a man on Arrakis, why can't they synthesize melange?

If you can show that trade is both profitable and feasible, it makes sense for the mother planet to stay in contact with colonies or trading posts abroad, and to take an interest in alien politics. Colonial rebellions, wars and alliances all become possible. But you may decide that interstellar trade is unprofitable — even though interstellar travel is technically possible. In that case, there will be no galactic civilizations. There will be no economic base for making war or forming governments across the stars.

There may, however, be other kinds of contacts. Maybe information and cultural exchange would be viable. Maybe Earth could send out colonies of humans who seldom or never contacted each other, but who formed self-sufficient communities on distant planets and asteroids. They would develop their own cultures and histories.

The rest of the chapter will assume that the technical and economic barriers to galactic civilization have been solved. That brings us to political problems.

Species Interaction

The most striking feature of galactic civilizations in SF is the mingling of alien and human cultures. As different civilizations break free of their native solar systems and spread across the galaxy, they may encounter alien civilizations who are also expanding the range of their own influence. This isn't as inevitable as it may at first seem. There might be as many as a half-a-trillion stars in the Milky Way. A galactic civilization could easily possess the technology to terraform planets or live in controlled artificial environments where there are no planets. There wouldn't necessarily be a pitched battle to claim rights to those few small stable suns that contain already inhabitable planets.

The more far-ranging the alien settlements are, the more likely that they will encounter humans. The more alien civilizations there are in the galaxy, the greater the chance that they will meet and be aware of each other. If there are actually very few, the chances of "accidentally" running into another spacefaring race isn't even as likely as being struck by a meteor. The best way of trying to connect with alien civilizations is to actively search for them.

Encounters between alien intelligences can take many forms. Would members of two radically different intelligent species even recognize each other as intelligent? The race inhabiting the surface of the neutron star in Robert Forward's *Dragon's Egg* is radically different from the human race with which it establishes communication. They are tiny and their life cycles are accelerated tremendously. Once communication begins they are able to absorb transmitted human knowledge at an incredible rate, so that they catch up with and overtake the human race in a matter of days. Another alien race might grow and think slowly, taking years to absorb or express a single thought, and yet, like trees, may live thousands of years. Communication between species this different from each other could be difficult and even impossible.

If you decide to avoid the whole problem of species interaction, you are in good company. The galaxies of Asimov's *Foundation* series and Herbert's *Dune* series assume that humans will encounter no other intelligent species when they go out into the galaxy. Larry Niven and Jerry Pournelle's *The Mote in God's Eye* is built around Earth's first contact with an alien species, after years of interstellar activity. If you confine your interstellar adventures to a small sector of space, it is even more plausible that no aliens will be encountered. You may find this frees you to focus more on human problems rather than spectacle. On the other hand, you may discover you can say more about humans when you are speaking through aliens.

Political Organization

A galactic civilization can be politically organized in a number of ways. These are usually based (even if only loosely) on the political models of past and present civilizations.

Your own attitudes and beliefs will affect the models you choose and the way you frame political conflicts. If you believe governmental issues boil down to a struggle between rich and poor, this will be reflected in your stories. If you believe that a strong central authority—an emperor or other charismatic authoritarian figure—is necessary for the creation of a strong society, this, too will be reflected in your stories. If you believe in a strong military, your heroes might be warriors. If you believe in diplomacy or science as the root of a nation's strength, your heroes might be ambassadors or scientists.

In any case, it will be helpful to closely examine historical models. Sometimes real historical events, such as the Crusades or the American Civil War, can provide ideas for galactic struggles among mingling alien species. The more you study, and the more obscure the events that inspire your fiction, the better equipped you'll be to dream up unique twists to these conflicts. Following are some of the general categories into which your civilization might fall.

Empires. By far, the most popular galactic civilizations in SF have been galactic empires. Like the Roman Empire under the Caesars, the Napoleonic Empire, or the British Empire of the nineteenth and early twentieth centuries, a galactic empire is a vast sphere of influence under the domination of a single people or select federation of peoples. Often, but not always, the ruling people themselves are dominated by a central all-powerful figure or elite group.

The inhabitants of a planet may be lured into the web of imperial influence because they believe the quality of their lives will improve, or they may be coerced into its domain by military force. The main difference between a federation and an empire is that the different peoples, planets and star systems allied to the federation have a say over the policies of the federation as a whole. In an empire, the power is centralized so much that the separate countries, planets or star systems under its dominance will be regulated by a representative of the emperor—a governor or viceroy who may be foreign-born and hostile to the traditions

THE WRITER'S GUIDE TO CREATING A SCIENCE FICTION UNIVERSE

of the creatures living there. Consider the treatment of the Spanish Empire toward the Central and South American natives. They burned the natives' religious artifacts and destroyed their cities. Human history is full of such insensitivities and brutalities — and these involve members of the same species living on the same planet. What drastic forms might it take when one species conquers another? In Ursula K. LeGuin's *The Word for World Is Forest*, the human settlers of an alien planet nearly annihilate the intelligent creatures who inhabit the planet's forests. Like the Europeans who conquered North America, their rationale is that they need the resources, they need the space, and they don't believe that the race in question is really civilized or intelligent.

An empire won't necessarily behave with such belligerence and cruelty. But the atrocities commited by a plundering empire have been used successfully in many SF stories, novels and films. Audiences seem to be drawn by the idea of a modest band of revolutionaries — including many different species from different planets — thwarting and defeating a powerful but decadent imperial reign. Frank Herbert's original *Dune*, aside from being one of the first great ecological SF epics, was a story of revolution that drew much of its power from its depiction of the cruel and power-mad Harkonnens, and from the rugged resourceful rebels who defeat them.

Republics. A republic is a state or government in which supreme power resides (at least officially) in those citizens who elect representatives. The chief of state is generally not a monarch, but is elected either by voting citizens or their elected representatives. The republic of Rome before the Caesars is an ancient example, the United States a modern one.

Republican institutions can sometimes cloak a decidedly nondemocratic state. In South Africa only 10 percent of the people have been allowed to vote, leaving nine-tenths of the population without any useful political voice. While those with the power to influence the governmental body feel the advantages of living in a democracy, most of the population is powerless. Even a dark oppressive state could still be considered a republic because of the influence governmental bodies have over the chief of state — whether he is a "benevolent" dictator or a bloodthirsty tyrant.

In its ideal state, where the general population is well informed and able to mold and influence governmental policy through democratic means, the republic *can* be the most egalitarian of states. But in societies divided along economic and racial lines, or where the vote is restricted, a republic can retain the title and still be a totalitarian state — one in which individual rights are under the complete domination of a centralized authority.

In SF the political struggles in republics are a fight to take control from an authoritarian regime. In a civilization that spans many solar systems and exploits stars and their associated planets and asteroids for riches and raw materials, whole planets can become ghettos, gulags or slave colonies. Millions or even billions of workers — a world of the underclass — can toil away under harsh miserable living conditions, providing resources for an upperclass that lives in unpolluted comfort on an Earthlike planet that could be in another solar system altogether. How much would these two very different populations know about each other? How might they react if they do encounter each other?

It might be difficult to form an interspecies republic. A republic requires the constant active cooperation of governing representatives. Two or more alien civilizations would have to be either very similar in nature or else familiar and tolerant of one another to exist in a political structure that requires so much interaction and negotiation.

Federations. It would be far easier for humans and aliens to merge their civilizations under a common political order by forming a federation. A federation can be nothing more than an alliance between nations, planets, colonies or solar systems, standing guard against a common enemy or striving for a common goal. It could be a single nation spanning many solar systems, with each participating species maintaining control over local matters while a central government would regulate the laws covering the nation as a whole.

As in a republic, this says very little about the quality of the lives of the individuals living within the federation. The difference is that while racial and economic factors may be the most critical dividing lines in a republic, in a federation it would be local custom and history. A federation made up of many species living in different solar systems (or even different sectors of the galaxy) would contain a tremendous variety of alien cultures, and there would be little need to sacrifice any of this to a common political identity. Beliefs or practices that one race within the federation holds and cherishes, another member race might find repellent and morally reprehensible. Because of the great distances between the planets on which these creatures live, there might be far fewer clashes than there would be if they had common borders or a mixing of cultures.

A federation could be made up of many different republics. Depending on the individual and collective histories you give the different alien races, you can juxtapose very similar or radically diverse systems of government within a single federation.

Earth's Place

However many species there are in your galaxy, you will probably want to have some human characters, if only to give readers someone to identify with. In a galaxy full of intelligent technological beings, what role does Earth, or the human community that originated on Earth, play in your stories?

Conquerer. Whether you feel great pride or disgust — or just plain ambivalence — about the record of human affairs, there is no doubt that we have done a thorough job in exploiting our landscapes, our resources and each other. What will our first encounter with an alien species be like? And what kind of precedent will that set for all future encounters?

The Utods from the Brian Aldiss novel *The Dark Light Years* are hideous obese creatures who live in their own filth. They are also a peaceful race, possessing great intelligence and ingenuity. Their encounter with human beings is a disaster from the start, with the humans opening fire and killing a welcoming party. When a specimen is brought to Earth it ends up on public display, where a debate over its intelligence depends less on the accomplishments of the Utods than it does on whether the captive measures up to the very human measures of intelligence applied to it.

How useful might an alien species be to an ambitious colonizing society of humans? Would they try to bargain or cooperate with them or just try to subjugate them to exploit their talents and abilities? What about a highly evolved race that stands between the humans and untold energy resources or the freedom to inhabit a rare Earthlike planet? Humans have been known to murder millions of people for living in the wrong place or following the wrong leaders or religious beliefs. And they have contributed to the extinction of many animal species. Humans are also known for great compassion, and sometimes this concern over the welfare of *others* — whether they be other humans or animals — is translated into government policy.

If the society that spreads out from our solar system to colonize the rest of the galaxy is aggressive, greedy or bloodthirsty, the chances are the human conquest of the galaxy will reflect these traits.

But what if humans aren't the most aggressive or technologically advanced species exploring the universe?

Oppressed. H.G. Wells introduced the idea of beings from another planet invading the Earth in his novel, *War of the Worlds*. These invaders are from Mars, and they are intent on the conquest of the Earth and the subjugation or elimination of the human race. Since the novel's publication in 1899, the theme has been one of SF's most popular. When SF characters ventured into space, the aliens they encountered were often full of devious intentions or just outright monsters. Just as often as humans are depicted as brutal conquerors, they are also portrayed as victims, the pawns of a far more powerful race, itself bent on plundering human colonies.

The motivations for conquest of the Earth or the human race would fall into the same range as humans' reasons for conquering alien races: need of resources, territory, elimination of competition.

What good would human beings be as slaves? What kinds of abilities do humans have that their alien conquerers can exploit? If it is their mechanical ingenuity, then humans must be educated and provided with an environment conducive to constructive thought. Would human beings be valuable slave labor to a race technologically advanced enough to use machines in their place?

As food, human beings provide only a temporary resource. Beyond the fact that alien chemistries might be too incompatible for such exchanges, there is the fact that human beings just do not make good cattle. Five billion human beings might be tempting morsels for aliens who could digest them. But humans generally only give birth to one baby at a time. Gestation lasts nine months and it takes many years for humans to reach full physical maturity. Even if gestation time could be shortened and growth quickened and increased, there are many animals already bred for food purposes, which, even in a wild state, would be more suitable. The idea of human beings as cattle is horrifying, but over the long run it might be an impractical enterprise for intelligent aliens unless they perfected techniques for shortening gestation and inducing multiple births.

When SF writers have imagined an oppressed or enslaved human race, they often envision it in one of two ways. In the first, humans are treated as they would be in a totalitarian state — with little or no freedom and subject to intense surveillance. In the second, humans are simply treated as animals. Just as our definitions of intelligence might be too limited to take in the unique genius of an alien race, that of alien invaders might categorize us as nothing more than industrious but unintelligent animals.

Ward. Just because the aliens are stronger or more technologically advanced doesn't mean they have to oppress us. They may treat us as a ward — a species they want to protect and nurture. Maybe they wish to groom us for some goal. The Overlords in Arthur C. Clarke's *Childhood's End* came to Earth to help humans make the leap to a higher state of being. In our own history, the United Nations has sometimes formed protectorates to help a former colony achieve nation status.

Be aware, however, that "ward" can be simply a euphemism for colony. The British Empire justified its existence for years by claiming to bring higher culture and peace to nations it considered less "civilized." An interesting conflict might arise between Terrans who consider themselves oppressed and alien rulers who think of Terrans as wards.

Colleague. Even within a galactic civilization full of war, there would be alliances between species. While a natural fear of "alienness" might color every interaction, cooperation could still be possible. This offers all kinds of opportunities for unusual interaction among humans and various alien species.

To make things easier, SF writers often make the size, respiratory and climatic requirements of the characters similar enough that they can coexist in the same rooms and landscapes without cumbersome life support. Of course, these conditions are usually identical to those found on Earth. Sometimes languages are translated through handy computerized translators; sometimes the range of vocal signals used are similar enough that aliens can learn each others' languages. This allows for easy interaction among various kinds of alien creatures.

On long-running television series like "Dr. Who" and "Star Trek," it is common to have a galaxy filled with creatures who all just happen to resemble humans and speak the same language. While this allows for a wider variety of traditional story lines, it stretches credibility a bit too far for most discriminating SF readers.

Given the wide variety of forms and environments in which life and intelligence can develop (as seen in chapter 8), you should try to exploit the unique attributes of your aliens in their relationships with humans. How would humans communicate with a race of philosophically advanced floaters living on a gas giant? What kind of translating device or intermediaries would they need? Would they breed a race of intermediaries? If they had a peaceful relationship with the creatures, what would that relationship be like after a thousand years of close interaction?

War and Peace

Because human and alien societies described in SF are so often a reflection and extension of real human societies, and because so many interactions between societies erupt into conflict and bloodshed, wars have become one of the staples of SF. The tradition began with Wells's *War of the Worlds*, and has continued since then.

Sometimes these wars are restricted to hostile factions of the same species, perhaps between those living on the surface of a planet and those who live in orbiting colonies. Who would have greater access to resources in such a struggle, the planetbound factions with an entire planet's mineral wealth, or the orbiting colonists able to mine and process the asteroids in zero gravity? Who would be a more vulnerable target, the planetbound people at the bottom of their gravity well, or the colonists in their brittle cylinders and toruses, just one puncture away from the vacuum of space? Who would be better equipped to endure long months of hardship? It might seem obvious that strong industrial resources can win a war, but these strengths aren't always accurately perceived by the opposing side — witness the breakaway Confederate states during the American Civil War, or the Japanese during World War II. The tenacity of a people cannot always

---

Uplift

One of the more interesting galactic civilizations in recent SF can be found in David Brin's Uplift novels, *Sundiver*, *Startide Rising* and *The Uplift War*. These novels combine the themes of ward, oppressed and colleague. In these novels an intelligent race will "adopt" a race that appears to be on the verge of true intelligence, and will *uplift* it through genetic engineering and education. A client race will then serve its patron for a period of indenture. In time it too may choose to uplift another species. This creates lineages of allied species stretched out across the galaxy. Former clients rebel against patrons, alliances are formed and broken according to a complex set of beliefs and traditions, behind which lies a single belief: that somewhere in the galaxy reside the Progenitors, the mythological race responsible for galactic culture and the original uplifts. Enter the human race: creatures who appear not to have any patrons at all, but have allegedly evolved intelligence and culture on their own. Not only that, they had already begun uplifting their sister species, the chimps and dolphins, long before they could have gotten the idea from the established galactic culture.

---

be accurately gauged by an enemy army. Technology itself can be overestimated by a strong technological power. In recent years these factors contributed to the overconfidence and miscalculation of the American military in Vietnam and the Soviets in Afghanistan.

Historical models can be very helpful in creating future wars between human beings. Wars between humans and aliens can be far trickier. How much do the two sides even know about each other? The war in Joe Haldeman's *The Forever War* is being fought between two species that know very little. In their first land battle, the humans aren't even sure what their enemy looks like. In the end, the war turns out to have been started through a series of misunderstandings by two paranoid, technologically precocious civilizations.

The conflicts that could lead to war have already been mentioned in this chapter: xenophobia (a fear and hatred of foreigners — or in this case aliens), greed, revolt of the underclasses. In SF, the stakes themselves are often the most thrilling and terrifying aspect. A warlike culture may have the potential to entirely wipe out an intelligent civilization. It could propel singularities

Creating an Imaginary Time Line

As you imagine the history of a galactic civilization, you might find it helpful to sketch out a historical time line. Wars, technological milestones, the introduction of new intelligent species into the community will be a few of its elements. Together, they will give you a clearer picture of the galaxy your characters inhabit.

You don't want to bog your story down with page after page of invented historical detail, but knowing the information yourself will add confidence to your storytelling. Historical detail can be revealed over time to explain a character's action, so that an alert reader, having picked up all the clues along the way, can finish your story and re-create at least some aspects of your time line.

into the core of the enemy's home planet, which would obliterate the entire planet within a few years. If a large star could be destabilized to the point of becoming a supernova, an entire solar system could be destroyed in a matter of hours.

Beings capable of sophisticated travel throughout the galaxy would also have the ability to design and use weapons that could work on a very large scale. They, in turn, would be vulnerable not only to an enemy with a superior technology but to one with a radically *different* kind of technology.

Wars fought over such vast distances might easily last hundreds or thousands of years. But a galactic civilization with many intelligent cultures could be built along alliances that are hundreds of thousands, even millions of years old. The possibilities for strife between the different societies within the galactic civilization are legion. Alliances could exist between two very different species in spite of the fact that they had been at war for hundreds of years. The alliance could be a *result* of that war and the treaty that ended it. Relationships between nations on our own planet are complicated, particularly when viewed in a long, historical context. To be convincing, a realistic galactic civilization would be built on historical relationships that are even older, more complicated and more varied.

Economics

An understanding of the economics of your spacefaring civilization is as important as understanding the food chains in your alien ecologies. If you have an orbital torus or cylinder—a huge piece of sophisticated technology—and it is inhabited by a poor, nearly starving population, your reader might be curious where the money came from to build the colony in the first place. Are these creatures the descendants of asteroid miners who depleted the resources that gave them the wealth to build the colony? As the section called "Why Connect?" suggested, there has to be a sound economic support for launching and keeping a society in space. A healthy economy might be inclined to support an otherwise unprofitable program of space exploration, but the money pouring into this expensive enterprise will last only as long as that economy remains stable. A galactic civilization will have to be self-sustaining, and its wealth and even its political disposition will mirror the ways in which the civilization supports itself.

In a civilization made up of many different intelligent species, each culture will have something distinctive to offer the galactic economy. For example, if the human race never finds a way to travel faster than the speed of light, its exploration of the galaxy might begin at a slow pace. But what if it stumbles upon an intelligent species that has mastered faster-than-light travel? Humans might court favor with these aliens to gain this valuable secret. Is it in the best interest of these aliens to reveal the secret? What do humans have to offer in return? What ingenious talent might these aliens recognize in human beings that they lack in themselves? Music? Art? The biogenetic creation of foodstuffs that could be tailored to any alien biochemistry? A killer instinct, marketed in the form of mercenary service? After finding an area of useful trade, would these aliens then reveal the secret of faster-than-light travel, or merely manufacture the ships for their human trade partners? Would the aliens themselves have to pilot the ships to keep the secret? Or would they make the ships fully automated, thereby giving the humans at least the illusion of independence in their space travels? In such a scenario, human beings would be passive commuters, moving throughout the galaxy without understanding what is transporting them. But they would still be exposed to a wide variety of cultures, markets and wonders.

Bruce Sterling, in his novel *Schismatrix* and in short stories collected in *Crystal Express*, describes an alien race of mercantilists called the Investors. They live for trade, for making deals;

they have established relationships with species throughout the galaxy and assimilated many elements of their technologies and cultures. On coming to Earth, they take advantage of the rivalry between two hostile human factions (the Mechanists and the Shapers) to stimulate ingenuity and trade. The Investors use human beings to turn a bigger profit, and the humans go along with it because it gives them access to the stars.

Cultural Implications

It is easy to become dependent on technology that one does not understand. Technology is proceeding at such a fast pace that it is difficult or impossible for most people to have a working understanding of even the most common modern appliances: the microwave oven, the VCR and the automobile. As society grows more complex, it will become even more difficult.

In a galactic civilization in which contributions have been made by a variety of alien races, all of whom had considerable technological histories before interacting with each other, the artifacts and traditions that permeate your characters' lives may seem incomprehensible to your readers. Only the most brilliant of your characters may have a clear grasp of where their culture and technology originated, how it works, or what it means. Yet, if these elements are important to your characters' lives, they will quickly adjust to them. Your characters might question the nature of an appliance or a food or a mode of travel bequeathed to them by an alien culture — or they might not. Whatever you choose, your reader will be interested in the variety of cultural influences, and they should all fit together.

Imagine a Galactic Library where the cultural history of dozens of different alien races is available to scholars. Thousands, perhaps millions of years of religion, philosophy, history, literature and science — the intellectual heritage of every known culture in the galactic civilization — are there for the study. The human contribution to this library, the scrolls, illuminated texts, books, magazines, videotapes, computer diskettes, CD-Roms, videodiscs, holographic epics and virtual realities, would take up one small section of this vast structure. The scholars could spend lifetimes studying the accumulated knowledge. Unless your characters are among these scholars, they may never have a clear picture of this combined heritage.

As the writer, however, you should have a reasonably clear picture of the history and cultural interactions that have shaped your galactic civilization. Not only will it make your fiction more convincing, it might provide you with enough background material for other stories or novels.

O

So far, this book has concentrated on space — what we call the "crown jewel of science fiction settings." We have traveled inside and outside the solar system, and made suggestions about how to design spaceships, planets, extraterrestrials and galactic civilizations.

But not all SF is set in space or on distant worlds. Much of the greatest science fiction is set on Earth in the future — twenty years from now, two hundred years from now, two million years from now. Space travel may well be a part of that future, but it need not be the center of your story. Even if you do write about space travel, you will want to have some idea of what things look like back home.

The rest of this book will help you design the world called Earth, as it will look in the future time of your stories. Many of the topics are also applicable to life aboard a spaceship or another planet. Among other things, the chapters cover future industry and agriculture, robots and computers, genetic engineering and ecological disasters. The final chapter takes a somewhat different tack, focusing on alternate Earths and alternate universes.

CHAPTER TEN

NANOTECHNOLOGY AND VIRTUAL REALITY

This chapter describes two technologies that are still in their early stages but are ripe with possibilities, both for the real world and for SF writers: nanotechnology and virtual reality. The chapter that follows, "Designing a Future," will cast a wider net, suggesting how future technology may affect all aspects of human existence, from food and energy to recreation and communication. In both chapters, the goal is not only to make predictions of what might come into existence, but to suggest ideas that will help you create entertaining, dramatic and plausible situations for your characters.

The Perils of Prediction

Nanotechnology (microscopic machines) and virtual reality (computer-simulated space) are two technologies now in their infancy that may eventually change the world. Like many such technologies, their implications are being played out first in the pages of SF. The atomic bomb, television, submarines and space travel were all predicted by SF long before they became background to our daily lives. The same can be expected for technologies like the ones in this chapter.

A word of caution, however: SF is as famous for its wrong predictions as it is for its right ones. SF writers predicted computers, but for the most part did not realize how quickly and thoroughly they would revolutionize daily life. Lester Del Rey's "Nerves" is a suspenseful evocation of a nuclear power disaster, but bears little resemblance to the actual accidents at Three Mile Island and Chernobyl.

One way to avoid making wrong predictions is to set your fiction in the far future. A story set thousands of years from now can be a safe way of avoiding error. You can set your story in a civilization that bears little resemblance to our own and has developed technology that appears magical to us. But such a society may have few hooks that allow the reader to identify with the characters, and it can be just as prone as any other story to creaky devices and implausibilities.

By writing about the near future (the next few decades) or even the middle future (the next few centuries), you risk being made obsolete by tomorrow's technological breakthrough or political revolution. But the quality of the fiction, not the accuracy of the predictions, is what makes for great SF. SF is not, finally, a literature of prophecy: Its classics sometimes stay in print well past the year in which the depicted events take place. Authors are forgiven for predicting future events that are far off the mark. One of the all-time great works of SF imagination is Olaf Stapledon's *First and Last Men*, his future history of the human race. Written in the 1930s, it picks up from the moment it was written and extends millions of years into the future. For contemporary readers the beginning chapters may seem distracting, because they depict events that obviously did not happen. But like all his predictions, Stapledon's vision of the twentieth century is a credible and fascinating one. It works as an interesting alternate history. Any near-future SF novel or story will ultimately end up as an alternate history, dealing with the past as it might have been.

For that very reason, it is worth making every effort to be as plausible as you can. Your story may not be accurate as a prophecy, but if the world you create is one that seems real, from the minutiae of home furnishings to the major social trends, readers will be more likely to continue reading it. The two topics in this chapter, nanotechnology and virtual reality, are likely to have wide-ranging impact on both the little details and big picture of the future.

Nanotechnology

Since the days of the earliest stone tools, human technology has been a bulk technology. A primitive human could take a stone consisting of trillions of trillions of atoms, and break away chips consisting of billions of trillions of atoms, eventually carving the stone into an ax head. It was the stone and what could be made from it that mattered; the individual atoms (even if primitive humans had known of them) were merely the infinitesimal building blocks of the stone.

Forty years ago, a computer with the power of a modern pocket calculator would have filled an entire room. Today there are wires in a pocket calculator one-tenth the width of a fine human hair. But the components of a pocket calculator still consist of billions or trillions of atoms. The technology is based on the manipulation of materials, not the individual atoms and molecules that make up the materials. Nanotechnology, or molecular technology, manipulates the atoms and molecules themselves.

Nanotechnology is currently an imaginary technology, but it is by no means based on imaginary science. Scientists understand how water holds a constant volume as it changes shape (molecules stick together in patterns and can slip over one another while remaining bound together), how rubber can be stretched (its molecules are kinked like springs), why glass shatters (because the atoms will separate before they can slip or stretch). Scientists also study protein, the primary engineering tool of living cells, and have observed how protein molecules are combined into particular sequences. Genetic engineers have built orderly molecule chains — DNA molecules — by directing proteins to add molecules in a specific sequence.

The aim of nanotechnology will be to manipulate individual molecules precisely and use them to build structures according to complex atomic specifications — in effect, molecular machines.

Simply put: Nanotechnology will allow us to *grow* materials and tools. It could (and possibly will) transform the world more radically than any technological breakthrough in history.

Medicine. Modern medicine operates on two scales. Most surgical procedures take place on the larger scale. A tumor is removed; an artery is inserted into the heart muscle to bypass a blockage. Looked at from a cellular level, however, these are blunt, destructive procedures, gashing through and destroying many cells in the process of entering and removing something from the body.

Drugs, on the other hand, work at the cellular level. Antibiotics will kill an invading army of unicellular organisms. Morphine molecules will bind to certain receptor molecules in brain cells, affecting the impulses that signal pain. But drugs are merely "dumped" into the body, orally or intravenously. Once inside the body they will just move through the bloodstream until they can attach themselves to the specific molecules they can affect.

Molecular machines will be designed to work in specific ways on specific groups of cells and tissues. They will be the size of viruses and bacteria but their compact design will allow them to perform more complex functions. A computer only a single micron wide could easily fit inside a cell and could potentially hold more information than the cell's DNA. It would be able to direct the molecular machines under its control to examine and rebuild damaged cells and tissues. The molecular machinery that exists naturally in cells routinely builds new cells to replace dying ones.

Nanomedical procedures will use molecular machines to destroy cancerous tumors, bacteria, viruses and parasites. They will clear arteries of fatty buildups. They will direct the replacement of damaged skin and muscle to prevent scarring.

Chemical imbalances and damaged molecular machinery build up in the body as a person ages, causing wrinkled skin and brittle bones. Nanotechnology could counteract this tendency toward breakdown in aging bodies, prolonging lives in the process.

Cryonics. Nanoagents would be useful in interrupting the metabolism of a human being in a long space flight. The astronaut would be infiltrated by nanoagents that would displace water and pack solidly around cells, stopping metabolism but preserving cell structures, leaving the astronaut in a state of biostasis, in which there would be no detectable signs of life, but none of the damage and decay associated with real death. At the end of a long space voyage, repair machines would enter the astronaut's tissues, remove the packing and replace it with water, repairing any damage that might have occurred in the tissues during biostasis, so that the astronaut could be revived.

Industry. Nanotechnology might have its greatest impact on industry. Because the nanoagents will build things from the molecular level on up, manufacturing will begin to resemble organic growth. For example, by bonding carbon atoms one on top of the other, you could create a diamond fiber, flexible and yet far stronger than any material used to create modern fibers.

Instead of the heavy spacesuits of traditional SF, your space travelers could wear a soft, flexible spacesuit, skintight and so comfortable that even when bending arms or legs, there would be no wrinkling or restraint. A material only a millimeter thick, woven from diamond fiber, could contain many active layers of nanomachinery and nanoelectronics. The material would be as strong as steel and yet programmed to feel soft. It could protect against injury and pain, but also be programmed to seem touch-sensitive by sending signals to the skin in response to force exerted from outside. The suit could also be programmed to amplify movements so that the astronaut could exert many times his or her normal force. The carbon dioxide exhaled within the helmet could be converted back to oxygen by a process similar to photosynthesis. The suit could also break down waste products and reassemble them into food products. Best of all, the suit could repair damages inflicted on it, so that it would not wear out.

An entire spaceship could be grown in a vat. Nanocomputers at the bottom of the vat would contain plans for the design and construction of the spaceship. The vat would be pumped full of a milky fluid containing nanoassemblers. Some of the assemblers would attach to various points on the nanocomputer "seed," receiving instructions to attach to other assemblers, forming specific patterns that, over the course of several hours, would grow into the spaceship. This scenario, described in greater detail in K. Eric Drexler's nonfiction book on nanotechnology, *The Engines of Creation*, was modified and used in Jeffrey Carver's novel, *From a Changeling Star*.

The most important limiting factor you will have in using nanotechnology in your own SF stories is with the atoms themselves. Nanotechnology will be able to manipulate atoms and molecules, but it will not be able to transform one element to another. It would be wrong science for nanoassemblers to magically transform deadly plutonium to harmless aluminum, or iron into gold. That would require rearranging the subatomic particles that make up atoms. Even the staunchest supporters of this future technology doubt that this will ever be possible, except through the processes of nuclear fission and fusion (see chapter 11).

The Dangers of Nanotechnology. Like any far-reaching technology such as nuclear power and genetic engineering, nanotechnology opens up as many threats as it does benefits. Consider the images that you can dream up from this one phrase: molecular warfare. Molecular warriors could be programmed to perform complex and multifaceted sweeps of destruction. Microscopic assassins, mind controllers and bugging devices are only some of the possibilities. In *From a Changeling Star* several competing nanoarmies battle for control of the mind and body of a famous physicist, with horrific results. His memory is fragmented, some of it is falsified, and his physical structure is even altered.

In Greg Bear's 1990 novel *Queen of Angels*, nanotechnology is the tool of a police state. Microscopic bugging devices are injected into wall paint, offering police the ability to mount a panoramic invasion of privacy. Machines comb the walls and floor of a murder scene like tiny dust mites, gathering and analyzing the most minute samples of debris.

Many of the dangers could be the result of error, incompetence or unexpected side effects. In the earliest days of any technology, scientists and manufacturers will make mistakes. As corporations race to be the first to exploit nanoagents, what mistakes might they make? Efforts to grow healthy new skin instead of scar tissue might produce a new form of skin, hideous to behold, perhaps with an intelligence of its own. And a building made of nanoagents might appear safe and solid. But something in the detailed instructions might be misread by the nanocomputers, resulting in subtle but potentially deadly differences in the final form of the building. What if the sections of the building designed for decomposing and recycling trash somehow "infect" other parts of the building? Because they are so small, what will happen to nanoagents that somehow escape their particular manufacturing area and free-float through the atmosphere?

Virtual Reality

The apparatus is crude and ungainly: a pair of goggles that resembles a skin diving mask, each eyepiece a tiny liquid crystal video monitor, stereo earphones, and a "data glove" with optical fibers sewn onto the fingers, capable of detecting the slightest finger movements. Electromagnetic sensors in both the glove and headset can read changes in position and orientation. If you turn your head, the image you see on your eye monitors will move accordingly, as though it were a real room or landscape. A movement of the hand will allow you to "step" forward or backward or "climb" up or down. If you reach your hand forward in what would be your line of sight, a hand will appear in the three-dimensional image of your eyepieces.

The whole idea of virtual reality is to immerse you into an illusory image. Instead of watching a two-dimensional movie or a three-dimensional holograph on a screen across the room, you become part of the illusion. A virtual reality environment can be investigated actively. You can move freely through it, picking up illusory objects, talking to computer-generated creatures.

A virtual room or landscape, with all its contents, is created by the system's software. The hardware would consist of the computer and the sensory-output devices — sight, sound, mobility, possibly even touch and smell.

Most of the potential of virtual reality, and most of the hype, are still within the realm of imaginary science. Currently, the quality of the computer graphics in virtual reality software is still primitive, at least ten years behind computer animation. The coordination of head movements to appropriate pans through the virtual environment is not nearly clean enough to give a convincing illusion that one is actually *in* that environment. Sometimes the data glove is difficult to control. Your hand may pass through an object instead of picking it up, and there is still no physical sensation of touching an actual solid object. Sensations like touch and smell can be just as critical in conveying the complete illusion as stereo vision and stereo sound. And of course there is the helmet itself, heavy and cumbersome.

Even without perfect realism, virtual reality can serve practical uses. With present technology, architects and clients can take tours through the virtual layouts of buildings, and can even modify these layouts as they move through them. Virtual reality has been used to simulate F-16 fighter jets and other aircraft. Crude as virtual reality still is, pilots-in-training have found simulated flight battles believable enough to increase heart rates dramatically.

If, as expected, virtual reality becomes more detailed, realistic and easy to use, it may become one of the most pervasive technologies of the early twenty-first century. Medical students could perform practice operations on virtual patients. Doctors could use virtual reality to construct a lifelike simulation of an actual patient; the imaging processes would be similar to those used in CT scans and magnetic resonance imaging. Working with such a model, a doctor in a virtual operating room could completely expose a tumor to study the best possible course for the real patient. Scale would not be a factor: As long as the image of the real patient contains enough data, the computer software could provide the appropriate resolution and modeling at many different scales. Doctors could therefore travel within gigantic virtual models of real patients, a virtual fantastic voyage. It would also be advantageous for the virtual image to respond to virtual courses of therapy in real, slow or speeded up time, and for the doctors to observe the potential results.

Virtual reality might also offer astronauts effective ways to work in space while never leaving the safety of their spaceships. The video helmet would give the astronaut a picture of what a robot saw as it repaired a satellite outside the ship. The astronaut's data gloves would control every nuance of the robot's movements. As the ship orbited a planet, robot explorers could comb the planet's surface, sending back data that would allow the astronauts to feel as though they were exploring the surface themselves.

The entertainment applications would be equally far-reaching. As in a role-playing game, a group of people would interact together in a virtual fantasyland that responds both to their own actions and to the actions of the game's software. The human beings who sit down to don the goggles and gloves (or whatever sensory accessories the game requires) might become reptilian or arthropodal aliens in the game, living in an environment unlike anything the player would encounter in real life. The quick thinking, hand-eye coordination, practice and research necessary to master the game might require months or years of training.

Much more vivid than a video game, virtual reality games

NANOTECHNOLOGY AND VIRTUAL REALITY

Virtual Games

Imagine sitting in a dark drab room with your fellow game players, totally withdrawn into the world within the light portable headsets. Better yet, you have a silicon wafer surgically implanted on the body. If the wafer is perforated and planted near a nerve trunk, nerves would grow through the perforations, interfacing the circuitry of the chip. To enter the game you have only to attach a cable to the chip, and you'll be plugged into the game.

You have the ability to fly through fantastic intricately detailed environments. You are in a pitched battle against a common foe, or battling each other. The fights are realistic and breathtaking, using sound effects and music to stir the emotions. Even without the nervous system-interface this would be possible via a bodysuit that relays a wide variety of physical sensations through a fiber optic circulatory system. (The suit could even be a variation of the nanoengineered suits mentioned earlier.) Perhaps you are fighting for your life, and perhaps you're wounded, frozen in the virtual fantasyworld, able to observe everything but unable to move through the environment yourself. Your bodysuit or nerve interface might be able to stimulate your pleasure center, causing ecstasy when you win; or, to make things interesting, it might punish you with pain when you lose.

You might even be killed. Your headset goes dead, the data gloves are useless, the bodysuit is inert. You pull off the headset and look around you only to find that you're in a dark, featureless room, sitting in a chair. All around you there are other people, sitting in chairs just like yours, mumbling into microphones, making strange convulsive gestures with their hands, jerking their heads back and forth, lost in the throes of a game whose rules and characters and battlefields can't even be guessed by anyone who hasn't experienced the world within the headset. For the gamers who prefer virtual realities to the world they were born in, to be deprived of the game might truly be hell.

could mold an unusual group of enthusiasts. It might even become a spectator sport, with a wide audience tuning in on a computer network to watch the virtual athletes.

Virtual Reality and SF. While virtual reality as a viable technology is a recent invention, the idea of a simulated, computer-controlled "reality" has been around for a while in SF. Variations on these ideas can be found in the novels of Philip K. Dick, including *Ubik* and *The Maze of Death*. William Gibson's cyber-punk trilogy, *Neuromancer, Count Zero* and *Mona Lisa Overdrive*, features a simulated three-dimensional world representing the data in the worldwide computer net, called "cyberspace." The characters in these novels also partake in a form of entertainment called "simstim." A character just pops a computer chip directly into the brain — like placing a CD into a disc player — and be-comes immersed in a movie of the senses.

Charles Platt's novel *The Silicon Man* takes the idea one step further. In this novel, a technology called Life-Scan allows a real human personality to be downloaded into a computer. As the brain is scanned, however, it is destroyed, so that in the end, the person is brain dead and their entire personality exists only as memory within the computer. These human beings exist in a virtual reality in which they are immortal, and able to interact with anyone else who's been downloaded and anyone who jacks in for a visit. The virtual reality in this novel has reached the point where it is indistinguishable from reality.

O

Whatever wonders or terrors your future world holds, its basic requirements will be as mundane as ours. It will need food to feed its people, energy to run its machines, factories to produce goods, vehicles of transportation, means of communication. The wonder and terror come in as you flesh out the technologies that will achieve these ends.

This chapter suggests some ideas you might think about as you design the future setting of your story. It treats the basics of any civilization — food, energy and so on — while also speculating about more farfetched but still entertaining SF notions, such as time travel and invisibility. It does not deal in depth with computers and genetic engineering; these will be discussed separately in the chapters that follow.

This is a book about science, and so the focus here is on technology. But it is just as important in designing your future world to think about social issues. If the advantages of advanced technology go only to a few nations, or to a small group within nations, what kinds of conflict can be expected between the haves and have-nots? If life expectancy dramatically increases, what kinds of conflict will arise between the older population and the young? If a new cheap technology endangers vested manufacturing interests, will they resist it? If advances in automation drastically cut the need for unskilled workers, and the educational system leaves people unprepared for the new workplace, how will society deal with a large class of the unemployed?

CHAPTER ELEVEN

DESIGNING A FUTURE

This kind of thinking points to conflict, which is unpleasant in real life but invaluable for a writer — since the whole basis of any kind of dramatic narrative is conflict. It is true that no matter how far you go in imagining the technology and society of the future, it is still only background: Your story will depend on the immediate human problems of your characters. But defining the background can go a long way toward defining the problems. The personality of Captain Ahab in *Moby Dick* is much more important than any of the facts Melville gives about whaling; but without the nineteenth-century whaling industry, there would have been no story.

Food Production

As for all living things, the most basic problem for human beings is finding enough to eat. Civilization depends on finding a workable solution to this problem — preferably a solution that creates enough surplus to pay for things like art, books, fashion, tall buildings and spaceships. Current agricultural methods can grow enough food to feed the entire planet — if only the technology and the food were more evenly distributed. Because they are not, the majority of the world's people still live lives of hunger and malnutrition.

Several factors in the future can affect the ability of humanity to maintain even this level of success in feeding itself. One is population growth. In the next century, the Earth's human population can be expected to increase, probably by several billion (see chapter 14). Feeding all these people may become harder because of climatic changes. The warming of the Earth as a result of increased carbon dioxide — the greenhouse effect — may radically alter the world climate in the next century, making deserts of farmland in some areas, swamping other areas with rising sea levels.

Some of the methods on which modern agriculture depends — selective breeding, heavy use of artificial fertilizers and pesticides — could backfire, since these techniques can be highly vulnerable to changes in climate or ecology. Genetic engineering — directly manipulating the genetic code of organisms — may prove to be a fast and efficient way of developing better crop strains. But it comes with its own dangers, as will be clear from the chapter called "Remodeling Humans."

Solving the Food Problem. One solution to future food shortages may be the reclaiming of desert lands for agriculture. Humans have been aiding in the expansion of deserts for thousands of years. This trend will have to be reversed. The deserts could be seeded with bioengineered plants capable of gathering water and creating a nutrient-rich soil with the help of engineered fungi. These plants would not be edible and the process of making the desert bloom might take a century or more. The moisture collected by the root systems of these plants could eventually create an evaporation-precipitation cycle, bringing rain to once arid lands. Food crops would be engineered specifically for the new climate and soil of these blooming deserts.

But in a world with a rising population of hungry people, is such a long-term program — with no immediate positive effects — really possible? Will the people in your world be willing to devote so much land and time to the seeding of deserts? How could these lands be protected from herdsmen who need to feed their cattle?

Crops such as wheat and rice, already the dominant food crops in the world, could be engineered to grow faster and bring bigger and more frequent yields. The plants could produce their own antibiotics to keep out pests and competing plant species. They could also be engineered to provide greater nutritional value — complete proteins and all essential vitamins. While few people would choose to live on an unvaried diet of "super rice," it might be an improvement for the billions of people who today live on little more than ordinary rice.

If high-protein plants were developed and accepted by cultures like ours that presently center their diets on meat, it would also reduce the need to devote so much land to crop production for the feeding of livestock. One of the unpleasant facts of the food chain is that you lose a factor of ten in energy as you move up from one level to another — from plants to herbivores to carnivores. This means more land is needed to supply meat for the table than vegetables and grains, a fact reflected in the prices at any supermarket.

Even so, meat-producers will probably stay in business. Genetic engineering might even produce more efficient livestock feed, perhaps in the form of single-celled proteins. These microorganisms, engineered from algae, fungi and bacteria, would live on (and recycle) a diet of wastes. They would feed cattle, sheep, pigs and poultry. In time, some strains could even be made suitable for human consumption.

Could livestock be engineered into boneless, brainless, immortal meat-making machines? This is a common feature of many SF futures, but it may be based on imaginary science. These vast masses of lean, harvestable meat would be engineered to produce a continual supply of a specific complex of tissues. But, like the cells in complete animals, these cells would eventually develop something called "cell senescence." Tissue rejuvenation would become less and less efficient as time goes on, with an increasing number of random errors in the DNA and RNA as the vital molecules were reproduced. The meat-making machine might grow old and die like a real animal. For a possible solution to this problem, see the section on medicine in this chapter.

A simple way to increase meat yields might be to engineer animals into giants. This was the original goal in H.G. Wells's *Food of the Gods*. The problem is that gravity puts a limit to how large animals can grow without changing their basic skeletal structure. This would not be such a big problem in water. Fish farms could hold genetically altered cod and perch two to ten times the size of their ancestors.

Seaweed could be a big part of the diet for future humans. If engineered to grow massively and rapidly in shallow waters, it could provide a valuable food resource. If grown in the open ocean there is no limit to how massive the seaweed crops could be, but they might be harder to harvest in deep waters and spark controversies over who had the right to reap the resources of the open sea, especially if it is at the expense of natural ecosystems.

As suggested earlier, conflict will be a part of any food-production schemes of the future. Bioengineering may result not in more food for the world, but more food for countries that can pay for it, and unexpected shocks to the ecology. Some people may call not for more technology, but for less: inexpensive agricultural methods on small plots of land with an emphasis on producing food for consumption by the grower. Those who advocate such a "small is beautiful" approach may come into growing conflict with large-scale agribusinesses seeking to exploit more and more land for profit.

Energy Production

The high-tech futures so popular in SF depend on a reliable source of energy. Currently, most of our energy needs are supplied by oil and coal, nonrenewable fossil fuels (fuel formed from the remains of organisms and having high carbon or hydrogen content). As time goes on, the available supplies of both dwindle, and it becomes more likely that any new sources found will be more inaccessible. Oil producers, having pumped dry the great underground lakes of oil, will have to drill deeper to find liquid crude. The oil might be bound up with other substances and so be more difficult to extract. As coal mines grow deeper, the energy required to carry coal to the surface will increase. The energy-producing industries will then become the largest consumers of energy.

Natural gas (a mixture of gases, chiefly methane, found in the Earth's crust) may come into wider use as an alternative to oil and coal. Eventually, however, the reserves of this substance will also dwindle. Civilization may come to rely increasingly on renewable resources such as hydropower (collected from flowing water), wind power (collected by wind farms, banks of windmills), and geothermal power (collected from natural heat sources such as volcanoes and geysers). Two other possible sources of energy, nuclear and solar, are described in detail below.

Your future world will be suffering from an energy shortage unless it exploits new sources of energy, practices greater energy conservation, or both. One way energy can be conserved is by inventing machines that run more efficiently—light bulbs that convert a greater percentage of electricity into light rather than heat. But there is a theoretical limit to how efficient machines can be. The second law of thermodynamics (see "The Three Laws of Thermodynamics," page 212) states that no machine can perfectly convert energy into work; some energy will always be released as waste heat, heat that cannot be reused. In other words, you cannot recycle energy indefinitely.

The second law of thermodynamics also means that civilization cannot go on doubling its energy consumption every ten years, as it has been doing in recent decades. Even with infinite energy sources, such a pattern would soon build up more waste heat in the atmosphere than could be radiated into space. With global warming already predicted because of carbon dioxide emissions, more heat is the last thing we need. Your future world will eventually have to slow down the rate at which it consumes energy.

That said, here are some possible energy sources for the future.

Nuclear Power. Among alternative energy sources, nuclear power is both the most frequently proposed and most controversial. Despite arguments about the dangers, there are already over 400 nuclear fission reactors in operation worldwide; in the

The Three Laws of Thermodynamics

Three little laws govern the conversion of energy from one form to another. They are:

1. The Law of Conservation of Energy. The total amount of energy in an isolated system does not change. In other words, if energy appears somewhere it must disappear from somewhere else. Put simply, there is no such thing as a free lunch.

2. The Law of Entropy. The disorder, or entropy, of an isolated system increases with time (or, at best, remains constant). Another way of stating this is that whenever work is done, some energy is converted into unusable, or waste, heat. It is impossible in principle to convert energy into work with perfect efficiency.

3. The Law of Absolute Zero. This third, more technical law, provides an absolute scale of values for measuring entropy, or the unavailability of energy to do work. It states that in any lowering of temperature, only part of the energy can be removed. Absolute zero, the state of zero energy, is unattainable.

United States alone, nuclear reactors provide more than 20 percent of domestic electricity.

When talking about nuclear power, it is important to distinguish between fission reactors (the kind that exist today) and fusion reactors (the kind that may be developed for practical use in the future). The mechanism behind both is the conversion of small amounts of mass into large amounts of energy. This is in keeping with Einstein's equation $E = Mc^2$, which states that mass and energy are equivalent, and that the energy locked up in mass is equal to the mass times the speed of light squared — a staggering piece of news for people looking for sources of abundant energy.

Nuclear power is based on the realization that the nuclei of atoms (the most massive part of the atom, consisting of protons and neutrons) can be split ("fissioned") into smaller nuclei, or fused into larger ones. When they split or are fused, some mass is converted into energy, which can be harnessed for use. A fission reactor works by taking "heavy" elements — elements such as uranium with large unstable nuclei — and splitting their atoms. A fusion reactor does the opposite: taking "light" elements, such as hydrogen, and fusing their atoms to form heavier ones.

Let's take each kind of reactor one at a time.

Fission Power. Fission occurs when neutrons strike the nucleus of an atom of a heavy element such as uranium or plutonium, causing the nucleus to split into two fission fragments, also releasing a large quantity of thermal energy (heat), gamma rays and two or more free neutrons. These free neutrons, in turn, strike other uranium nuclei, setting off a chain reaction. Billions of uranium nuclei can "fission" in a fraction of a second during a chain reaction.

This is the source of power generated by all existing nuclear power plants. Uranium-235 is bombarded with neutrons, setting off a series of fissions. The reaction is controlled with rods made of a material such as boron or cadmium that absorbs neutrons; these control rods can be moved into or out of the reactor core. Water or gas (usually carbon dioxide) is used to cool the reactor. The thermal energy released by the reaction is used to heat water and convert it to steam. This high-pressured steam drives a turbine, creating mechanical energy that is converted to electricity by means of a generator.

There are several dangers to such a process. If the control rods malfunction, too many neutrons will fire into the core, increasing the fissions and releasing too much thermal energy and radiation. If the cooling system fails, the reactor could overheat. Radioactive materials could leak into the atmosphere. In the worst-case scenario, an uncontrolled reaction or "meltdown" could take place, in which the reactor core would melt its way into the earth.

Even without such an accident, the fission products left over from the reaction — including plutonium — accumulate in the reactor core. Plutonium is intensely radioactive, and will remain so for thousands of years. No one has yet come up with a practical way of disposing of all the nuclear wastes that build up dramatically in fission power plants. Consequently, nuclear power stations that use fission may be phased out if fusion reactors become a reality.

Frederik Pohl's novel *Chernobyl*, a dramatization of the nuclear accident in the Russian city of that name, details the real-life horrors caused by a nuclear meltdown. Michael Swanwick's

In the Drift presents an SF portrait of the American Northeast in the wake of a massive nuclear accident.

Fusion Power. As noted in chapter 5, nuclear fusion provides the self-sustaining energy that powers the stars. Under great pressure and high temperature, nuclear reactions occur that fuse lighter elements into heavier elements, releasing a substantial amount of energy in the process. If this kind of energy could be harnessed, it would be cheap, clean and almost limitless. Among other advantages, the main component of fusion fuel is one of the most abundant elements in nature: deuterium, a heavy form of hydrogen that is easily extracted from water. Deuterium and tritium (another isotope of hydrogen) would fuse to produce helium, neutrons and energy.

The major problem with fusion power is getting deuterium to the high temperature needed to ignite it. Because atomic nuclei are positively charged, they naturally repel each other; to get nuclei to fuse, you have to overcome their repulsive force. To do that, you must increase their kinetic energy — that is, heat them up. The necessary temperature for a working fusion reactor is about 200 million °C.

Particle accelerators can produce small-scale fusion reactions as neutrons are hurled at near-light speed against mixtures of deuterium and tritium. But it isn't a sustained reaction. When the accelerator is turned off, the reaction stops. Also, the amount of energy required to power the particle beam is millions of times greater than the amount released in the fusion reaction.

To be economically viable, a reactor has to produce more energy than it takes to run it. That means the fusion reaction must be sustained — which means the reactor walls have to be able to withstand the heating process and the energy release without melting or vaporizing.

Most probably, a fusion reactor would not rely on a solid inner wall that could melt or vaporize. Fuel, heated by electric current, would take the form of plasma, a cloud of electrically charged particles contained by a magnetic field. The magnetic field would be generated by a torus, a doughnut-shaped structure inside a building-size machine. Such a reactor is called a tokamak. As in fission reactors, a tokamak would heat water to drive turbines and generate electricity.

A powerful computer would be needed to predict and correct fluctuations in the fusion process. The coils generating the mag-

Fusion Prospects

At present, several countries are experimenting with fusion reactors. The Joint European Torus, or Jet, an experimental fusion reactor in Oxfordshire, England, has generated brief pulses of nearly 2 million watts — still only a fraction of the energy needed to be commercially successful. The International Thermonuclear Experimental Reactor, a joint venture between the United States, Europe, Russia and Japan, is an effort to build a working tokamak early in the twenty-first century. If it succeeds, the ten-story multibillion dollar machine will be the first fusion reactor to operate continuously.

---

netic fields would need to withstand very high temperatures. The outer walls would need to be protected from the "exhaust" of fusion reactions: stray neutrons, which, if released, could cause radiation hazards.

If you want to avoid the headaches of "hot" fusion, you could invent a "cold" fusion process — a process where fusion occurs at much lower temperatures. Such a process would have to be based on imaginary science. Even as speculation, this idea has been discredited ever since some Utah scientists claimed to have achieved fusion at room temperature with an experiment that was never successfully reproduced.

Solar Power. Living things on Earth have been tapping nuclear fusion for energy for billions of years in the form of sunlight. Sunlight fuels the chemical reactions that cause photosynthesis, making plant and all other life on this planet possible. It can be tapped to generate electricity by illuminating photovoltaic cells, which can then power satellites and heat houses. But the ability to tap sunlight for electricity is dependent on our ability to collect it. In arid climates with little cloud cover, it is relatively easy to collect the solar power needed for a single house. This would be harder in a crowded urban environment with frequent cloudy weather.

Solar energy would more easily be collected above the atmosphere — in space. Space colonists could build large solar mirrors to collect the sunlight, which would be four times as energetic as that received on the surface. The array of mirrors could be very large, so a space colony would be able to get most of its electricity from the sun. With thriving solar colonies in place, it would also be possible to direct solar mirrors so that the sun's energy, converted to easily collectible microwaves, could be transmitted to the Earth's surface. Dishes collecting the incoming microwaves would have to be spread out over a large area, but it is believed that the microwaves themselves would not be a health hazard. The collecting antennas could be spread across unpopulated areas or placed on artificial islands in the sea.

Biopower. Could future scientists engineer "biological batteries" that generate electricity? Electric catfish and electric eels have organs composed of modified muscle tissue and spinal nerves that can give brief electric shocks. The electric eel can discharge up to 650 volts. Living, bioluminescent strips, sheets and globes might be engineered to provide lighting and power for small appliances.

In addition to being an important food resource, giant seaweed and other kinds of genetically engineered plants could provide a much-needed alternative to dwindling fossil fuels. As the energy needs of powerful nations are often more critical and endangered than their food supplies, the open seas might be seeded to provide material for hydrocarbon fuel rather than for food. An ideological battle might begin between poor nations wanting to grow food and rich ones wanting to harvest fuel. What kind of conflict could arise from these opposing needs?

Artificial Photosynthesis. This process is a form of solar power modeled on the most basic process of life: photosynthesis, the process by which plants convert sunlight into food. Plants do so in cell components called chloroplasts; these contain "photochemical reaction centers" that use solar energy to synthesize compounds called ADP and NADPH, which in turn convert atmospheric carbon dioxide into carbohydrates, or sugars. If scientists can reproduce this process in the laboratory (as they are now trying to do), they may be able to create assemblies of photosynthetic cells that produce liquid fuels like hydrogen and methane. Like plants, these generators (either genetically or chemically engineered) would require only sunlight, water and carbon dioxide — in the process, drawing off some of the carbon dioxide that is contributing to global warming.

Imaginary Energy. Moving into the realm of imaginary science, some writers have speculated on the use of tiny black holes as a form of power, tapping the energy of their enormous tidal effects. This would require the capture or creation of singularities, and there is no known way of accomplishing either. Also, the same problems that would occur in housing a fusion reactor would be multiplied drastically. How could the enormous pressures be applied to create a black hole? Perhaps nuclear fusion technology might someday be so advanced that the possibility of compressing the fuel into a singularity (or maybe a cosmic string in the form of a loop) would be within reach.

Also, there is the matter-antimatter reaction, the most efficient form of energy theoretically possible. Subatomic particles of matter and antimatter are often forced to collide in giant accelerators. In such a collision, both particles are destroyed and *all* matter is transformed into energy. On an industrial scale, the some problems would arise that were noted in chapter 2: How can antimatter be produced in sufficient quantities and kept isolated from regular matter until the appropriate time? For now, this too is in the realm of imaginary science.

The Politics of Energy. In our present world there is a great disparity between energy-rich and energy-poor societies. Without efficient affordable energy, poor countries can never keep up with technologically richer ones. The gulf separating them threatens to grow wider all the time. In creating a future Earth, you might see this problem resolved by going to one or another extreme: 1) part of the world has mastered new, highly effective energy sources while the rest of the world has slipped back into a pre-industrial agrarian society; 2) the energy needs of the world are distributed across a World Grid with all available sources of power (solar, fusion, fossil) combined to provide all countries with the necessary energy.

Achieving the second of these alternatives wouldn't have to be the result of a grand, unified stance among the different governments of the world. It could arise gradually, spreading from country to country, eventually spanning entire continents. It might come to be controlled by a single company, with the energy needs of entire continents, maybe even the whole world, in the hands of one, all-powerful CEO.

Weapons

Cold War or not, weapons will probably be a part of the human future. As the final arbiter of social conflicts, they are always in demand and are immensely profitable for those who manufacture them. Throughout the twentieth century, modern technology has increased their lethal effectiveness to the point where they can kill every person on Earth many times over, and a single battle can kill as many people as used to die in entire wars. At the same time, new weapons and defenses make older weapons and defenses obsolete (as the lopsidedness of the war between Iraq and the United States made clear), so that a few countries work to develop ever "smarter" weapons while others shop on the international arms market for the best ones they can get. This pattern may well be part of the future worlds you create. Here are some of the weapons that may figure in these worlds.

Nuclear Weapons. For nearly fifty years, the threat of nuclear war has been one of humankind's biggest fears. The effects of limited or widespread use of nuclear weapons will be detailed in chapter 14. For now it's important to note one thing: As long as the knowledge of building nuclear weapons exists, and as long as there is fissionable material — such as the plutonium wastes from nuclear reactors — available to fuel the reactions in the weapons, nuclear war will *always* be a threat. During the Cold War it was common to talk about "mutual assured destruction" between the United States and the Soviet Union. Such an exchange could threaten all life on Earth — for now and all time. Whether or not two antagonistic superpowers ever again hold the entire world hostage to their own economic and ideological squabbles, that possibility still exists.

As of this writing, no civilian or military targets have been destroyed by nuclear bombs since Hiroshima and Nagasaki in 1945. But as conflicts continue, there is the chance that someone somewhere will use nuclear force on an enemy. If that enemy also possesses nuclear weapons, the devastation will be mutual. And the aftereffects of fallout will impact around the world.

A nuclear weapon could be put together by a terrorist group, and an entire city destroyed as a "political statement." In this case, a fission (atomic) bomb is far more likely to be used than a fusion (thermonuclear) bomb. A fission bomb requires only the fissionable material (plutonium waste would be the easiest to obtain) and the technology to build the triggering device. The bomb must be built quickly, because uranium and plutonium decay at such speed that a small amount might simply melt away. Enough fissionable fuel is needed to achieve supercritical mass, along with a triggering system that would smash pieces of the fissionable material together with precisely timed conventional explosives. This would cause a runaway chain reaction, releasing tremendous energy.

A fusion bomb is more technically difficult. It incorporates a fission bomb as one of its components. The heat from the explosion of this component triggers a fusion reaction, forcing atoms of lithium or hydrogen isotopes to fuse into heavier elements. A fusion or thermonuclear bomb releases vastly more energy than a fission or atomic bomb. An atomic bomb releases energy equivalent to several thousand tons of TNT (kilotons). A thermonuclear bomb releases energy equivalent to several *million* tons (megatons). There is no theoretical limit to how big a nuclear explosion can be. The record so far is 58 megatons, exploded in a Soviet test in 1961.

The nuclear weapons built by the superpowers are loaded onto missiles that can be launched from the ground, submarines or bombers. A ballistic missile is a chemical rocket that, once launched, follows a predetermined parabolic flight path — curving up from its launchpad and down to its target. A cruise missile is actually a pilotless aircraft that has computers enabling it to seek and destroy its target. Missiles can carry multiple independently targeted warheads — multiple thermonuclear bombs.

Defense systems against nuclear missiles — such as the system of Earth- and space-based lasers, rockets and particle beams envisioned by the U.S. Strategic Defense Initiative ("Star Wars") — may become a part of the future. But these are unlikely to provide a perfect leak-proof shield against a full-scale missile attack, and they would provide no defense against bombs dropped from radar-evading aircraft or carried into town by a terrorist.

Chemical and Biological Warfare. Plagues and poisons may be even more difficult to control. Defoliants (which burn chemically) and nerve gases (usually made up of two harmless chemicals lethal only when mixed) have already been used throughout the great wars of the twentieth century. A lethal dose of nerve gas will kill in a matter of minutes. Attacking the central nervous system, it induces sweating, vomiting, filling of the lungs with mucus, respiratory failure and then paralysis. Chemical weapons in the future could be designed to cause all sorts of agonizing, horrifying forms of death. Or, if the enemy is trying to attack but not destroy civilians, chemical weapons might only induce a temporary illness or madness.

Biological warfare would probably resemble natural plagues. An enemy could unleash a plague upon a city or entire country without ever declaring war, and the source of the plague might never be traced. The antagonists in a plague war might not be the official governments of sovereign nations. They might be secret cartels, spreading their devastation quietly, without laying claim to their victories. Only an advanced medical technology could deal effectively with a plague war. In the days, weeks or months it took to develop an immune serum, millions of people could die.

It would be difficult to control the spread of biological weapons. How do you prevent the plague you've unleashed from attacking your own people? Immunize them beforehand? A widespread immunization program would attract a lot of attention. The anonymity of the attack would be lost, and public knowledge of the immunization might be coupled with the enemy's acquisition of the immune serum.

There are all kinds of likely candidates for plague warfare. Mutant forms of familiar diseases, super-pneumonias or influenzas, would be as practical, though perhaps not as colorful, as any other. An extremely advanced genetic technology could tailor a disease with a complex series of symptoms designed to terrorize the enemy.

Nanotechnology would offer an even more deadly artful form of mass murder. Nanoagents could reduce their victims to a deadly ooze, or rebuild them into superpowered but mindless, obedient slaves. The most outrageous megomaniacal dreams of an insane leader might be realized with the use of nanoagents, inducing specific, irresistible behaviors in the afflicted enemy.

Lasers. The idea of the death ray was standard in SF when the first lasers were demonstrated in 1960. Lasers (an acronym for "Light Amplification by Stimulated Emission or Radiation") lent a new respectability to the death ray, even though most scientists at the time scoffed at the idea that a laser could be used as a weapon of destruction. The efficiency of modern lasers makes certain forms of the old-fashioned death ray seem perfectly plausible.

Lasers work by pumping energy continuously into certain kinds of material (ruby, for example) so that large numbers of electrons are balanced at a high energy level. They are "eager" to drop back to a normal ground state, and in doing so, each electron releases its excess energy by throwing out a photon. Each photon stimulates other energized atoms, causing a chain reaction of identical photons. The resulting surge of light is reflected back and forth between precisely placed mirrors, becoming amplified in the process. If one of these mirrors is partially transparent, this intense beam of light will escape.

The laser is powerful because its light is coherent. Unlike ordinary light, the waves of a beam of laser light are all of the same amplitude (height) and frequency (width), traveling in the same direction. In other words, they are focused to an extraordinary degree. A laser beam can travel thousands of miles without dispersing. It can be focused into a microscopic area, producing intense heat for precisely timed intervals. Hence, eye surgeons use laser beams to repair retinas so quickly that surrounding tissues are not affected. The precision and heat of a laser, however, also make it an excellent potential weapon.

The more powerful the energy pumping into the laser material, the more destructive a laser can be. A rare-earth element known as neodymium is currently the most widely used laser material. Energy sources vary: fluorescing organic dyes, gas discharges (usually a mixture of helium and neon), chemicals, electrical currents from semiconducting materials, and — most efficiently — electrons from a particle accelerator which pass through a powerful magnetic field and strike the laser material at nearly the speed of light. Only the largest and most cumbersome lasers can presently tap into the energy of a particle accelerator.

As of yet, no one has developed a workable laser handgun. But the practical applications of lasers are so widespread — cutting and welding, radar, communications, surgery — that lasers can only become more efficient and advanced as time goes on.

Laser light can be powerful enough to vaporize a small amount of any substance. In the vacuum of outer space, lasers work even more efficiently, as there is no atmosphere to soak up power and scatter the beam. Whether or not lasers ever replace handguns, they could become important battlefield weapons, able to destroy tanks and bring down planes. In space they could be used as killer satellites, perhaps designed originally as defensive weapons — for intercepting missiles — and later strengthened into offensive weapons.

Lasers are generally restricted to low energy radiation, such as infrared or visible light. A gamma ray laser (graser) would tap into the more energetic shifts in the atomic nucleus. Gamma ray photons are millions of times as energetic as those of visible light. At present there's no energy source powerful enough to fuel a graser, but if there was, it would be a very deadly weapon. Even from a great range, a few billion megawatts of graser power could destroy a planet or even blow up a sun.

Particle Beams. These are essentially particle accelerators used as weapons. Charged particles (electrons or protons) are accelerated to high speeds by magnetic fields, then discharged as a destructive beam. It is believed that these devices are less efficient than lasers, with more opportunities for snafus. The particles tend to spread and diffuse their energy; the beam can be deflected by a magnetic field. However, in your future, some of the problems may have been worked out, and the beams might be used as an alternative to lasers.

Hurled Debris. Larry Niven has stated that, "Anything worth doing in space can be turned into a weapon." Mass drivers or coil guns (see chapter 2), which use magnetic fields to hurl cargo, could easily be converted to offensive weapons. Originally designed to throw their cargo from the Moon into a safe orbital pattern around the Earth, they could be redirected to hurl chunks of rock directly at the Earth, aiming for major cities or coastal seas.

An object moving through space at relativistic speeds would devastate an Earthlike planet. A ten-ton missile would have a mass seventy times greater if traveling at nearly the speed of light. If it were to strike a planet, that mass would be converted to the energy of a 22 million megaton explosion, smashing continents and stripping away portions of the atmosphere. Since it would be traveling at nearly the speed of light, it would be nearly impossible to prepare or defend against the attack.

A large chunk of antimatter might also be directed toward the Earth by squirting gas at it. Annihilation reactions between the antimatter asteroid and the gas molecules would power the antimatter, pushing it toward Earth. A ten-ton antimatter asteroid reacting with ten tons of matter on the Earth's surface would cause a 400,000 megaton explosion.

Black Holes. In Greg Bear's *The Forge of God*, two small black holes are hurled into the Earth's core, eventually bringing about its destruction (see chapter 5). Two colliding black holes, each of them with a mass equal to the Sun's, would unleash 29 percent of their combined mass as radiation, elementary particles and antiparticles. This explosion, which would unleash more energy than the Sun will emit over the course of its lifetime, could easily destroy the entire solar system. All that would remain would be a single larger black hole.

Force Fields. SF has traditionally made use of all kinds of force fields. Most of them utilize electromagnetic force, which causes the attraction and repulsion of magnets and holds together the charged particles of atoms in all chemicals. Using gigantic magnets, a magnetic force field could be erected that could melt all metal objects that came into contact with it, no matter how quickly or slowly the object was moving. But this would be a cumbersome energy-draining defensive measure, and not nearly as mobile or cost-effective as a laser-radar antimissile system.

It would be wrong science to give your characters individual protection within an electromagnetic force field. An electrostatic field might be able to repel bullets, but it would have to carry such a powerful charge that it would probably electrocute the person it was designed to protect. It would also be wrong science to use gravity as a force field. An artificial gravity field would require the creation of mass/energy, and quite a bit of it at that. It takes the gravity of an entire planet just to hold you to the ground.

Effective force fields that are relatively safe, not tied to cumbersome hardware and able to protect a person or object of any size, would have to come under the heading of imaginary science, using an as yet undiscovered force. If your story uses such a force field, beware of giving it too much detail.

Communications

Ever since Marshall McLuhan published *Understanding Media*, people have theorized that the world is becoming a "global village" — a world where experience and information are shared without regard for distance. The unifying factor in this world is communications technology. With the help of fiber optics, digital processing, computers, and whatever else your future age invents, your characters may live in a bath of words and images pouring to and from everywhere. Your characters may swim at ease in this world — or they may feel that they are drowning.

Modern telecommunications depend on the fact that waves, traveling either through wires or space, can carry information. A telephone system translates sound waves into a pulsing electric current, carried by wire to a receiver that converts the signals back into sound. A radio system modulates electromagnetic waves so that they exactly copy the pattern of sound waves; the waves are then beamed through space to a receiver, which converts them back into sound. Broadcast television works much the same way, but conveys images as well as sound. The TV receiver converts the waves into a series of tiny dots (called pixels), forming hundreds of horizontal lines that the human eye integrates into a coherent picture.

Both wire and broadcast communication have limitations. Copper wire can only carry a few messages at a time. The number of broadcast channels available is limited by the range of wavelengths that can be efficiently modulated and distinguished. And until a few decades ago, the reach of TV and radio signals was limited by the curve of the Earth.

Several innovations helped solve these problems. By bouncing radio and TV signals against satellites in Earth's orbit, the signals could travel around the world, allowing instant global communication. The use of coaxial cables — cables in which two conductors share the same axis — increased the number of TV channels that a TV set could receive.

Perhaps the most promising innovation for the future is fiber optics. Optical fibers are glass tubes finer than a human hair. Light is introduced into the fiber at such an angle that it does not escape, but bounces inside the tube all the way from transmitter to receiver. The light inside the fiber is modulated to carry information — voice messages, data, images. A bundle of optical fibers is cheaper and less bulky than copper-wire cables and can carry much more information. Already, telephone companies around the world are laying fiber optic cables as the information pipeline of the future.

Complicating the telecommunications story is the fact that telephones are not just used for sound anymore. Computer networks are now pushing torrents of data across phone lines in digital form. This means they translate information into binary digits, ones and zeroes, known as bits. (Compact disc and laser-disc players also depend on this technology.) At the moment, standard modems send data over phone lines at only 2,400 bits per second — too slow to easily transmit books and video images. In the future, billions of bits (gigabits) per second may travel over fiber optic cables. For reference, a twenty-volume encyclopedia occupies about 1 gigabit; a television signal requires about 1/20 of a gigabit per second.

Improvements in fiber optics technology mean that people with modems — or with sophisticated videophones — will be able to talk to neighbors, go to meetings, tour other countries, shop, do research, manipulate machinery at a distant factory, and watch (and edit) TV. Fiber optics networks can be "patched" through to radios and satellites, allowing for mobile communication anywhere in the world. Laser beams may be used as broadcast channels. Because laser light has a much higher frequency than radio and TV waves, more channels can be created. It is even possible that every person on Earth might have his or her own personal wavelength.

It is up to you to determine just how far telecommunications has gone in your future world. In stories set in the next few decades, you can expect people to carry communicators considerably more sophisticated than beepers. These devices might be able to take down not just phone numbers but whole documents and video images; they might double as cellular phones or be plugged into jacks as conventional phones. In the more distant future, pocket devices might also serve as stand-alone computers, workstations and two-way videophones.

As with any other technology, the riches of advanced communications may become fairly evenly distributed throughout the world (the way television and soft drinks are), or they may mainly serve wealthy nations and individuals. In your future world, it may be that only a highly educated technocratic class fully exploits the information that is available, while most people are confined to being consumers of entertainment.

Another potential problem is the oversupply of information. Your culture may depend on knowbots (software robots programmed into phones and computers) that act as personal secretaries: weeding out unwanted information, marking the most important messages and data. If sufficiently intelligent, these knowbots might come to wield as much power as doorkeepers to an emperor — and might use their power to serve interests of their own.

Finally, communications advances might reduce privacy in undesirable ways. If you think a ringing telephone is intrusive, what about a world where personal communicators are implanted in your brain and cannot be turned off — where bosses, police and research scientists can always find you?

Satellites

As mentioned above, artificial satellites orbiting the Earth will be an important part of future telecommunications. But they will have other uses as well.

The first artificial satellite, Sputnik, was launched in 1957. Within five years, communications satellites were bouncing television and telephone signals across the Atlantic Ocean. Satellites now provide international communications, military intelligence, astronomical observatories (free of atmospheric disturbances), and detailed meteorological information. They might one day be used as military lasers or solar power stations. They come in many shapes and sizes: drums with flat solar panels extended like wings; cubes, oblongs, spheres. Most satellites are powered by purple-colored solar cells made of silicon.

Military "spy" satellites typically travel in a low Earth orbit, several hundred miles above the surface. Communications and weather satellites usually travel in a geosynchronous orbit, 22,238 miles above the surface. The orbital period exactly matches the 24-hour rotational period of the Earth. The satellite therefore stays at a fixed longitude, though it may move up and down in latitude during the day. In a geostationary orbit, the satellite stays at a fixed longitude and latitude. To an observer on Earth, the satellite appears to stand still at a single point in the sky.

If a building material strong enough could be developed (perhaps made from strings of carbon atoms manufactured by nanoassemblers), a tower could be built from the Earth's surface to the satellite itself. Arthur C. Clarke's novel *The Fountains of Paradise* is about such a project, a fusion-powered space elevator that could carry freight and passengers to a spaceport at the end of the line. This would provide an inexpensive alternative for transporting people and materials into orbit. But the material from which it was made would have to be strong enough not only to support whatever payload it carried, but its own weight over thousands of kilometers.

Transportation

Like everything else in this chapter, the future of transportation depends on the availability of energy. If personal automobiles continue to depend on fossil fuels, finite reserves that, even at their cleanest, foul the atmosphere, the long-term future of these devices is rather shaky.

Electric cars do exist, but as yet they are not efficient enough to travel at highway speeds, and they need recharging too often to make long trips possible. Access to solar power cannot yet provide electric cars with the energy they need, so the batteries generally need recharging from household outlets, which still derive most of their energy from fossil fuels. The long-term future of electric cars depends not only on improving the efficiency of their own power sources but a diversification of sources for all electrical power — solar, fusion, geothermal.

Using imaginary science, you could have personal transport vehicles, no larger than modern automobiles, that contain their own fusion reactors, needing nothing more than deuterium (or water from which to cull deuterium). Fusion technology would have to be very advanced in such a society, and this would reflect the energy availability in all aspects of that society. Can you think of ways that nanotechnology or genetic engineering might aid in the development of a compact power source within the car?

Computerized cars could be connected to traffic networks that control the safe flow of traffic. Drivers might be relieved of some driving responsibility, while being able to interact with the traffic network through a monitor and keyboard. A fully automated car wouldn't need windows, but could instead offer a variety of leisure activities to ease the monotony of long-distance travel. Perhaps windows would be an option for those with a claustrophobic nature. Bringing the vehicles and roads under the jurisdiction of such a traffic net might seem a controversial step for future societies. It is likely that the change would occur gradually rather than as the result of a swift, traumatic overhaul.

Flying Cars. Flying cars have always been popular in SF. These would diminish traffic by spreading the available "roads" into three dimensions. Would all drivers (or computers within the flying cars) be hooked up to an air traffic control net that prevented midair collisions? Perhaps using lasers or radio beams as signposts, the skies might become highways as complicated and as organized as those paved across the ground.

On what principles would these vehicles fly? Electromagnetic forces could suspend the car above the ground, eliminating much of the wear that affects roads and vehicles. Trains are already proposed that may "fly" on such magnetic cushions in the near future. But the ability to travel anywhere at adjustable altitudes requires, for the moment, wings like an airplane or blades like a helicopter, along with a lot of energy. These flying machines counteract the force of gravity by making use of aerodynamic lift: that is, by temporarily inducing a low-pressure area above the wing or blade, so that the aircraft is "sucked" upward.

Flying cars not based on such principles, but rather on some kind of "antigravity" field, are pure imaginary science. There is no known way to "block" gravity waves, as a window shade blocks out light. Any substance used to block gravity would itself have mass and be subject to gravity.

An advanced plastics technology might give us materials that could trap slippery helium atoms. This would make helium a viable alternative to the more dangerous hydrogen, and bring back floating airships. They would not move as quickly as planes or helicopters, but they would be more fuel-efficient, and their slow speeds might make commuter air travel safer.

Which brings us to this point: How much traveling will your characters really need to do? Already, fax machines and conference calling allow people to transact business over long distances with more immediacy than any kind of travel would ever allow. With computer terminals in their houses, many people can already work from home. Advanced telecommunications, combined with virtual reality, would allow participants — scattered all across the Earth and in orbit — to have a meeting in a virtual boardroom. It may be that in the future, travel will be less important than communication.

One more point: What if your future society is energy-poor? What if the world has drifted back into a pre-industrial state? Will humans revert to the modes of transportation common five or six hundred years ago? Maybe, but with one difference: bicycles. Even if none of the technological advances in this chapter come to pass, this simple nineteenth-century machine might make all the difference in the world.

Factory Production

One of the biggest changes of the industrial age was the creation of a large urban working class, most of whom worked in factories. As we enter the post-industrial age, two factors have acted to reverse that trend: the automation of factories and improved information processing. More and more factory work is done by robots, decreasing the number of human workers. Computers allow for tighter control and greater access to inventory, so that the inventories themselves can be smaller and more customized to buyer demands, which also means fewer workers. If these trends continue, human workers in factories are likely to be highly educated technicians, needing frequent re-education as customer needs change and technology advances.

Virtual technology could create a strange kind of hybrid: mass-produced but handmade artwork and gadgetry. After all, the special quality of handmade artifacts lies in the complexities of design a skilled craftsman can add — on a whim — to a pair of shoes, a sculpture. A craftsman could be hooked up by computer to a factory. He would be handmaking a single, *virtual* object, while the fiber optic network connecting the craftsman to the factory floor would be orchestrating an entire factory of sensitive robot arms to duplicate every movement as they made the *real* counterparts to that object, perhaps hundreds at a time.

With nanotechnology, the computers that control the manufacturing process could be microscopic. A factory might resemble a vast soup kitchen, as nanoagents inside vats build complex vehicles and household appliances . . . or androids.

Finally, Von Neumann machines might someday revolutionize industry. These are machines capable of replicating themselves using available raw materials. (You are a kind of organic Von Neumann machine.) Sophisticated computers could make possible Von Neumann power generators, construction robots and terraforming robots. With exponential growth, they would rapidly increase in numbers — until some programmed limit or dwindling resources made them stop replicating.

Medicine

The preoccupations of future medicine can be divided into these categories: fighting disease, increasing longevity, improving the human body. A fourth, striving to make the human body independent of traditional biological needs, is covered in chapter 13, "Remodeling Humans."

Disease. Understanding of the way diseases are transmitted and how they attack the human body is one of modern medicine's great achievements. The more research that goes into studying the protozoa, bacteria and viruses that cause deadly disease, the better prepared we are to fight not only known diseases but those as yet undiscovered. Genetic engineering and nanotechnology could virtually eliminate the threat of known diseases by fighting disease-causing germs according to strategies specified by the engineers. However, these technologies and our ever-increasing understanding of how diseases work will also increase the chances that military leaders will demand new diseases, designed to spread death or debilitation, also according to specific strategies. The offensive and defensive lines of battle of future wars might be drawn at the molecular, cellular level. If wars are fought in this way, eliminating disease from the world may never be possible.

Lasers and fiber optics will probably become more and more widespread as surgical tools. Lasers allow for microscopic precision in cutting. A fiber optic cable inserted in the knee is already being used for noninvasive orthopedic procedures. In a technique called arthroscopy, the fiber optic cable relays images to a video monitor so the surgeon can see the inside of the knee. Surgical instruments can be inserted through the same tube as the fiber optic cable and used to repair injuries. These techniques will only become more sophisticated. So will computer modeling of injured and diseased areas to provide guides for treatment.

Longevity. One of the side effects of living a long life is that over the course of many years, copying errors in DNA and RNA increase, so that the cells in the human body are more and more likely to be faulty and inefficient. This is often called "cell senescence." An artificial phagocyte (a cell that engulfs and destroys foreign particles) could be developed to work as a weeder in the human body, identifying cells in the human body whose DNA was deficient in the manufacturing of important proteins. These could then be replaced with cells from cryogenically preserved tissue culture (cloned with cells created in the patient's youth). Or, more conveniently, a method could be developed for rehabilitating the DNA in the faulty cells. This could help extend human life span and improve the quality of life for the elderly. People could retain the flexibility, healing ability and acute senses that otherwise erode over time because of copying errors in the cells.

Improvement. Life expectancy would also be increased by not only maintaining but *improving* the body's abilities. Whether done with artificial organs and limbs, or with living, genetically engineered replacements, it would increase the chances that someone could live a long and vigorous life.

Plastic surgery, which alters facial features, replaces scar tissue with healthy grafts, and can change the shape of the body, could become a noninvasive procedure. Engineered cells or nanomachines injected into the body could work these changes from the inside, making someone taller, stronger, leaner, more attractive. It would also be possible to increase the intellectual capabilities of the patient by modifying the architecture of the brain. For more information on this, refer to the previous chapter on "Nanotechnology and Virtual Reality" and to the chapter on "Remodeling Humans."

Education

We are presently only at the dawn of education in the computer age. Many children are learning to use computers in school, but how will the computer itself affect the way subject matter is taught?

Interactive programs that use laser discs slaved to computers are allowing students to use video and audio materials in conjunction with text material on the computer monitor. The hardware is too expensive for many classrooms right now, but there's a possibility that in the not-too-distant future, teachers (or the students themselves) will be controlling such multimedia or hypermedia lessons with computers. A student might begin by reading about D-Day, then go to a video map showing troop movements on the beaches of Normandy, then to an animated simulation of the weapons used in the battle, then to an audio of Franklin D. Roosevelt. No two students would follow exactly the same path.

Virtual reality would take these interactive methods several steps further, plunging students into digital reenactments of historical events, into a cyberspace where mathematical equations and the physical entities they represent swim around them. In a world where entertainment is highly seductive, it may be necessary to use elaborate means like these to lure students into learning. What would a classroom look like in this kind of society? Would the students even need to be present in a centralized location?

The molecular technologies discussed throughout this chapter might also have an effect on education, implanting information with nanocomputers or enhancing the brain's ability to absorb and analyze information through genetic engineering.

Recreation

Three-dimensional entertainments, such as holographic movies, are common in SF. (Holograms are 3-D images formed by coherent radiation from a laser and photographic plates.) These could be contained in a box or projected onto a flat open surface. However, virtual reality, which could simulate (and overtake) reality more convincingly than holographics, might become the primary entertainment medium. Stories could be told in virtual reality, with the viewer as an uninvolved spectator or participant. Music, which even now is tied to visuals in music videos, could become part of a mind-expanding virtual reality experience, accompanied by visuals that have no counterpart in everyday reality.

Genetic engineering and cyborg technology could change sports by focusing on the kinds of individuals best suited to certain sports and magnifying those traits in all participants. Athletes would be augmented biologically or mechanically to be better ball players or more spectacular gymnasts. Athletes could be designed for these activities from the moment of their conception, with every moment of their lives dedicated to the pursuit of excellence in their sport. This will result in a class of athletes who are fundamentally unlike the rest of humanity. Their adaptations might appear grotesque outside the stadium, but their special abilities would make for thrilling sport. These sports might pit human athletes against robots or other machines. The amount of violence in these games — which can vary from none at all to death for the losers — would be a good indicator of the aggressive tendencies of their societies.

In space colonies, where centrifugal force could determine the pull of "pseudo-gravity," sports could be developed for play in low gravity or even zero gravity. Imagine a large sphere of water along the zero gravity axis of a spinning cylinder. The audience is seated along the inner rim, experiencing full Earth gravity. The athletes hover "above" them, where the gravity is minimal or nonexistent. Can you dream up a sport that uses the globe of water? It would be easy to break through and swim inside of it, but there would be no sense of up and down, only an awareness of the distance to the inner surface of the globe. For a primer in swimming on such a globe, see Arthur C. Clarke's *2061: Odyssey Three*.

Most of the ideas discussed so far in this chapter are theoretically possible according to known scientific principles. But some of the most-beloved technologies in SF are hopelessly dependent on imaginary science and will probably remain popular just the same.

Time Travel

Everyone on Earth time travels, but usually in one direction only (forward) and at the same constant rate. Modern physics provides some theoretical alternatives. Accelerated time travel into the future is possible because of the relativistic effects of space flight at speeds near the speed of light (see chapter 4), though that method offers no way to make a round trip back to one's starting time. There is also speculation that traveling through a wormhole (in one black hole and out the other) would bring the traveler not merely into another part of the universe, but in a different time, as well (see chapter 5).

But time travel in the traditional SF sense is strictly imaginary science. In these stories, travelers have control of a device that can take them to a precise time in the future or past. Sometimes the location can be changed, or, as in the case of H.G. Wells's *The Time Machine*, the machine stays rooted in one spot as time moves forward or backward. The subject of *time* — what is it, how does it differ from what we experience as a sequence of ordered events, how can our misconceptions of time blind us to possible avenues of escape — all take on philosophical dimensions in books on time travel, but one fundamental point remains: We know of no practical way that we can travel into the past. Except for the metaphorical time machine of memory, time travel appears to be a strictly one-way experience for us.

Still, the "what if?" nature of SF demands the option to travel back in time, to alter future events, to solve ancient riddles, to meet prehistoric beasts, to observe our ancient ancestors. The methods by which this is accomplished should remain vague, because the only thing that will damage the illusion is the over-detailed depiction of a device or a description that obviously includes wrong science. You will also have to set rules about paradoxes — changing history in a way that affects the time traveler's present state. Can your time travelers change the past at all, or are they only passive observers? If they can change the past, what happens if they kill their own grandfather? What if they use the knowledge of the future to change the future? These topics are well-worn, but after looking at what's already been written, you may come up with a new story that uses some of the same old principles as a familiar background.

Gregory Benford's novel *Timescape* makes use of tachyons. These are hypothetical particles, as yet undetected, that travel faster than light. In *Timescape*, physicists have discovered that they also travel backward in time. In 1997, the scientists transmit tachyons across space to the exact point in Earth's galactic orbit where Earth would have been in 1962. There another physicist picks up their apparently random signals and discovers that they are sending him a warning. Benford went to great pains to make this novel plausible, and it remains one of the most realistic time travel novels in all of SF.

Invisibility

Invisibility has been a popular theme in stories and legends throughout history. H.G. Wells turned it into a SF device, introducing a technique by which a man was able to chemically bleach his entire body white (including his blood) and then, using a mysterious form of radiation, lower the refractive index of his body to that of the surrounding air. By doing this, he disappears from sight, just as a frosted glass will almost disappear in water because the refractive index of water and glass is so close, reducing the amount of distortion or reflection of light to almost zero.

But for the refractive index of two materials to be so close, their density has to be close, which obviously is not the case with air and human tissue.

No one has come up with a convincing method for achieving invisibility. SF writers have imagined techniques by which someone could seem to be invisible. Algis Burdrys's "All for Love" and Poul Anderson's "My Object All Sublime" are among the many stories in which light is somehow bent around the invisible device, where it emerges at the corresponding point on the far side. This would appear as a kind of lensing effect, so that, if nothing else, the invisible device or character would be seen as a distortion moving through space.

Once again, nanotechnology could present an efficient answer to the problem of invisibility. A nanodesigned suit, made from a material that is full of tiny video monitors and cameras, all of them tied to a central computer, could create the illusion on the surface of the suit of what is on the other side of it. This would be an extremely advanced piece of technology, and it is doubtful that even then it would offer a perfect illusion. But it might be sufficient for certain low-light situations and is still far more plausible than anything requiring the flesh, bones, blood and organs of the human body to become completely transparent.

Matter Transmission

Teleportation or matter transmission is a concept so popular in SF that few writers ever stop to explain it. It refers to the instantaneous transportation of matter from one point to another. This is often done by converting travelers or cargo into energy, beaming the energy at light speed to a different spot, then converting the energy back into matter. This is the principle behind the famed transporter on "Star Trek" ("Beam me up, Scotty") and the experiment that ends in disaster in the movie The Fly.

In some ways, the process seems plausible. Almost any physical entity can be reduced to information (a house to a blueprint, living tissue to DNA patterns); almost any information can be carried by waves (radio, light, sound). Theoretically, a piece of cargo could be "scanned" by a computer; complete information could be carried by cables or laser beams to a receiving port, where the information would be used to build a duplicate of the cargo. This is basically how a fax machine works.

However, just like a fax machine, this would be an "information duplicator," not a matter transmitter. The original cargo would still be sitting in its home port, just as your original paper is still sitting in your office after you send a fax. If such a method were used on people, Captain Kirk would still be sitting on his starship, while a duplicate Kirk walks around the planet surface. This assumes that the people on the planet have enough raw materials and technology to reconstruct all of Kirk's tissues, down to the memories in his brain and the number of gray hairs on his head. It also assumes that the volume of information needed to characterize the precise present state of a complex organism can ever be comprehended.

If your matter transmitter actually beams the person—not just information about the person—from one place to another, then the traveler's atoms have to be converted to energy. Einstein was very clear on this: Such a process would release energy equivalent to the mass times the speed of light squared. Presumably you don't want an annihilation explosion every time you use your transmitter. So perhaps the original copy of the traveler is destroyed (reduced to gas or liquid) on the transmitting platform. Then a single surviving copy can be reconstructed at the other end, according to transmitted information.

Simply breaking the person down into component atoms and beaming those will not work. The atoms will have the same mass as the person, and be just as difficult to accelerate to near-light speed.

If your culture has developed a matter transmitter, you have to expect that they will exploit it in every way possible. If they are able to synthesize instantly almost anything from raw materials, then there will no longer be much need (if any) for trade in finished goods. Why import champagne, medicine and luxury cars if you can reconstruct these things from information in a few seconds?

Another possible form of matter transmission is through wormholes. If your society possesses the ability to create black holes and cosmic strings, maybe they have also developed a technology in which wormholes (see chapter 4, "Starships") can connect various ports. Your characters might be able to move from one specific location to another, leapfrogging (or worming) their way toward a final destination. This is imaginary science of a tall order, but some writers have found ways to explain it. Dan Simmons, in his novels *Hyperion* and *The Fall of Hyperion*, credits these and many other inventions to the enigmatic civilization at the galaxy's core. They are gifts whose technologies exceed any human understanding.

In one of the most durable classics of SF, Alfred Bester's *The Stars My Destination*, characters travel from one place to another by jaunting, which simply means concentrating on the destination and transporting themselves there by will of thought alone. Is this imaginary science or wrong science? Well, it might be preferable to call it *no science at all*, since the idea that the neurophysiology of the brain can have such a drastic effect on the material world is purely mystical. However, Bester succeeds by fitting this mystical ability into a realistic SF future and creating the kind of broad implications with it that are so necessary to make believable SF.

If you are interested not in transmitting matter but in transforming it — synthesizing whatever you need from a few simple elements — see the section on "Matter Transformers" in chapter 4, "Starships."

Expect Magic

To close this chapter, remember Arthur C. Clarke's famous dictum: "Any sufficiently advanced technology is indistinguishable from magic." From the viewpoint of scientists in 1900, some of today's technology would be comprehensible (television, submarines, airplanes) but some of it (lasers, nuclear reactors, memory chips) could only be considered magic. John Barnes has speculated that in each new surge of technological advance, 90 percent will be what you might project from existing science, and 10 percent will be "magic": inventions based on facts that are not yet known. Since, as Barnes suggests, there may be three or four technological surges per century, each century that you project into the future will be more and more "magical" to the present eye. The lesson is: In designing the future, begin with present science, but don't forget the element of magic.

O

Of all the machines that fascinate SF writers, none is more enchanting than a machine that thinks. The excessively logical robot, the android that broods on its own existence, the computer gone mad are all familiar favorites. Now the computer revolution has brought some of these possibilities within reach — and opened the way to possibilities once undreamed of in SF. Science fiction writers today have to keep up with the constant changes in computer science to make sure intelligent machines are not made obsolete. Here are the facts on the state of the art and ideas for the future.

Computers

Computers today do many amazing things, but they are not yet completely "intelligent." They store and process data at superhuman speeds, but to our knowledge they are still not conscious entities capable of creative thought.

CHAPTER TWELVE

INTELLIGENT

MACHINES

Yet even without sentience, computers have changed our lives. They have done so in ways largely unpredicted by earlier SF. At one time, computers in SF were massive machines, some (as in Clifford Simak's *Limiting Factor*) so huge that they covered entire worlds. Often these computers were symbols of a single all-consuming repressive institution, controlling every facet of every person's life. Sometimes these global computers were in the service of tyrants, sometimes the computers *were* the tyrants, supplanting human influence.

The real computer revolution, however, has been far more egalitarian, replacing slide rules, pinball games and typewriters in many people's lives. The home computer, the electronic keyboard, the inventory software used by retail stores, the programmable microwave oven — these and many other consumer goods have found a comfortable place in people's daily routines. The computerized traffic control systems that monitor the flow of city traffic or automated buildings such as the new city hall in Tokyo are not the totalitarian monoliths portrayed in pre-computer revolution SF. Even though most of the world's nuclear arsenals are under computer control, the computers themselves are still controlled by human beings, and the threat of nuclear war is still usually considered a *political* threat perpetrated by world leaders, not their computers.

The interweaving of computers into people's daily lives is something that can be expected to continue. In your description of the future, it will be an important starting point. How else will computers affect our homes, jobs, schools, cities? What kinds of conflict will arise between people aided by computers and people who are not? The Gulf War showed what can happen when a nation with a computerized military confronts a nation that relies on vintage tanks and artillery. Could a similar technological rift happen on the home front — between rich computerized suburbs and poor pre-computer neighborhoods?

If you want to write about a global computer, you might extrapolate from the systems used by large international banks. Gradually, the world economy is developing a network in which information can be transmitted between any two points in milliseconds. This global computer was not created intentionally. Financial service houses and international banks have invested great sums of money designing their own hardware and software in order to have an edge over their competition. The complex links between them were formed after the fact, in response to the demands of business itself. This global system can be expected to grow, and other global systems — in police work, research, etc. — may develop.

Two factors might create havoc in global systems, computer-controlled cities, buildings and military defense structures: sentience (a computer becoming self-aware and deciding to take matters into its own hands) and computer error or failure. Computer failures have already interrupted telecommunications services and brought air travel to a complete halt for hours at a stretch in large sectors of the U.S. In a future society where computers regulate many more aspects of society and people's personal lives than they do now, and are more intricately interconnected, what would be the repercussions of a major computer failure? If a global computer network were to connect every computer in the world, and this computer somehow achieved sentience, what might it think of the human beings it services and how might it seek to change them?

One of the most popular conventions to have entered SF since the computer revolution is the idea of the Net, in which television, libraries, radio, telecommunications, personal and corporate computers are all integrated into one massive system to which everyone has a certain amount of access. For most people, it is no more than an entertainment center and a simple home computer. But all computer information is connected, and any piece of information is therefore (at least theoretically) accessible to whoever is ingenious enough to uncover it. One of the major preoccupations of SF in the 1980s was speculation on the ways in which human civilization would transform as it began to operate like a vast, intricately connected Net. Since the Net would be formed by accretion, with many distinct units being linked as need or opportunity arose, it would not be the result of a coherent plan or model. It might not even be possible for future experts to create a model of the Net if it grew quickly enough and contained many labyrinthine passageways of information.

Nanotechnology would bring computers down to the microscopic level. Tiny molecular computers could perform surgery and help in the construction of complex pieces of machinery — spaceships, hivelike buildings of incredibly durable materials, and supercomputers with intricate, neural-like networks.

Nanotechnology (as detailed in chapter 10) might also offer a plausible linkup between brain and computer. William Gibson's novels *Neuromancer*, *Count Zero* and *Mona Lisa Overdrive* introduced SF readers to "console cowboys" who could link their brains to their computers, sending them on a mind trip through an analogous computer reality called cyberspace where the data of the Net was laid out in a colorful 3-D spacescape. Gibson never fully rationalized the precise mechanisms that would allow the console cowboys to "jack-in" to cyberspace, but molecular computers, negotiating the neural pathways of the brain and somehow slaved to a larger computer, would be one way for mind and computer to merge.

Artificial Intelligence

By far the most popular computers in SF are those that interact with human characters in a conversational patter that might lead the reader to believe that the computer possesses a humanlike personality—whether it really does or not. Mike, the computer in Robert Heinlein's *The Moon Is a Harsh Mistress*, is an example. So is HAL, the computer from Arthur C. Clarke's *2001: A Space Odyssey* and its sequels.

Can a machine think? How would we know if one did? In some ways, the computer has already advanced far beyond the capacity of a human mind. It can compute more factors faster and can display more sophisticated models of complex systems — the cell, economics, even weather. But a computer, in spite of its speed and agility, still has shortcomings. For one thing, it performs its computations one step at a time. The human brain, on the other hand, is a network, billions of neurons functioning simultaneously. This *parallelism* allows the brain to adapt to many diverse experiences, to look at the world and create an ever-changing picture of it.

Scientists still haven't clearly mapped out brain function. But the fact that the human brain exists at all makes the idea of an artificial intelligence plausible. Would it also be a complex network, with electronic versions of neurons and synapses? Or could it achieve true humanlike intelligence through simpler mechanisms?

The standard test for determining whether a machine thinks was proposed by British mathematician Alan Turing in 1950. In the "Turing Test," a computer is asked conversational questions on any subject by a human seated at the keyboard. If the human cannot tell whether the answers come from a machine or a person, then the computer can be considered intelligent.

So far, no computer has completely passed the test. Philanthropist Hugh Loebner has offered a $100,000 prize for a machine that passes. Some scientists are skeptical that any machine will ever succeed; others are trying diligently. One scientist argues that to duplicate human intelligence requires a machine with the processing power of the human brain — about 10 trillion calculations per second (10 "teraflops" in computer jargon). Today's most advanced parallel computers reach about 100 billion calculations per second. The necessary advance in speed, however, might come within the first decades of the twenty-first century.

Your story, however, does not have to take the Turing Test for granted. It may not be true that merely passing the test is a sign of intelligence. It may be that a computer could fail the test but actually have a form of sentience.

In SF, the fundamental bridge that a machine must cross to achieve true humanlike intelligence is *self-awareness*, when the machine begins to reflect philosophically about its condition. And yet, some human beings seem incapable of philosophical reflection. In the works of Philip K. Dick, among others, there is often the ironic comparison between androids who have achieved self-awareness (often with tragic results) and the humans who haven't. While no existing computer is on the brink of self-awareness, SF writers have always been fascinated by the possibility.

Clarke's HAL illustrates how fruitful this subject can be. In the first novel, HAL is the dominant personality and his actions ultimately appear to be those of a confused paranoid human being as he sabotages the astronauts' mission. As he is slowly disconnected he exhibits something that resembles real fear. But did Clarke really see HAL as a self-aware computer? In *2010* the reader is told how HAL's sabotage of the earlier mission was the result of ambiguous programming, creating an unresolvable conflict, a paradox. Is HAL just an extremely complex computer who can imitate human emotions so well that when it does experience some kind of computer failure, it only *appears* to be a nervous breakdown? In *2061: Odyssey Three*, HAL returns as a spiritual noncorporeal presence that would seem to make him a self-aware being: a soul that once resided in a computer. There are no easy answers to this question, either for the characters or the reader.

In Greg Bear's *Queen of Angels*, a computerized mission is sent to Alpha Centauri. One of the things the ship's computer, AXIS, is programmed to study is the life-forms that might exist on the planets orbiting Alpha Centauri B. It is also prepared to attempt communication with any possible intelligent life-forms. Upon arriving at its destination, studying the life-forms there and discovering no signs of intelligence, AXIS begins to spiral into a depression. It *feels* its whole purpose was to establish communication with another intelligent entity; finding none, it realizes that forever after, AXIS will be alone. AXIS is sad and lonely and very obviously self-aware, and it took this unforeseen tragedy to make that point obvious. Back on Earth, AXIS's sister computer JILL also experiences a moment of revelatory self-awareness. In capturing this moment, Bear has written some of the most painfully eye-opening passages in the history of SF—worth reading for anyone wishing to write about computer sentience.

Robots

Even before Karel Capek coined the word robot in his play *R.U.R.* in 1920, people speculated about manlike machines. An 1868 issue of *Beadle's Library* had a cover illustration for a story titled "The Huge Hunter: or, The Steam Man of the Prairies," depicting a steam-operated robot in a smoke-belching top hat pulling a wagon with passengers across the American wilderness. Ambrose Bierce's story "Moxon's Master," which dates from the late 1800s, tells the story of an inventor who builds a thinking man-shaped machine. When Moxon beats his creation in a game of chess, the machine becomes enraged, strangles him and explodes.

Robots today are nothing like the robots of fiction. Typically found in industry and entertainment, robots are capable of performing a series of tasks over and over with great precision—assembling an automobile unit; moving like a dinosaur. Most industrial robots are made in Japan, which currently produces more than 75,000 robots a year. But such robots can only follow the specific commands set by their software; they are incapable of reacting to unexpected events. Ask the robot in the factory to take over your spot while you go to the washroom, and it will be helpless.

Even so, robots can be very useful. Personal household robots may be priced within the reach of consumers within the next decade. And within certain constraints, they are capable of adapting quickly to changing environments. These abilities are sometimes showcased in athletic events. The All-Japan Robot Sumo Wrestling Tournament is a yearly competition between six-pound chihuahua-sized robots that look like a cross between a bulldozer and a bug. Japan has also introduced an International Robot Olympics, which includes events such as wall following and obstacle avoidance—two things that are much harder for robots than for humans.

In SF, robots are usually autonomous, relying on nothing but their own circuitry to perform their tasks. But real robots are often remote controlled—and may be for a long time. You can use such robots for exotic jobs in your fiction. The space probes sent to Jupiter, Mars and Venus are essentially radio-controlled robots, responding to computer and operator instructions from Earth. Space station inhabitants and colonists on other planets will probably make use of descendants of these robots.

If you are writing about undersea research, remote-controlled robots will also come in handy. Robots now routinely assist in deep ocean salvage and exploration. A robot is lowered overboard in a cage, then released. A fiber optic cable connects the robot to the ship at sea level. A shipboard operator transmits commands through the cable. The robot's video camera and sonar send back images. The robot's manipulator arm, equipped with metal wrist and gripper, can perform both heavy and delicate tasks: lifting wreckage, picking up small coins. Sea-resistant materials are used: ceramic to resist ocean pressure; titanium to guard against corrosion; Kevlar — a lightweight polymer with the strength of steel — to fortify the cables.

Sometimes SF stories assume that a human needs to be sent on a dangerous job, when a robot can do the job just as well. Your story will be more realistic if you think like a mission planner. Does the task require the costs and risks entailed by a human agent? If not, how sophisticated does the robotic agent have to be? Where and how do human agents fit in? When might humans have to intervene? Virtual reality might be a useful way for humans to monitor robots working in dangerous situations. Important information would be transmitted to the astronaut's headset, and the robot's movements could then be slaved to the data glove.

Intelligent Robots

Of course, many SF writers are only interested in robots for their minds. If you want your robot to think, you will have to take into account the same issues raised in the section on "Artificial Intelligence." The robot will have to do all that a sentient computer can do — plus perform physical tasks and fit into a mobile body roughly designed like a human's.

Such a robot might have aluminum bones, rubber muscles with nylon skin, sensors to detect heat and light, "touch" pads that measure position and force. Its computer will be able to learn from experience and make complex judgments. Things that seem simple to us will be hard for the robot. Think of the complexity that goes into moving an apartment of furniture: picking up and balancing different pieces, navigating the stairs, avoiding scratches, figuring out how to arrange all the pieces in the truck. How would trainers try to educate their robot pupils?

Your thinking robot might not contain its computer inside its body. It might respond by radio or cable to a computer in a laboratory. In fact, an intelligent computer could control a team of robots. The computer would be the "brain" of the robots; the robots would be the computer's arms, legs and senses. Computer centers in different locations could communicate by modem and share the robots. This computer-robot system could operate throughout a large area – a city, a country, even the world. Would the computer-robot system be helpful to humans – or would it become a danger?

There have been many menacing intelligent robots in SF, but there are just as many sympathetic figures. Sometimes, because they are programmed for just and nonviolent behavior, they appear nobler than the human characters. And because they often resemble human beings, they can interact with humans in a wide variety of situations. While they are sometimes portrayed as having emotions as complex as human beings, they are often given a simplicity of character more reminiscent of domestic pets.

Isaac Asimov has written a number of stories and novels about robots throughout his career. Early on he devised what he called the "Three Laws of Robotics":

1. A robot may not injure a human being or, through inaction, allow a human being to come to harm.
2. A robot must obey the orders given it by human beings except where such orders would conflict with the First Law.
3. A robot must protect its own existence as long as such protection does not conflict with the First or Second Law.

On first glance, this seems like good fail-safe programming for a robot. But because of their logicality, Asimov's robots often interpret the Three Laws in strange ways.

Brian Aldiss's classic story *Who Can Replace a Man* shows how oddly robots can behave. In this story, a group of agricultural robots discovers one morning that their human masters have disappeared. The robots conclude that the humans "have broken down," not just those for whom they worked, but all humans everywhere. This group of agricultural robots, which are already divided into a class society because of their grade levels and responsibilities, decide that they will take over — they will govern themselves. Because they already have an established hierarchy, they are quickly able to organize themselves and leave the farm. Along the way, their confidence grows and they find a new sense of purpose. They decide that it is better that humans have died out, robots are far better equipped to run the world (even though they're receiving word that robots are battling each other for control of the city). At the end, however, they find a man. He is alone, wandering in the mountains, feverish and ravaged with starvation. They bear down on him. He turns to them and without even thinking, demands that they bring him food. "Yes, master," one replies. "Immediately!"

In SF, there is usually no doubt that a robot is not human. Whether it is covered in metal, plastic or ceramics, whether it has a male or a female name, whether it is painfully logical and without personality, or programmed to banter like a clever human being, or is in fact self-aware, to be a robot is to be a machine. Often SF writers will use the odd words and actions of robots to shed light on human behavior or to make a pointed statement on our relationships with the machines we think are serving us.

Sometimes, however, a robot will be a perfect likeness of a human being and will blend inconspicuously into the crowd. This is the point where definitions begin to blur.

Androids

Androids have been defined in many ways. For our purposes, an android is an artificial intelligent being that looks human. Anyone who has seen industrial robots knows there are far more efficient ways to design such beings. But the idea of an intelligent machine in a fully mobile humanoid form is a persistent one.

In SF, androids can walk among human beings and communicate effectively. They are often laborers, replacing or at least supplementing a human work force. Underneath its humanlike skin, the android may be a complicated tangle of machine parts. But it might contain an arrangement of "organs" nearly resembling human organs in function. If a human brain, the most complex piece of matter known, could be duplicated through technology and housed inside a human-sized head, then the rest of the android's "organs" could be designed as well. Then, rather than needing to recharge or collect sunlight to keep running, it would simply eat something its body could break down and use as fuel while excreting the waste. The android might even eat normal human food.

Even using nanotechnology, however, it would require quite an advanced technology to duplicate all the complex functions of the human brain, skin and vital organs. And the question arises: Why bother? What function could an android serve that a human, computer or robot could not serve just as effectively? Would they be works of art, works of pure science, secret agents, secret police?

Perhaps the simple fact that humans dream of simulating themselves in mechanical form is enough motivation for an advanced society to design one. In that case, social and ethical questions arise. Would an android that resembles a human being in shape, speech and manner be looked upon as a machine, or more like an animal or even a human? An android designed to work in research or business or diplomacy might be more effective if it appears human. But if the android is designed to take on dangerous or self-destructive tasks, it might be better not to give it a human appearance or personality. People might form pressure groups to protest against mistreatment of androids. The androids themselves might rebel.

Achieving self-awareness might not be intentional. An android with a complex "brain" programmed to learn might begin to recognize and fear its own mortality; it might fall in love; it might realize that its greatest enemies are the humans who believe an android is beneath them. An android might lose itself in human society, trying to fit in, seeking revenge, trying to hide its real identity while it wrestles with the problems of existence.

Cyborgs

Clearly, there are many obstacles to developing genuine artificial intelligence for computers, robots and androids. It may be there is no way for a machine to simulate the human brain perfectly. But if you can't make a machine-brain, you may still be able to put a brain inside a machine. That is the principle behind cyborgs, or cybernetic organisms.

Cybernetics is the comparative study of computers and the human nervous system. A cyborg is a human being integrated with (or into) a mechanical system. In its most extreme form, a cyborg might be a human brain implanted into any number of machines: a robot, an automated factory or a starship. As the term indicates, these cyborgs would ideally contain complex computer/nervous system interfaces that at the present time are strictly in the realm of imaginary science. But in spite of this, cyborgs appear to be far likelier to be a real part of the future than androids.

Electronic prosthetics and medical implants already exist that place machine elements inside a human being. The next chapter, "Remodeling Humans," will say more on that subject. But the fully integrated machine-human belongs in this chapter, because stories about cyborgs deal with many of the same issues as stories about androids and robots. Is a cyborg human? How do its mental experiences — heightened by computer microcircuits and sensors — differ from those of a human?

Again as with robots and androids, the question must be asked: Why build a cyborg? In Frederik Pohl's *Man-Plus*, astronauts volunteer to be transformed into cyborgs for use on missions to Mars. But why would any healthy human agree to have his body so transformed? Why would he sacrifice his own limbs and senses — even for better ones? How would his wife take it? How would his self-image be affected? Why would he not feel that he had been made a monster? *Man-Plus* deals imaginatively with just such conflicts.

There are other ways to get your human being meshed with a machine. The human subject may be a dying man who becomes a cyborg to save his life. The human subject may be a prisoner who is forced to become a cyborg. Maybe in a future age, people simply think their bodies are ugly and impractical, and prefer to become cyborgs. The Mechanists from Bruce Sterling's story collection *Crystal Express* and novel *Schismatrix* offer a variety of looks at a future human society in which cyborgs constitute the majority.

Human-Machine Relations

Chapters 10 and 11 detail the many technological advances that might occur in human society in the near and far futures. From the household appliances that mold personal lives, to the military hardware that will change the strategy and the rhetoric of defense, to the breakthroughs that will change the way human beings look at the world, and finally, to the intelligent machines that help human beings run the world — these changes will shape the psychology of your characters. Will your readers be horrified by what this technology has done to the human condition? More important, will this horror be something that is apparent to your characters, or will they look back upon the late twentieth century as a barbaric or frivolous or wasteful era? If your characters are enslaved by their technology and yearning to break free of their bonds, how will they envision the alternative they yearn for? The chances are that they'll be struggling for the kind of life that might seem as alien or repugnant to modern readers as the oppressed society they're trying to escape. If an aristocrat from the late eighteenth century could see how the great discoveries of the Age of Reason had molded life two hundred years down the line, would he be horrified by the state of the world? It is very likely that he would be. And yet, how many modern people really yearn to be living two hundred years ago, even in the richest countries in Europe? In a way, modern people are enslaved by their own technologies, but more often than not these are benevolent forms of enslavement that spoil and soften people. They also serve to make people of advanced technological societies less and less like people in impoverished "backward" societies. At the same time, enough technology leaks over into Third World economies to make even the poorest people far different from their ancestors two or three generations ago.

Supercomputers and androids may cause deeper, subtler changes in the human psyche, as they offer analogs to, and deviations from what we ordinarily think of as the human mind. But unless the machines actually take over, forcing changes on human beings that no humans can protest, even these most complex areas of technology will be under the jurisdiction of human decision-making.

Cyborgs, because they represent subtle integrations of flesh with metal, plastic and ceramics, create a more unsettling picture of technology's invasion into the human form. And as nanotechnology is used to interface the human with machine form, it will become increasingly difficult to distinguish where the flesh ends and the machine begins.

SF readers will always be interested in stories about machines in the image of humans. But just as interesting are stories about how humans themselves may be remodeled. That is the subject of the next chapter.

○

Throughout most of history, human mastery of nature has meant the mastery of nature *outside* the body. Tools, clothing, buildings, dams, ships and spaceships are all ways of manipulating the outside world to better suit the human form. But humans today stand at the threshold of a world where they can change the human form itself. How this radical shift in focus can be a part of your science fiction is the subject of this chapter.

Some distinctions are necessary. Tattoos, athletic exercise, surgery and wooden legs are all ancient ways of altering an individual human form. Sophisticated prosthetics are an outgrowth of this tradition and are described in this chapter. But alterations done to an *individual* will never pass on to an individual's descendants — unless the alterations are done at the genetic level, in the sex cells or fertilized eggs that set the pattern for future generations.

Natural selection is one way of achieving this kind of remodeling. Gene variations are selected in the natural "struggle for survival" when some individuals succeed better than their competitors in reproducing; over many generations, a whole species can be remodeled this way. It is slow but effective, and it is touched on in this chapter

CHAPTER THIRTEEN

REMODELING

HUMANS

(a fuller treatment can be found in chapter 7). Then there is artificial selection. Since civilization began, breeders have been practicing this method when they allow only plants or animals with desired traits to reproduce. Domestic dogs and cats are animals "remodeled" from wild ancestors.

In just the last few decades, a momentous new tool for remodeling has been found. Scientists now understand that a molecule called DNA, found in every living cell, carries the information that directs the development of an organism. Scientists can now directly manipulate this DNA. The technology is still in its infancy, but in the world of your SF stories, genetic engineering (perhaps combined with nanotechnology) may have succeeded in remodeling any number of species, including humans.

Genetic engineering may bring many benefits, but it is also dangerous. It is subject to human error, greed and ignorance. It raises ethical and religious questions that may never be answered to everyone's satisfaction. Like the industrial revolution that led to the warming of the atmosphere and the degradation of the ozone layer, the bioengineering revolution will be carried out without full awareness of all the consequences—and may one day be a source of deep regret. But like the industrial revolution, it will probably happen. It is worth exploring in your fiction.

Are We Evolving?

Before speculating on how humans might alter themselves, it is worth asking whether nature is already altering us. Is the human species still evolving?

Studies of blood proteins in humans and chimps reveal that they shared a common ancestor as recently as six to eight million years ago. The oldest *australopithecus* fossils, which reveal a strange mixture of human and apelike features, are around four million years old. "Modern" humans appeared less than a hundred thousand years ago.

Once humans began making tools, they were solving problems through reshaping the environment. We didn't need sharp claws and the speed of a cheetah because our arms were just strong enough to hurl spears after our prey. We didn't need to alter our teeth as the environments changed and our food sources changed. We decided what we would eat, processed it with fire and tools, and even began controlling the growth of the plants and animals we chose. Natural selection ceased—if only for a short time—to exercise control on our evolutionary direction. But have humans stopped evolving?

The answer is yes—for the moment. Since the end of the last ice age and the beginning of agriculture, we have stalled natural selection and have managed to retain a form little different from our ancestors thirty or forty thousand years ago. (This isn't unusual—many species reach equilibrium and stay there for millions of years.) If our civilization falls apart, if for some reason humans are reduced to a wandering hunter-gathering lifestyle once again, nature will again weed out individuals unfit for the harshness of a particular climate or ecosystem. Natural selection will again remodel humans to fit the environment.

But if civilization continues to advance as it has been, with humans exercising more and more control over the environment, evolution will soon become a matter of conscious human direction. Not only will humans determine their own evolutionary path, they will be able to remodel plants, animals and microorganisms.

Natural Remodeling

Before speculating on how humans might remodel themselves, it might help to imagine the possible courses human evolution could take if natural selection were still the determining factor. The genetic variation among the races of humanity is an obvious example. Early modern humans migrated across Africa, to Eurasia and the Americas. They scattered into what became isolated communities. Within the races there is wide variation in skin and hair color, and between the races there is far more of a difference. These differences developed as a result of natural selection choosing pigmentation levels, among other things, to increase the hardiness of the people living in widely divergent climatic regions.

But modern technology makes most of these differences superfluous. Human populations were never separated for long enough to make interbreeding impossible, and the differences in climate have never been enough to make transitions to new climates too difficult. The racial modifications within the species are minor and may continue to blur in the future. If standards of beauty were to remain constant for hundreds or thousands of years, sexual selection might remodel men and women into a narrower range of facial and body types. But these standards will probably continue to change from generation to generation.

Nutritional standards have an enormous influence on the physical form. In the early 1800s, as rural populations in England began drifting into industrialized cities, their diet became worse. The result was that the average height of English men and women decreased over the next two generations. In Germany in 1920, the average height of a man was 5 feet 7 inches. Now the average height is 5 feet 11 inches. The average height of men and women in the U.S. has been increasing slowly over the last 100 years. But these changes are caused by nutritional factors, and do not affect the genetic information passed from generation to generation. Therefore they aren't true evolutionary changes.

If an extraterrestrial species with advanced technology were to colonize or even attempt terraforming Earth to suit their own environmental needs, the selective pressures on the small populations of human survivors could be very intense. As the Earth was slowly, painstakingly transformed, the humans would have to be transformed too, or perish.

As the sun ages (see chapter 3), its changes will affect the evolution of all life on Earth. Gene Wolfe, in his *Book of the New Sun* series, envisions a world that is rich with the mysterious residue of millions of years of human civilization and environments full of strange creatures that may be either remnants of genetically engineered forms or the products of natural selection. But the human beings are little different from contemporary humans. In Brian Aldiss's classic *The Long Afternoon of Earth* (aka *Hothouse*), Earth in the far future is a place suitable more for plants than for animals. One side of the planet faces the sun at all times, and it is bombarded, unprotected, by ultraviolet radiation. Vegetation flourishes in this environment, having gradually evolved into gigantic active forms, while the animals — less able to adjust to the rise in temperatures and UV radiation — are disappearing. Human beings are small climbing animals, still possessing intelligence and rudimentary tribal societies, but restructured for life within the worldwide tangle of vegetation, with green skin to camouflage them from free-moving predatory plants.

Cybernetic People

The previous chapter considered the possibility of a human brain inside a machine body. But for the near future, it is more plausible to think of humans who are partly composed of machines. The use of prosthetics — artificial replacements for missing parts of the body — is a natural outgrowth of the human inclination toward toolmaking. Once we are able to manipulate these prosthetics with agility, and once we can design not only new limbs, but new artificial organs, we are well on our way to being able to design cybernetic people.

Transplants. Mechanical systems designed to replace failed or destroyed body parts are already being used on human beings. People suffering from kidney disease have for years been using dialysis machines to clean impurities out of their bloodstreams. In the 1980s surgeons had limited success replacing damaged hearts with artificial ones.

Dialysis machines are getting smaller all the time, and those used now are fairly portable. The patient can remain permanently plugged into the machine but still walk about. Ideally, of course, the kidney machine would be no larger than a real kidney (or a pair of kidneys), and it could be permanently implanted inside the patient's body. Luckily for those who've needed them over the years, a patient doesn't have to be permanently hooked up to a dialysis machine. The procedure may take several hours, but once the procedure has ended, the patient is free to go until the next appointment.

An artificial heart *has* to be housed within the body, because the patient will need to use it every second of his or her life. So far, implanted artificial hearts have not had a terribly impressive record. One of the biggest difficulties has been the need for an external power supply to keep the heart pumping. The point on the chest at which the power lines enter the body are susceptible to infection. For an artificial heart to be truly successful it would need its own permanent power supply, perhaps a tiny nuclear engine using energy supplied by decaying plutonium. Many heart patients would probably not consider carrying plutonium around in their bodies (even if it was safely housed). And in a world where some nonnuclear nation would do anything to get hold of a supply of plutonium, it might not be a very good idea to have heart patients walking around with their own miniature stockpiles. Another thing an artificial heart would need is a biosensor—a device that could tell the heart to beat faster when the body needs more oxygen.

Prosthetics. Modern prosthetic limbs are far more sophisticated than the peg legs of storybook pirates. If the patient's vestigial arm or leg has enough muscular control at the tip that connects to the prosthetic limb, it can manipulate the control system in the prosthetic limb. Some prosthetics are sensitive to electrical impulses caused by twitches in the muscles; some have microcomputers that increase control. These advances allow some patients to play sports even though they've lost a leg, or to work as carpenters or artists even though they've lost an arm.

All of these advances require manipulation of the muscles that connect to the limb. But what if these muscles are degenerated? Ideally, the prosthetic limb would be linked directly to the nervous system of the wearer. The brain could then have direct control over the artificial limb. This would require biosensors, able to translate signals from the brain to the limb and back again.

Brain Implants. Any surgically inserted brain implants that can be designed in the near future are likely to be less complex than the brain itself. The on-off switches that control computers are affected by far fewer factors than the neurons of the brain, each of which is intricately linked by thousands of synapses, so that the information and instructions processed by the brain at any given moment are controlled by a far more complex set of wiring. Would the brain *play* the brain implant, giving it instructions, or would the brain implant be a more integral part of the system? If the implant were sufficiently complex, could it be almost a twin, a companion or counselor with an independent personality, inside the human brain?

A simpler kind of brain implant could be used to control a prosthetic limb. If a human brain can have direct control over a piece of machinery, are there any limits to the size and complexity of the machine it can control? If we can produce an artificial arm that is more versatile and more powerful than a real arm, that delivers as much or more sensual pleasure, and can be manipulated with the same ease with which a brain uses a real arm, people might choose to have the inferior outmoded limbs removed and replaced with powerful pleasant-feeling prosthetics. Why stop at a single arm or leg?

Another possibility of brain implants is that they'd allow a human being to "jack into" a computer, which would allow them to control an automated factory. This person would be like a floor supervisor able to monitor and control the actions of every robotic aspect of the factory. He or she would just come to work, plug into the computer for the duration of the shift and then go home. Such personnel could even work from home over a computer network. A manager in San Francisco could oversee a plant in Singapore. This has the advantage of using the strengths of both computers and human brains in one integrated system.

Brain implants that can create effective meshing between the human mind and a computer might be able to do more than control factors outside the mind. A data file containing great amounts of information (technical, scientific, historical, biographical — whatever suits the needs of your characters) could just be "loaded," allowing the person temporary or even permanent access to information and skills that might have taken years to learn in the traditional manner. This would allow people to augment their personalities and expertise to fit particular situations — for example, allowing an ambassador to speak a number of alien languages and follow alien protocols without lengthy drilling, guiding a surgeon through a difficult, unfamiliar operation, helping soldiers negotiate dangerous terrain.

Mind Control. Brain implants may introduce a kind of involuntary "programming." Used as a form of mind control, brain implants could be an effective way of controlling a hostile population. Soldiers dominated by computer instructions might serve as a colonial army, acting coldly to subjugate or destroy their own people. Their original personalities could be subdued or destroyed entirely, or selectively destroyed so that only certain aspects remained (intimate knowledge valuable to those controlling their minds, such as the layout of a town or military installation).

A brainwashed subjugated population is one of the primary images in SF. In a century that has seen an increasing interest in psychological warfare and the emergence of oppressive totalitarian states, dystopian novels such as Yevgeny Zamyatin's *We* and George Orwell's *1984* projected these traits into the future, implying a global tyranny full of brow-beaten brainwashed people. At the same time, Aldous Huxley's *Brave New World* depicted a future civilization so lulled by extravagant sensory pleasures that they have willingly degenerated into a state of dreamy submission.

In a society where brain-computer connections are very advanced, people might regularly jack programs into their brain implants to learn new work skills, games, languages and immerse themselves in vivid fantasies. This easy access to the human mind could be dangerous if it fell into the wrong hands. In *The Three Stigmata of Palmer Eldritch*, Philip K. Dick wrote of a hallucinogenic drug that offered vivid illusions of immortality. Yet these hallucinations also introduced an omnipresent patriarchal image of the drug's manufacturer, Palmer Eldritch, so to engrain into every user's mind the God-like love and power of the man. The aim was to get everyone who took the drug (potentially every human being in the solar system) to love and worship Palmer Eldritch. His conquest of human civilization would then be simple — a popular movement, the will of the people.

Whether or not a drug could control so many aspects of a

hallucination, it might be fairly easy to code the same kind of subliminal messages into computer programs for brain implants, so that an entire population would willingly but unknowingly become slave to an idea or a megalomaniacal personality. The victims of this kind of mind control wouldn't need to be an oppressed populace or prisoners of war. They could be members of a prosperous consumer society, being gradually molded and transformed by messages and images hidden in the harmless entertainment they plug into their brains.

Genetic Engineering

Genetic engineering is the direct modification of chromosomes to produce permanent changes in a species or variety. It can be used to force existing organisms to produce new products. Potentially, it could be used to create entirely new organisms.

In a way, human beings have been engineering genes for thousands of years by selecting the individuals whose genes are passed from one generation to the next. The "gene pool" of any domesticated plant or animal represents only those variations that human beings have allowed to survive. Any individual born with unwanted physical or behavioral characteristics isn't permitted to reproduce.

As human beings have come to understand not only the laws of heredity but the actual mechanics of genetics, we've reached a point at which we will soon be able to manipulate the genetic building blocks of plants and animals, giving rise—in a single generation—to radically altered creatures and new species.

Basic Genetics. Genes are instructions, transmitted by inheritance, on how to build an organism. Composed of an organic compound called deoxyribonucleic acid (DNA), genes control the formation of proteins, the building blocks of life. Every cell in an organism's body contains a complete set of genes in threadlike structures called chromosomes, found in the cell nucleus. Each chromosome contains many genes, or units of inheritance; each gene directs the formation of a particular polypeptide (a chain of ten or more amino acids; proteins are long polypeptides). A single gene can influence many physical characteristics in the organism. Every characteristic in the organism can be influenced by many genes.

There are twenty-three matched pairs of chromosomes in a

normal human cell. The entire set of an organism's chromosomes is called its "genome." The "Human Genome Project," currently underway, is an enormous multi-billion dollar project, attempting to "sequence" all twenty-three human chromosomes – to find out where all the genes are located and what they all do.

It is important to note that not all genes are active all the time. When a gene is actively producing a protein, that gene is "expressed"; when it is not, it is "dormant." The DNA in a chromosome provides instructions as to when a certain gene should be expressed. Every cell in the body contains genes that explain how to make thyroid hormones, but those genes are only active in the cells of the thyroid gland.

In organisms that reproduce sexually, one chromosome in each matched pair comes from the mother, one from the father. The chromosomes in each pair contain the same pattern of genes, but the nature of the genes may differ. The alternative forms of a gene are called alleles. One allele is often dominant while the other one is recessive; in such a pair of genes, only the dominant trait is expressed. A person would have to have two recessive genes for the recessive trait to be expressed.

Altering DNA. Genetic engineers use enzymes called "restriction enzymes" to chop a particular gene out of the DNA of one organism and insert it into the DNA of another. This process is known as gene splicing. It requires that the scientists know the specific function of a particular gene, how to pluck it from DNA, insert it into the DNA of the recipient organism, and switch it on in the appropriate cells. This allows the latter organism to make a protein it could not have made otherwise, so that certain physical traits can be transferred from one kind of organism to another. So far it has been very successful with bacteria: For example, bacteria can be genetically altered so that they can produce a human hormone. Gene splicing is more difficult with more complex creatures, because their cells are far more specialized, and only certain genes are supposed to switch on in any particular cell. Ultimately, scientists will be able to redesign organisms by radically transforming the genetic information in egg cells. So far it is a crude process, but once scientists can control how many copies of the gene are inserted, and where they attach themselves to the chromosomes in the nuclei of the egg cells, the possibilities are almost endless.

Methods of Gene Splicing. There are three ways to transfer genes

A Tour Through a Genetics Laboratory

The business of tinkering with life has come a long way since the movie images of Dr. Frankenstein's castle laboratory, cluttered with arc lamps and bottled brains. Actual genetic engineering laboratories have a modern and antiseptic look. Here are some of the sights you might encounter in a laboratory dedicated to altering bacteria so that they produce a human hormone.

1. Research and Development (R&D) and Preparation. Here bacteria are prepared to become bioproduct factories. This phase takes place in cluttered labs where work space is staked out amid instruments and equipment. A freezer contains enzymes used to cut and paste DNA. The most important types of enzymes are DNA polymerase (to build DNA), ligase (to anneal or soften), and endonuclease (to cut). Equipment in this lab includes culturing media and ovens (to grow bacteria), constant temperature baths, and lots of glassware and high-purity chemicals. Enzyme is dispensed with microdispensing pipettors (glass tubes), capable of doling out quantities as small as a millionth of a liter.

This lab also contains a DNA sequencer and synthesizer used to investigate which DNA sequence (or gene) directs the making of the hormone you want. These are computer-controlled box-like instruments sitting on counters or tables. Sequencing requires cleavage and reaction of the DNA sample with dye-labeled DNA base mixtures; the instrument reads the dyes by laser and the data is interpreted by computer.

All this cutting, pasting and sequencing produces chemical and biohazard waste. Strong steel vessels called autoclaves are used to contain the waste. Where there is any chance that altered bacteria might leak into the environment (or that unknown DNA might contaminate the bacteria), special air filters, clean suits and masks are used. The next three phases of the process take place in separate labs, each dedicated to one phase.

2. Cooking. This is the production phase, in which the altered bacteria produce the desired hormones. The bacteria live in "cooking" units or fermenters, closed cylinders of steel and glass surrounded by pipes, wiring, heaters, gauges and meters. In these sophisticated stills (from 1-2,000 liters in volume) the bacteria are kept reproducing merrily, producing human hormone in the process. Temperature, pH and nutrients are kept at optimal levels for unrestricted growth.

3. Separation. This is the harvesting phase. Like trees and apples in a field, the bacteria and product are in the same liquid media and have to be separated. The most popular method is to use a centrifuge followed by a trip through a size exclusion column. This contains gels or solids that allow hormone solution to pass while bacterial bodies and other contaminants are kept out. It is connected to the fermenter or to the front end of the purification system.

4. Purification. This is the refinement phase. Here you separate the hormones further from impurities in the solution. You might use a fancier, faster centrifuge resembling a flying saucer to get out the cruder gunk. Then you pump the solution through a purification system consisting of filters and a column full of liquid or solid packing that separates components based on tiny chemical differences. (The process is called chromatography.) The whole setup looks like larger and smaller boxes with keyboards attached by tubing. The final hormone product is stored in a −20° C freezer until ready for use.

5. Analysis. This phase, which might share lab space with the R&D division, tests hormone products for purity and analyzes impurities. A liquid chromatography system is the main work horse of the lab; techniques such as gas chromatography and UV radiation detection are also used.

---

into the chromosomes of a different organism. The first involves inserting the gene into the DNA of a virus. A virus is a microorganism with no reproductive machinery of its own; it lives by taking over the machinery of other cells. Scientists infect cultured cells with the viral DNA, creating colonies of cultured cells whose chromosomes contain the foreign gene.

The second method involves injecting the gene directly into cell cultures, which also results in a colony of cultured cells containing the foreign gene.

In the third method, the gene is injected directly into the nucleus of a fertilized egg, after which the egg is returned to the womb. The result is an organism with the foreign gene in every cell, so that an entire breeding population will contain a gene for a specific trait.

New Humans

The most drastic use of genetic engineering (the one least likely in the near future) is the transformation of human beings into new species: varieties so different from ordinary humans that the two cannot interbreed. SF writers have been speculating on the possible uses of such new species for decades. In a series of stories collected under the title *The Seedling Stars*, James Blish wrote of human beings spreading throughout the galaxy. Each colony was made up of a human species custom engineered to survive and thrive on a particular kind of planet. In "Surface Tension," humans take on the form of minute underwater organisms on planet Hydrot. In "The Thing in the Attic" humans are engineered into small tree-living creatures on the jungle planet of Tellura. Both of these examples take place on Earthlike planets.

The total genetic engineering of humans into creatures capable of living on alien worlds is often called pantropy. Could altered humans survive in the atmospheres of gas giants like Jupiter? If so, they would probably be designed much like the gigantic alien floaters described in chapter 5. Since terraforming might be possible on smaller rocky worlds such as Mars, pantropy might not be necessary. The environment would be customized to suit human needs and would be changing over the course of two or three generations, making the altered humans obsolete by the time the planet became inhabitable by normal humans. In a massive colonization of new planets, terraforming and pantropy might be used together, with each new generation of humans engineered for abilities appropriate to the timetable of the planet's transformation.

Would such people be accorded the same rights as "normal" human beings? In space this might not present a problem. Humans designed to live in zero gravity vacuum conditions might be isolated from normals. They might have long arms, short legs with hands instead of feet, and a supple flexible spine, all to allow them better maneuverability in space. They would require a thick reinforced skin to protect them from the effects of zero pressure, radiation and temperature extremes. They might have four lungs, two of them used as internal reservoirs for oxygen and waste carbon dioxide. All pores and orifices would need to be tightly sealable, including protective outer lenses for the eyes.

If they are oppressed by the normals, who consider them freakish subhuman laborers, they might start a revolution to gain their independence. But once the revolution was won, they might have little contact with "normals."

But new forms of humans could be engineered here on Earth,

too. If the oceans became vast farms, with enclosed schools of fish and kelp beds that could thrive at great depths, a crew of human laborers might be engineered into aquatic forms. They might have gills as well as lungs, a thick layer of subcutaneous fat, protection against the deadly "bends" and against the corrosive saltwater, webbed extremities, chemoreceptors that would serve as a sense of smell underwater, and possibly even an echo-location system to guide them in the darkness of the deep seas.

A human might also be engineered into a flying creature. Such a human would have to be small and lightweight, probably no more than twenty to twenty-five pounds, and it would have large membranous wings extending from all or part of the hands — like those of the pterosaurs. Could these creatures retain manual dexterity?

One problem with flying humans is that no matter how hollow and lightweight the skeleton, they would probably need full function of their brains, which in normal human beings is big enough to cause aerodynamic problems for any flying creature. What would be the practical reasons for winged humans? They might just be the result of an artistic urge, rare and well-protected creatures. They could be designed to live on a planet with a lower gravity, which would allow them to be heavier and brainier without sacrificing aerodynamic skills.

Genetic engineering might also be used for more subtle transformations in humans, raising intelligence or athletic ability, and increasing longevity.

Clones

Cloning is a type of bioengineering that does not involve altering the genetic sequence. In nature, a clone is an organism produced asexually by a single parent; its DNA is an exact copy of the parent. In science fiction, a clone is an organism grown from a body cell of an adult organism. This has not yet been accomplished with humans, but there is no reason in principle why it could not be. Every body cell — skin, saliva, blood — contains the genetic blueprint for a complete organism. The trick is to get a donor's body cell to behave like a fertilized egg cell, so that it develops into an embryo. The resulting embryo would grow into an exact twin — a clone — of the donor.

The fertilized egg could be implanted into a surrogate

mother, where it would be carried to term. This method is already in use with eggs that are fertilized in the laboratory using donated sperm (a technique, incidentally, which not long ago was pure science fiction). Or the embryo could be grown in an artificial womb, a technique that may someday be developed.

It is wrong science for a clone to be the same age as the donor. Clones would grow at exactly the same rate as any other human being. An old man's newly born clone would be an infant—an infant identical in genetic structure to the donor, but with his own life still to live. Since environment has a lot to do with how people turn out, the clone might become a very different person from the donor.

It is also wrong science for clones to have a mystical or telepathic connection any different from the connection between identical twins. After all, identical twins are clones of each other, having developed from a single fertilized egg cell. And it is wrong science to say that a clone is not a human being. Clones may be *treated* differently by society, but in their biological makeup, clones will be just as human as their donors.

Why would clones be desirable? Some people may not be content to have a child who has only *half* their genes; they may seek a kind of immortality by generating perfect copies of themselves. Society may also use cloning to bring to life famous people of the past—the frightening premise of Ira Levin's *The Boys From Brazil*, in which a Nazi scientist makes clones of Adolph Hitler. They might also use clones to multiply the numbers of endangered species or even restore extinct species—the premise of Michael Crichton's *Jurassic Park*, in which dinosaur blood cells, preserved in the bodies of insects that were trapped in amber, are used to clone living dinosaurs.

Regeneration

Clones may also be useful in regenerating lost or diseased body parts. The plausibility of this goal comes from the fact that many organisms have remarkable powers of regeneration. Plants are able to grow new individuals from single cells. If a planarian worm or a starfish is sliced into several pieces, each slice will grow into a new individual. Some salamanders can regrow lost limbs, and lizards can grow new tails. But tissue regeneration among birds and mammals is very limited.

Scientists can already get nerve cells to reproduce in the laboratory, and grow new skin tissue from cell cultures to be grafted onto burn victims. If they could learn to activate the genes that make a complete arm or finger grow, accident victims would be able to grow back dismembered limbs. This is where clones come in. If humans could clone themselves, they might be able to stash younger, more fit versions of themselves in cryonic suspension. These could then be used for spare parts — compatible perfect replacements for diseased organs and limbs. While this type of genetic engineering might be gradually accepted, people might object to it on moral grounds, claiming that the clones used for spare parts were living human beings with the same rights as any other.

Remodeling Other Species

Society would probably find it more acceptable to engineer animals and plants rather than humans for commercial, ecological or medical uses. For speculations on some of these new uses, see the chapter on "Designing a Future."

Scientists might try "uplifting" certain species, especially whales and the great apes, giving them near-human intelligence and the ability to speak. In Michael Bishop's novel *Transfigurations*, a chimp/baboon hybrid is endowed with a high intelligence. While it cannot speak, it has a fluent command of sign language, which it teaches to an apelike alien. In this way the humans are able to make at least some rudimentary communication with the alien. In David Brin's "uplift" novels (see the chapter on "Galactic Civilizations") humans have genetically altered chimps and dolphins into intelligent articulate creatures who seem to be equal to humans in almost every way. In small experimental communities, many animals might be molded into intelligent forms. Mammals and even birds could be uplifted for purely aesthetic reasons.

This, too, might cause discomfort and controversy among human beings unable to accept the idea that other animals could be the intellectual equals of human beings. Some people might see a large-brained bird able to carry on a simple conversation as an evil devious creature, even if the bird could only attain the intelligence of a five-year-old child. A hostile ignorant population might embark on a wholesale slaughter — genocide committed against a species that was on the brink or even beyond the brink of achieving true intelligence.

One way of resurrecting long-dead forms of life is to work with the DNA of their closest living relatives. In the case of dinosaurs, this would be either crocodiles or birds, whose DNA could be modified to transform them into living replicas of dinosaurs. These creatures wouldn't need to behave as real dinosaurs did; ferocious-looking Tyrannosaurus replicas could be engineered to behave as peaceful plant eaters.

Biomechanics

Just as people who've lost limbs in accidents can use prosthetic limbs, genetically engineered humans might be born *requiring* advanced specialized prosthetics. Military research might lead to the creation of armless, legless humans who grow up operating an increasingly complex array of computerized limbs, weapons and sensory devices. They would not need to be trained as adults to use the wings or infrared lenses or tactical nuclear devices with which they are meshed; it would have been ingrained into them from earliest childhood. Terraform engineers on inhospitable worlds or asteroid miners might also be organic, thinking components of a larger machine. The machine would be helpless — inert — without its human component. The symbiotic relationship between the two parts of this biomechanical construct might be totally unlike the usual relationships between humans and machines, or even between humans. They might think of themselves as a single entity.

The emerging technologies of genetic engineering and nanotechnology could meet and overlap to create striking hybrids. Both deal with the ability to create large structures from fundamental building blocks: cells and molecules. Nanomachines could assist in genetic engineering by entering into cells and hunting for flaws in the DNA. It's even possible to imagine a world where there is no clear distinction between the living organism and machine.

Perhaps successful cloning of human beings will require nanoagents to assist in the orderly reproduction and differentiation of the developing cells. The creation of human biomachines could be an outgrowth of this procedure. A human could be born with a high-speed computer that works separately from but in cooperation with an organic brain, or a complex construct that is part human brain and part computer, or a skeleton reinforced with a strong synthetic material that grows and develops as the human does. Many SF writers have imagined starship captains or navigators as disembodied human brains connected to the ship by electronics. A biomechanical starship captain might be the biological aspect of the starship itself: living, thinking tissue meshed into the fabric of the ship at a microscopic level. A human might be 50 percent machine and still look more organic than robotic: a complex molecular construct with a human mind and a fine mixture of living and mechanical features. Appliances, weapons and homes could all be living things, with the same fine mixture of living and mechanical features. What possibilities could this advanced hybrid technology offer? What could be the potential problems?

Genetic Art

In a society in which genetic engineering has reached an advanced level and there is little controversy over its practical applications in medicine and agriculture, the practice of genetic art might become popular. The organisms created by these genetic artists might serve no practical purpose. Instead of an abstract sculpture, the genetic artist might design and grow a strange "abstract" living organism. These organisms might be short-lived mindless creations, beautiful to look at but serving no purpose other than giving aesthetic pleasure. They might be durable life-forms with long life spans, growing the whole time in ways that not even the artist can predict. Instead of pets and art prints, people might have examples of genetic art in their houses: colorful, cute, able to make adorable cooing sounds and small enough to fit on a mantelpiece.

Maybe there would be controversy surrounding the moral limits of genetic art. When does it become cruel to bring a creature into the world for the purpose of providing idle pleasures for the rich? In a hostile warlike society, one of the appeals of genetic art might be the satisfaction of knowing that your attractive wall hanging can think and suffer and die.

Often the aims of the artistic avant-garde run counter to the popular taste and morality of the rest of society. Some artists like to think of their creations as dangerous. How would this tendency manifest itself in genetic art?

Frankensteins

Advanced genetic engineering would allow for the creation of nightmarish organisms. Not all the hazards resulting from engineered organisms would come from those intended to be dangerous, such as those used for bacterial warfare. A bacteria engineered to digest cellulose might prove hardy enough to escape laboratory conditions and survive in the open. There it could devastate food crops, grass and trees, causing famine and massive disruption in the food chain.

Victor Frankenstein did not set out to create a monster. He wanted to bring life to an assemblage of dead body parts, to create a new man. The result was a tragic creature, filled with the same emotions as normal human beings, but ostracized from society. By all definitions of what was human, he was considered an inhuman monster. And so, in a very human way, he acted like a monster. In the same way, the greatest threat of genetic engineering may not be what it would do to carefully monitored microorganisms, but what it might do to human beings.

Like any other science, genetic engineering of humans will proceed by trial and error. What will happen to all the "errors": the humans whose DNA has been botched by experiments? Will such "industrial accidents" be aborted as fetuses; will they be destroyed at birth? What if the errors are not immediately apparent, but only develop when the experimental subject is an adult? How many misshapen, diseased, mutated subjects will be created on the road to making better humans? What will their legal rights be? If they have no legal recourse, what private vengeance will they exact?

Even if genetic engineering goes exactly as planned, monsters may be created. What if the aquatic people designed to tend kelp beds are a slave race and are scorned by the normals? The aquatics might have all the intelligence and range of emotion of the normals but be treated as little more than animals. Their hatred of the normals could turn into a full-scale revolution. Aquatic people might be able to take control of drinking water or threaten the safety of a major oceanic crop. Because their appearance may be repulsive to the normals, just the thought of them coming ashore or on board ships and slaughtering normals would terrify the normals even more than a traditional enemy.

What if humans engineered for greater intellectual or athletic ability happen to become psychopaths? Maybe drugs or therapy will one day be able to eliminate violent, destructive behavior in murderers or potential murderers. But the metabolism of the engineered individuals might be able to override these drugs. Perhaps their intellectual ability will make them immune to therapy or conditioning.

An entire society, after generations of genetic tinkering with the human form and mind, might seem to us like monsters. Traditions, religious beliefs, their attitudes toward each other and toward other living things might all be shaped by factors that stem from the ways their genetic makeup has been altered. If humans spread out through the solar system and beyond, communities might be out of contact for generations at a time. Contact between humans who still resemble us physically and psychologically, and humans whose physical adaptations to a particular environment have created a strange and frightening society, might seem nearly as alien as a meeting between humans and extraterrestrials. Humans whose forms have veered too far from the human norm might seem like (and be treated as) monsters even if their society was more civilized.

Animals engineered for police or military purposes might be so intelligent and bloodthirsty that not even their human masters could control them. Also, guard animals might be engineered to look horrifying though they are docile unless threatened. Animals engineered for specific ecological purposes, such as assisting in the terraforming of a planet, might prove dangerous when introduced into other ecologies.

Greg Bear's *Blood Music* is the story of Vergil I. Ulam, a brilliant but troubled and careless researcher in the biotech industry. On his own he begins experimenting with B cells from his own blood. (B cells are lymphocytes — white blood cells — which bind to germs and produce antibodies.) But Vergil's experimental B cells, which he calls noocytes (noos from the Greek word for mind), are able to use DNA as tiny cellular computers. He soon realizes that the noocytes have a kind of rudimentary intelligence. They can learn and communicate. *Blood Music* tells the story of what happens when the noocytes begin exploring — and transforming — the outside world.

Better Humans?

How much would advanced humans, hundreds or thousands of years from now, resemble us? Would they resemble us at all? It may be hard to imagine a society allowing human embryos to be transformed into creatures that appear radically strange, alien. These practices would probably be introduced gradually. More and more birth defects could be eliminated by altering the DNA of the unborn embryo, or augmenting it with nanomachines that would develop along with the baby. More sensitive prosthetics would allow accident victims to not merely live normal lives, but to excel as they never could have with their weaker, more limited real appendages or organs. As generations passed it would become clear that these kinds of alterations of the human body could actually improve the quality of life. Parents might insist that genetic or synthetic molecular alterations be made to their developing embryos as in Robert Reed's *Black Milk*. People might opt to augment themselves with all kinds of prosthetic devices. As generations passed, the changes could multiply, and the old-fashioned, raw-stock humans might seem quaint and poorly equipped for the "good life." It might be that such improvements would be too expensive for all but an upper class. After generations, that upper class would be superhuman — more handsome, taller, stronger, healthier, smarter than anyone alive today — while lower classes would consist of the old unimproved stock.

Ectogenesis. One very critical change could be ectogenesis, the development of the embryo and fetus outside the mother's body, in an artificial womb (already touched upon in the discussion of clones). A fetus in an artificial womb could more easily be monitored and manipulated. This might seem like a perversion in most modern human societies, even though it would be safer for the mother and safer for the fetus (once the technology for ectogenesis was perfected). An ancient bond between mother and baby would be broken. How would this affect the treatment of children by their genetic parents?

The controversies over the morality of ectogenesis might be debated for a long time, but if it improves the overall health of human beings (and eliminates the unpleasantness of pregnancy and childbirth), this controversy may eventually be subdued by popular demand.

Ectogenesis would allow many modifications to take place in

humans. A newborn baby's head is so large (to accommodate the human brain) that oftentimes it can barely fit down the birth canal. Biologists have said the human brain couldn't get any larger without making natural birth impossible. Embryos in an artificial womb would have no such constraints. Their brain could be larger, the neck and shoulders strengthened to accommodate it, and the intellectual capacity of the individual would then be increased. Molecular machines developing upon or within the embryos wouldn't cause any accidental harm to the mother.

Improved humans wouldn't necessarily be adapted for special environments such as the ocean or space or the surface of alien planets. They could just be more efficient versions of modern humans. The neck could not only be strengthened, but could contain tiny backup lungs and heart to supply oxygen to the brain in an emergency. Stronger, more flexible materials could be used to make or reinforce the skeleton. All humans could be born with genes that cause severed limbs to regenerate, and with tougher skin at areas that are now vulnerable.

Metabolism could be improved. New enzymes in the stomach and pancreas would allow the digestion of materials such as cellulose that humans cannot currently digest. This would widen the variety of foodstuffs humans could eat.

The enormous potential of genetic engineering could lead not just to minor adjustments in the human form—making it stronger or smarter or more able to thrive in an inhospitable environment—it could be the force that drives human beings through a major evolutionary change.

Arthur C. Clarke in *Childhood's End* wrote of the next great evolutionary step of humankind as the shedding of physical form altogether and the merging into a single, great thinking entity. This is also close to the final stage of development of the noocytes in *Blood Music*. If genetic engineering and nanotechnology begin to interact in complex ways, finally merging into a single science—the manipulation of self-replicating matter—the distinctions between humans and machines will eventually disappear. A human being might be its own habitat and ecology: a single, self-sufficient, thinking whole. Humans might become unrecognizable, something beyond biology and technology altogether.

○

Science fiction doesn't predict the future. It can envision a better, higher road toward the future, or it can show the results of current trends, played out for good or ill in an imagined future. SF writers ask, "What if . . .?" and proceed to imagine answers. Which trends in modern life, which breakthroughs in science, technology, government and religion will be the dominant forces in our world 20, 100, or 10,000 years from now? Which small, seemingly insignificant undercurrents will mold the future into something completely unexpected?

Looking back through history and ahead to the future, only one trend is certain, and that is *upheaval*. Here then, is a look at some of the upheavals that will shape our futures and may influence the worlds you design in your fiction. It runs the gamut from political and social changes to wars, ecological shifts, killer meteorites, and the death of the Sun.

Future Nations

CHAPTER FOURTEEN
FUTURE SHOCKS

When asked to define who they are, most people will get around to some kind of national identity. People think of themselves as Americans or Germans or Senegalese or Taiwanese. Their nations are defined by central government, region, common language and/or tradition. They think of the world map as an array of such nation-states, neatly delineated.

The recent collapse of the Soviet Union demonstrates the actual fluidity of such ties. After the collapse, people who were once considered Soviets received recognition as Ukrainians or Latvians. In place of civil conflict, national identity may be unclear over long periods. People may disagree on whether their nation is Croatia or Yugoslavia, Namibia or South Africa. In flourishing empires, people of many ethnic groups may consider themselves parts of a much larger unit. In decaying ones, the units of identity get smaller and smaller.

In writing SF, you have to expect that such processes of change will continue. New nations will be created; old ones will fragment and form new combinations. You also have to expect that time may prove your particular scenario wrong. How many SF stories were based on the premise of a flourishing Soviet Union in the twenty-first century?

You may also expect that national ties will become less important. The modern nation-state, after all, is a relatively recent invention: "England" would have been a hard concept to explain to a resident of the British Isles in the fifth century. At that time, the "Angles" or "English" were one of several invading Germanic tribes, and identity was defined by loyalty to kinsmen. Future forms of political organization may be as alien to us as the "United Kingdom" would have been to the fifth-century Briton.

One of the forces that may weaken national ties is communication. As the world becomes a "global village" united by television, telephone, fax and modem, people may be less inclined to see themselves as members of separate nations. The need for global cooperation on such issues as war and peace, energy and the environment may strengthen the movement toward "one-world" organization—based either on the United Nations or on some successor to it. On the other hand, nation-states will probably survive as long as separate populations have conflicting interests. And political leaders will always be ready to use fear of foreigners as a way of gaining popular support.

Corporate Empires

One of the forces that may weaken national ties is the growth of multinational corporations. A bank or corporation can choose as its own home base whatever country is least likely to impose high taxes or government regulations. It can carry out its operations wherever the labor is cheapest and the resources most abundant. It can sell its product wherever there are people with cash in hand. A corporation may depend on the unique expertise of many people in different parts of the world to produce a certain product. In poor countries, it may supply for its workers many of the products and services they might otherwise do without— food, housing, electrical power, sewage, police protection. The corporation thus gets involved in the social welfare of these countries, even as it develops a compelling interest in the economic health of the countries where its money is lent or its products are sold. As the corporation grows in wealth, it may seek to exert influence over the governments of these countries. The government, in turn, will court the favor of a corporation that provides many jobs or performs vital services.

These developments have deep roots in history. The rise of industry in the early nineteenth century shook a centuries-old system of wealth, making millionaires of people from modest origins, some of whom eclipsed the power of those whose wealth came from inherited titles, fortunes or lands. It also created a new kind of working class: urban, literate and dependent on the company for their standard of living—sometimes for their lives.

A corporation that develops an innovative product or process of manufacturing stands a good chance of spreading its influence throughout the world. The more powerful the corporation, the more power they exert on governments. If the company pulls out its operation, the country could suffer a rise in unemployment among its labor force and a disastrous loss of revenue. In time, privately held corporate power could be more significant than any publicly elected, tax-financed government.

A corporation that exploits zero gravity manufacturing or the raw materials of the asteroid belt or runs a World Power Grid (see chapter 7) could conceivably become more powerful than all the world's nations put together. Company policy and the beliefs of an ambitious, unelected CEO would impact on people's lives all over the world—or the solar system.

At the same time, an educated, affluent society will make greater demands on its government and major corporations. Nuclear accidents such as Three Mile Island and Chernobyl, chemical disasters such as Union Carbide's accident in Bhopal, India, and the *Exxon Valdez* oil spill have brought corporate practices under greater scrutiny than ever. Does a company aid in the development of standards of living in Third World countries in which it builds its factories? Or does it exploit them and destroy their environment? How safe are the citizens of a community bordering a nuclear power plant?

Current trends seem to indicate that companies are being forced by governments and pressure groups to show more responsibility to the public and to the environment. Does this work with or against the increasing internationalization of corporations?

Power Blocs

Centers of Power. Three major power blocs are expected to dominate the world economy of the near future: the North American free-trade zone (Canada, the U.S. and Mexico), the European Community, and the rapidly developing area of the Pacific Rim. Geographically, it would make sense that the countries of Central and South America would ally themselves with North America, and that the newly opened-up countries in Eastern Europe would join the European Community. What part the nations of the former Soviet Union will play is still unclear.

Japan's power in the Pacific (and in the world) is great, but it is of great strategic importance for them to ally themselves with their neighbors, the greatest and most problematic of which is China. The future of China's one billion people will depend on what happens to the Communist state that still governs them.

What about Australia and New Zealand? Their nearest markets are along the Pacific Rim, but their emotional bonds are tied more strongly to North America and Europe. And where will the developing nations in Africa and the Middle East fit into this scheme? Debts in many African countries are so great that unless the debts are at least partially forgiven, they may never gain a foothold in the world economy. And the Middle East often seems to be at war with itself, making the possibility of economic unity seem less and less likely.

Wild Cards. There are wild cards scattered throughout the world, countries that, out of ideological differences (Cuba) or longstanding feuds (India and Pakistan), seem unable to function in harmony with their closest neighbors. Yet alliances that once seemed impossible are all around us: Three of the bulwarks of today's European Community—England, France and Germany—have a long and bloody history of wars between them. The Hundred Years War fought between Britain and France (which was actually closer to 120 years) may have ended over 500 years ago, but in your own stories you might be writing of events that occur 500 or even 1,000 years in the future.

Rich and Poor. What about the entity called the "Third World"? This term refers to the poor nations of Asia, Africa and Latin America, united by a common history of colonization and exploitation from the West (the "First World") and the Soviet bloc (the "Second World"). But the term has perhaps become outdated now that the Second World has formally ceased to exist.

As for the rich Western nations of the First World, they must now incorporate their poor cousins in Eastern Europe, and compete with their wealthy Asian rival, Japan. Some former Third World nations, such as Singapore, South Korea and Taiwan, have fast-growing manufacturing economies.

Even so, distinctions between rich and poor nations will probably remain part of the future globe. One common speculation is to expect a division between the rich Northern countries and the poor Southern ones. But there will probably be some countries that do not fit the geographic pattern, and every country will have its own division, more or less sharp, between rich and poor citizens.

What new movements or ideologies will arise to channel the frustrations of those who, for whatever reason, are unsatisfied with things as they are? What old ideologies will be resurrected with a new face? Will a new discovery or industry bring power to Africa or South America, as oil fields did for the Middle East? And what will become of the United States — at once the world's greatest debtor nation and sole military superpower?

Some of the most interesting speculations in SF are the seemingly harebrained projections writers make about the future — especially if they can then be explained in a plausible manner. A study of history is sometimes the most inspiring guide.

Population Growth

Barring some planetary catastrophe, the human population can be expected to keep growing. Like all species, the human population grows exponentially unless something, such as famine or predation, slows it down. This means that the number of people in each generation is proportionately larger than the number of people in the last. In the last few decades, the annual rate of increase has been about 2 percent: There are 2 percent more people each year than there were the year before. Like a compound-interest savings account, that "2 percent" amounts to a larger figure every year that the "principal" gets bigger.

There is a simple formula that gives a rough idea for how long any population, growing exponentially, will take to double:

$$\text{Doubling Time} = \frac{70}{\text{\% annual increase}}$$

In the case of 2 percent annual increase, the 1990 world population of 5.3 billion would double to 10.6 billion in 35 years — by 2025. By 2130, the population would be 85 billion.

There is a natural limit to population growth: the point at which an ecosystem reaches its carrying capacity, the maximum number of organisms it can feed. At that point, famine and disease will kill off the excess numbers, and the population will level off. We do not know just what the Earth's carrying capacity for humans is: We increase it by developing better agricultural methods and clearing more land. But eventually, the sheer mass of humanity would be more than the Earth could support. At the 2 percent annual rate of increase, the world population would be 6.3 *trillion* by 2600 A.D. — and there would be only 2.5 square feet of room per person on the entire land surface of the Earth. To get some idea of what that would be like, read *A Torrent of Faces* by James Blish and Norman L. Knight, in which the human population reaches a trillion.

Fortunately, humans can check their population growth in ways other than famine, epidemic and war. Birth control, sex education and high living standards have reduced population growth in developed nations to zero or less. Worldwide, population growth shows signs of slowing: The U.N. currently predicts a population of only 8.2 billion in 2025. A global policy consensus can eventually stabilize the population at some healthy level. Poverty is the greatest factor in overpopulation: People are likely to have more children where life expectancy is low and ignorance and hunger are great. In a nutshell, the exact population of your future society is up to you to determine.

Totalitarian States

The totalitarian nightmare seems to many people to have diminished with the fall of the Soviet Union. Clearly, some people argue, representative government and personal liberty are good business, and the wave of the future. The future projected in Orwell's *1984* — where an all-powerful state controls every aspect of its citizens' lives through terror and propaganda — seems to be unlikely. It is economically unviable; it invites condemnation and resistance; and modern telecommunications make it almost impossible to shut out the voice of the outside world.

Still, the rest of history is a long time, and anything can

happen. Modern technology may make it easier for a state to fulfill some of the old fantasies of totalitarian control. In Aldous Huxley's *Brave New World*, people are controlled from conception through biotechnology, conditioning and psychotropic drugs — all techniques that are more fully developed now than in the 1930s, when Huxley wrote. All of the technologies described in the previous chapters — computers, implants, virtual technology, nanotechnology, genetic engineering — could be used to the same end.

The two questions to figure out, if you choose to write a dystopia, or negative utopia, are *why* and *how*. Why did the state begin exerting such control? How did people let it happen? Why is the system profitable for the state? How is the apparatus of control paid for? As for the citizens, are they deluded, drugged and pleasure-loving? Are they cowed and fearful? How does the state maintain its control? What challenges might overthrow it?

Nuclear War

Nuclear war is another threat that may seem to have diminished with the demise of the Soviet Union. Most SF scenarios of the past imagined an apocalyptic war between the United States and the Soviet Union, in which both sides unleashed enough missiles to wipe out all life on Earth or at least all of human civilization. Consequently, as the nuclear threat between the two has eased, the threat of nuclear holocaust has retreated *just a little bit*. Why hasn't it retreated more? Because in the meantime, the rest of the world has begun building a nuclear arsenal.

As of this writing, the following countries have the bomb: the United States, France, the United Kingdom, China, Russia, and several former member republics of the defunct Soviet Union. Israel, India and South Africa "probably" have the bomb, though they have not as yet officially declared themselves nuclear powers. Many other developed nations have the technological capability: Canada, Germany, Italy, Sweden, Switzerland, the Netherlands, Finland, Belgium, Taiwan, South Korea and Japan. It is widely suspected that Pakistan, Iraq and North Korea have secret programs to develop a nuclear arsenal.

In imagining the countries that would be responsible for world nuclear annihilation in the future, the list of suspects is growing. Some countries, notably Algeria, Libya, Syria and Iran,

THE WRITER'S GUIDE TO CREATING A SCIENCE FICTION UNIVERSE

may now feel a need to have a nuclear arsenal but so far aren't technologically prepared to undertake it. As the amount of plutonium waste from nuclear power plants increases, it will also be easier for terrorist groups to construct small nuclear weapons. If terrorist groups can steal plutonium for the reaction material in nuclear devices, the nuclear threat becomes one of not only incoming missiles, but suicide bombers with bulky satchels on board trains and in automobiles and in the lobbies of government buildings. It may someday be possible for a nuclear war to be conducted as a precisely coordinated hit by a terrorist group inconspicuous as they carry bombs to their targets.

The Aftermath. A major nuclear war would decimate the populations of the warring countries, devastate vital communications and service networks, poison the water and atmosphere, increase the incidence of certain forms of cancer and cause mutations. (See "Nuclear Devastation," page 284, for more.) Nuclear radiation has highly toxic effects. In the form of "fallout" — radioactive isotopes carried through the atmosphere as dust — this radiation could persist for thousands of years.

In recent years, nuclear winter has been proposed as an equally devastating effect of nuclear war. According to this hypothesis (debated by some scientists), the heat produced by the enormous fireballs of nuclear blasts would ignite great fires, burning cities and forests, and sending several hundred million tons of soot, dust and smoke into the atmosphere. The heat would carry this material high into the atmosphere, where it would drift for weeks, forming a uniform belt of particles, blocking out all but a fraction of the sunlight. Surface temperatures would drop 11 to 22 degrees C (20 to 40 degrees F). Semidarkness and subfreezing temperatures would combine with radiation from nuclear fallout to disrupt plant photosynthesis, killing off much of the Earth's plant life.

The combined effects of the resulting famine, high radiation and the collapse of industrial, medical and transportation infrastructures could devastate human and animal populations. The degree of death resulting from starvation, exposure and disease is still disputed by scientists, and would of course depend on the severity of the nuclear conflict. But it demonstrates that even an isolated nuclear conflict — between two Middle Eastern countries for example — would have negative environmental effects all over the world.

Other Wars, Other Aftermaths

Nuclear weapons aren't the only threat wars could bring to world civilization. See chapter 11 for details on chemical and biological weapons — the two most likely alternatives to nuclear conflict — as well as space-based weapons that could be used in war.

War is one of SF's major preoccupations. This is due in part to the fact that many (if not *most*) SF novels are adventures, and the war story has been one of the most popular forms of adventure going back to Homer's *Iliad*. But SF deals with wars that haven't been fought yet, using weapons that haven't been invented yet, often against foes we haven't even discovered yet. See chapter 9 for how our human tendencies for war could spread throughout the galaxy, or how we might be trapped in a fight with an alien species more warlike than we are. See chapter 11 for a look at the types of weapons with which these future wars could be fought.

SF is preoccupied not just with war, but with the aftereffects of war. Who will survive the nuclear holocaust or the world plague? Can civilization be rebuilt? What kind of wasteland will the world become in the aftermath of the war?

Walter M. Miller's *A Canticle for Leibowitz* is the story of the fall and rise and fall of science and technology, as seen through the eyes of the monks of a Catholic monastery in North America in the aftermath of a world-devastating nuclear war. Enough generations have passed so that the history and technology of civilization just before the war have been reduced to tall tales and misrepresentations. Many people look upon science as a scourge, an evil that corrupted mankind. The book is in three parts: first, the naive, post-scientific world immediately following the war; second, the rebirth of science and the serious study of pre-War culture; third, the high-tech world that results from this rebirth and the nuclear war that results from it. Miller did not see science as the evil that many of his characters believed it to be, but he did show how the worst aggressive tendencies in humans can be brought to devastating extremes through science and technology.

Books like *A Canticle for Liebowitz*, Kim Stanley Robinson's *The Wild Shore* and David Brin's *The Postman* take a more hopeful tone than most works of this type. SF books and films are filled with post-nuclear wastelands. Often these post-war societies are brutal and inclined to react violently at the hint of anything scien-

Nuclear Devastation

If you're going to write about a nuclear war and its aftermath, the best place to begin your research is Jonathan Schell's nonfiction book *The Fate of the Earth*. Schell describes in precise, chilling detail the projected consequences of full-scale nuclear war. *Warday* by Whitely Strieber and James Kunetka is a well-imagined fictional account of life in America five years after a "limited" nuclear war.

Schell's book is perhaps most famous for describing the effects of a one-megaton bomb exploded 8,500 feet above the Empire State Building (actual nuclear warheads may reach 20 megatons). The bomb's blast wave would utterly crush every building within a radius of about four miles from ground zero, and heavily damage buildings as far as eight miles away (as far out as Staten Island). Winds in the area would reach hundreds of miles per hour, die down in a few seconds, and then blow steadily and strongly in the opposite direction.

For ten seconds, a mile-wide fireball (the thermal pulse) would rise brilliantly into the sky, igniting everything below that was flammable, melting metal and glass. People nine miles away would suffer third-degree burns, probably lethal ones. Mass fires would break out in all five boroughs and New Jersey, to a radius of nine and one-half miles. After the fireball, a mushroom cloud of dust and smoke, twelve miles wide, would darken the sky. Its plume, carried by the wind and perhaps by a dirty rain, would drop radioactive fallout throughout the next twenty-four hours. Within tens of miles, all exposed survivors would die over the next few hours and weeks.

Radiation sickness as a result of fallout would kill about half of exposed adults as far as 150 miles downwind. The initial symptoms of radiation sickness include *petechiae* (small spots on the skin caused by hemorrhages), vomiting, fever and thirst. A latency period of hours or days may follow, when the victim seems to have recovered. In fact, however, production of blood cells is dropping, including the white blood cells that guard against infection and the platelets that aid in clotting. In the final stage, which may last hours or weeks, the victim may suffer loss of hair and teeth, diarrhea, and internal bleeding. Not all victims will die, but in the months and years that follow, the survivors will suffer from abnormal rates of cancer and birth defects.

The many small fires would become a mass fire. Depending on wind conditions, they might coalesce into a conflagration, a winddriven wall of flame, or a firestorm, a fire that sucks surrounding air toward a central point of extreme heat, suffocating or burning anyone who tried to hide in shelters.

In a nuclear attack on a single large city, people would be killed and maimed by the millions — by fire, crushing, radiation. An electromagnetic pulse would knock out electrical equipment for miles around. In an attack on a whole country, large sections of the country would be illuminated by flashes of white light brighter than the Sun. Blast waves, thermal and electromagnetic pulses, and mass fires would level the country's infrastructure, leaving only ruins and rubble for those who survived.

---

tific. Examples are Norman Spinrad's *Songs From the Stars*, Wilson Tucker's *The Long, Loud Silence* and Edmund Cooper's *The Cloud Walker*.

It's clearer in SF films than books that one of the fascinations with this genre is the idea that the post-nuclear world, with its reduced populations, its wastelands of mutants (who sometimes, in a popular application of wrong science, seem to transform uniform populations within a few years of the bombing), and its savagery, is an *opportunity* for heavily armed, rapacious survivalists to bring order, rebuild society, or exercise mass acts of terrorism on the rest of the populace.

Ecological Nightmares

The history of the Earth is full of ecological catastrophes. Wave after wave of extinctions have been caused by changes in the environment. The introduction of massive amounts of atmospheric oxygen poisoned many of Earth's bacteria some 3 billion years ago. Something — perhaps an asteroid or comet striking the Earth — wiped out the dinosaurs and many aquatic forms of life 65 million years ago. Life-forms grew plentiful or perished as the ice caps advanced and retreated throughout the ice ages. The legacy of these catastrophes is extinction, which wipes out many plants and animals and offers new advantages to those creatures left to fill the emptied niches in the environment. It's what made it possible for primitive primates to eventually evolve into humans, and it could easily bring about our downfall as well. Some of these ecological changes — a new ice age or a collision with an asteroid — are natural. But many of them — greenhouse warming, ozone depletion, the release of deadly poisons into our water and atmosphere, ice cap melting and the subsequent flooding of lowland areas — would be the result of human interference with a naturally evolving world ecology. Humans tend to focus on these because we believe that if we caused these problems, we can surely solve them. Is this true? And might it also be possible to affect natural events — deflecting an asteroid, preventing the advance of glaciers?

Greenhouse Hell. The temperature of Venus is far hotter than Earth's. Mars's temperature is far lower. As suggested in chapter 6, this can't be explained away as simply a result of their relative distances from the Sun. Rays of visible light filter through our atmosphere and heat the Earth's surface. The visible light is converted into long-wave infrared radiation reflected from the Earth's surface. These rays would bounce back into space if they weren't absorbed by water vapor and molecules of carbon dioxide in the atmosphere. The vapor and the CO_2 reflect the infrared radiation back to the Earth as heat, serving to contain heat like the glass roof of a greenhouse. If it weren't for this greenhouse effect, Earth's average temperature would be about -73 degrees C (-100 degrees F). Even the oceans would freeze. Mars has less CO_2 in its atmosphere (although CO_2 constitutes a higher percentage of Mars's thin atmosphere) and no water vapor. Its temperatures can get as cold as -125 degrees C. Venus, on the other hand, has so much CO_2 in its thick atmosphere that the greenhouse effect has had a runaway effect on the temperature, giving Venus the hottest surface of any planet in the solar system.

The CO_2 that warms the Earth makes up less than one percent of the atmosphere. A small rise in CO_2 level in the atmosphere can have dramatic effects.

Modern industrial societies burn great quantities of fossil fuels (oil, coal and natural gas), which release CO_2 into the atmosphere. Unchecked, this process will (and may already have begun to) intensify the greenhouse effect, so that more infrared radiation is reradiated to the Earth's surface, raising the surface temperature even more. In addition, human activities also release chlorofluorocarbons, methane and nitrous oxide, and these may aggravate the greenhouse effect.

Many scientists believe that the greenhouse effect will cause changes in climate patterns all around the world. If temperatures rise just 5 degrees C (which some scientists believe it could by the mid-twenty-first century), it would alter drought and rainfall patterns (causing widespread famine), increase the size and frequency of hurricanes, and melt polar ice caps and mountain glaciers.

Most of the ice in the Arctic Circle is already underwater, so a massive melting there wouldn't have too great an effect in raising sea level. But Antarctic ice is landlocked, and currently has no effect on world sea level. If parts of the Antarctic ice were to melt, many coastal cities such as Miami and New York and low-lying countries like Bangladesh would be flooded. If both the Greenland and Antarctic ice caps melted, the world's oceans would rise about 200 feet. In New York, only the tops of the tallest buildings would rise like islands out of the water.

The melting of the ice caps would decrease the Earth's albedo, the degree to which it reflects away the solar radiation it receives. That effect would contribute to global warming, which would in turn melt the ice caps further.

To counteract the greenhouse effect, scientists may try to remove excess carbon dioxide from the atmosphere. One strategy is to increase the amount of plant life that consumes CO_2. Algae growth might be promoted in the Antarctic Ocean by fertilizing it with iron. Seaweed could be farmed on giant ocean grids spanning hundreds or thousands of square miles. Stored carbon dioxide might be ejected into the ocean depths, where it is believed that high pressure might solidify it (though it might eventually bubble to the surface). Another alternative is to increase the Earth's albedo, by inducing white cloud formation or spreading reflective balloons high in the atmosphere.

Whatever remedies your future society tries, global warming will be a problem as long as fossil fuels are burned and the hunger for energy continues unabated. Energy conservation on a massive scale may be the wisest course — and the most politically difficult one.

Ozone Depletion. Earth's ozone layer, between 10 and 50 km (6 and 30 miles) from the surface, forms a protective barrier from harmful ultraviolet rays. Without the ozone layer, the amount of UV radiation would be enough to increase drastically the rates of cancer and mutation. Yet, though it performs a vital protective function, the amount of ozone (O_3) that makes up this shield is small. If the entire ozone layer were under the atmospheric pressure at sea level, it would only be a few millimeters thick.

The ozone layer has for many years been under attack from chlorofluorocarbons (CFCs), which are used to clean microchips, as refrigerants and in the manufacture of styrofoam. These chemicals have been building up in the atmosphere. The chemical most deadly to the ozone layer is chlorine monoxide, which has been found in high concentrations over Antarctica and more recently, over parts of Canada and New England. The high concentrations of chlorine monoxide over Antarctica are thought to be responsible for the hole in the ozone layer there, and scientists believe that the erosion of ozone in other parts of the world — everywhere but the tropics — is also caused by these chlorine compounds.

The reason that Antarctica and colder regions of the northern hemisphere have shown signs of ozone erosion first is that in these regions the cold air forms cloud particles that help convert harmless chlorine-containing compounds into chlorine monoxide. In the presence of bright sunlight, these molecules will destroy ozone. In recent years the ozone in Antarctica has almost disappeared during the late winter months.

Even though many countries have tried to ban the use of chlorofluorocarbons, these bans have yet to go into effect. The U.S. has put a time limit on the use of CFCs, attempting to phase them out by the year 1995. In the meantime, the buildup of chlorine monoxide in the stratosphere increases.

If this trend is not reversed soon, it may drastically affect life by the early twenty-first century. Protection against the Sun's harmful UV rays will be even more important than it is now, so that people might not be able to expose their skin to direct sunlight without a very high risk of skin cancer.

The Montreal Protocol is an international treaty trying to phase out the use of CFCs everywhere in the world by 2000.

Air Pollution. Ozone depletion is only one result of air pollution that will be affecting society in the future. According to the Standards of the U.S. Clean Air Act, the air in Los Angeles, California, is already unfit to breathe one out of every two days. This pollution is caused by the gas, coal and oil that industries burn as fuel, discharging hundreds of toxic contaminants into the air. Sulfur dioxide expelled from power plants and nitrogen dioxide exhaust from automobiles are altered by gases in the atmosphere, where they become corrosive acids such as sulphuric acid. Lakes, rivers, soil and whole forests are damaged by precipitation of these chemicals in the form of acid rain. Many aquatic species cannot survive in highly acidic conditions.

Most industrialized areas of the world are subjected to this kind of pollution. Even as the wealthier countries move into less polluting technologies and impose stricter regulations on waste-producing industries, it may be difficult to regulate the toxic discharges of industries in developing Third World nations.

Water Pollution. The global water cycle works like this: Water evaporates from the ocean, rises to form clouds that pass over continental areas, releasing rain and snow, which flows into lakes and rivers and back into the ocean. Pollutants that affect the water in one part of the cycle can spread to affect all parts of the water cycle. Herbicides and pesticides can find their way into the food chain in rivers and lakes. Poisonous and carcinogenic chemicals called PCBs, discharged by industrial plants up until their ban in 1976, can still be found in animal life in places like the Fox River in Wisconsin, where they've become concentrated in river sediments.

Half the population of the United States and Europe uses groundwater — water that flows through the porous spaces beneath the surface. Chemicals from buried wastes can seep into the groundwater, contaminating it.

One difference between air and water pollution as it affects the future in which your stories take place is that water pollution can be fought more effectively. Not only can industrial regulations diminish or eliminate the release of pollutants that might get into the water supply, but the water itself can be cleaned in Waste Treatment Plants. The dangerous chemicals that accumulate in the water can be removed, though at considerable cost. Air pollution is a much greater problem because even if chlorofluorocarbons were banned tomorrow, there is no known way to artificially repair the damage done to the ozone layer. Global warming and increased UV radiation are bound to affect conditions on Earth indefinitely.

Ice Ages. During the ice ages that have occurred several times in Earth's history, thick sheets of ice covered vast land areas. Simply stated, an ice age is a condition in which, over a continuous span of time, the surface of the Earth receives heavier snowfalls in winter than can be melted away the following summer. A drop in world temperature of ten to fifteen degrees (59 degrees F is the current world average) can trigger this kind of long-term accumulation, and over thousands of years the effect on world climates can be extreme and for many life-forms, catastrophic. During the most recent ice age, which lasted from 120,000 to 10,000 years ago, glaciers nearly two miles thick covered areas of the northern United States, Europe and Asia. Because of the lowered temperatures and because so much water was locked up in year-round deposits of ice, there was far less rainfall than there is today, so that even tropical areas not heavily affected by glaciation or lowered temperatures suffered from arid conditions. It's estimated that during the height of the last ice age, the sea level dropped as much as 400 feet.

As mentioned in chapters 6 and 7, it is believed that ice ages are caused by a complex interaction of a number of factors, many of them astronomical. First, there is the shape of the Earth's orbit around the Sun, which varies considerably over a cycle of 100,000 years. During that time the orbit will stretch from a nearly circular shape to a more elliptical one and then back again. At its most elliptical, the Earth can be as much as 11,350,000 miles further away from the Sun than when in its more circular shape. Second, there is the tilt of the Earth. The axis of the Earth is never perpendicular to the orbital plane. Depending on which part of its yearly orbit the Earth is in, the northern or southern hemisphere is tilted toward or away from the Sun. This is what causes the change in seasons. Over cycles of 41,000 years, the angle of the tilt changes. The more extreme the tilt, the more extreme the seasonal variations. Third, there is the wobble of the Earth's axis, which completes a circuit every 23,000 years. Right now, the northern hemisphere is closest to the Sun during its winter, which causes milder winters and cooler summers. Eleven thousand years ago (at the end of the most recent ice age) the arrangement was exactly the opposite: The northern hemisphere was closest to the Sun in summer, causing warmer summers and cooler winters.

Because these three astronomical factors are not in sync with each other, their interaction on the Earth's climate is complex. When the cooling affects of the orbital stretch, orbital tilt and orbital wobble coincide, the climate will be suffering from its most severe periods of cooling and the resultant ice accumulation.

The rise of human civilization is an interglacial event, beginning at the end of the last ice age. Within the next 1,000 to 10,000 years, it's likely that the Earth will enter a new ice age.

An increased greenhouse effect might counteract the astronomical factors, lessening the impact of the ice age. The greenhouse effect might eliminate the ice age altogether. But there are far safer, more controllable methods of melting the glaciers as they advance across the landscape. Clean ice has an albedo of 85 to 90 percent, which means that of all the solar radiation that hits it, only 10 to 15 percent is absorbed. By spreading dark, light-absorbing dust atop the ice, the albedo goes down and less light is reflected into space. The sunlight can therefore melt more of the ice. To concentrate the sunlight strategically, solar mirrors in space could direct light energy to specific problem areas.

However, if civilization were to collapse — if temperatures were to lower and the glaciers began to advance at the tail end of a devastating nuclear war or plague — human beings might not be prepared to fight the ice age at all.

Killer Meteorites

Many geologists believe that 65 million years ago, at the end of the Cretaceous Period, a huge meteorite or comet, perhaps ten miles wide, crashed into the Earth, setting off a chain of events that exterminated many forms of aquatic life, and ended the reign of the most successful terrestrial vertebrates of all time — the dinosaurs. While no definite impact site has ever been confirmed (Iceland and the Caribbean-Gulf of Mexico region are two possibilities), an element called iridium, which is rare on Earth but concentrated in meteorites, has been discovered as a thin, discrete layer separating the Cretaceous from the following period (the Tertiary) in many fossil sites.

This impact would have sent up a huge cloud that blocked the sunlight, killing off plant life, with repercussions spreading throughout the world food web. If such an object were to strike in the ocean it could have punched a hole through the oceanic crust, causing a massive volcanic eruption. The cloud would then be full of ash, and bring on something resembling a nuclear winter.

Even before it hit the Earth, it would cause extensive damage. As it sped through the atmosphere, it would ionize air molecules and generate an acidic rainfall that could have been as strong as battery acid.

Whether or not such an impact killed the dinosaurs, the danger of an impact from a comet or a meteorite is very real. The asteroid Icarus came within 6.5 million km of Earth in 1968. Had it struck the Earth (at an estimated velocity of 40,000 kph), Icarus — which is a small asteroid only one km across — would have set off an explosion greater than all the nuclear stockpiles in the world.

A society with a strong presence in space might be able to thwart a meteorite or comet from striking the Earth. If lasers could be fired at just one side of the approaching object, boiling that side so that the vapor pressure nudges its trajectory, it could be diverted from the Earth entirely.

Lucifer's Hammer by Larry Niven and Jerry Pournelle, and *Shiva Descending* by Gregory Benford and William Rotsler are two superior novels dealing with this subject.

The Death of the Sun

About five billion years in the future, most of the hydrogen at the Sun's core will have fused to helium, which will start to contract under its own weight. The heat produced from this contraction will ignite the surrounding shell of hydrogen. The Sun will begin to expand, heating up the Earth. Over the course of a few million years the heat from the expanding Sun will kill off all exposed life, evaporate the oceans and burn away the atmosphere. Eventually the expanding Sun will swallow Mercury, Venus, Earth and possibly even Mars, as the helium at the Sun's core fuses to carbon. In another hundred million years the helium will all have fused to carbon; the Sun will compress into a white dwarf star, while the outer envelope drifts off into space.

Will human beings survive to witness the death of the Sun? So far, no species of multicellular life has survived even one billion years. Unless civilization remains relatively stable for the next five billion years, humans will probably have evolved into something nearly unrecognizable. To adjust to the changes that will overtake the Earth during the next few billion years, perhaps humanity will engineer itself into one or several different types of forms. See chapter 13 for speculations on the varieties of engineered humans that might exist in the future.

Meteorites: What Are the Odds?

Don't go buying a lot of meteorite insurance yet. The odds that an asteroid of at least six-tenths of a mile—one large enough to cause global repercussions—will hit the Earth during a person's lifetime have been calculated as 1 in 7,000. The probability that such an object will strike in a given year is 1 in 500,000. The odds that you personally will be killed by a meteorite are virtually infinitesimal.

Still, over the long periods described by SF, a major impact *somewhere* on Earth is a distinct possibility. Here are the estimated frequencies for different sizes of asteroids, calculated by a NASA team of scientists in 1992:

- 33 feet to 328 feet: The frequency of these is decades to centuries. They produce fireballs (many times greater than those of nuclear bombs) as they burn up in the atmosphere, radiating shock waves that can be felt on the ground. The explosion that rocked Siberia in 1908 is believed to have been caused by such a fireball.
- 328 feet to 3,280 feet (0.62 miles): These arrive on a time scale of thousands of years. They can survive atmospheric burning to strike Earth and form a crater. The force might equal a 50-megaton blast.
- 0.62 miles and up: One of these hits landmasses about once every 300,000 years. The dust thrown up by impact can affect the climate for years or decades.
- 6.21 miles to 9.31 miles: This is the type of object believed responsible for the mass extinctions 65 million years ago. Their frequency is in the tens of millions of years.

Maybe humanity will die off in the meantime and another type of creature will evolve intelligence, the descendant of a modest, unlikely creature that lives among us even now. While the dinosaurs evolved throughout their 130 million year reign, the mammals were a quiet, marginal class of animal in comparison. There may be intelligence of a very different sort upon the Earth that faces the dying Sun.

○

SF isn't just about the future, or what's happening in another part of the galaxy. Many of the worlds SF writers build are alternate versions of the present — or even the past. Some of the worlds don't even exist in our universe, but rather in parallel universes that are only slightly different from our own, or else in universes where even the laws of physics are different. Sometimes these different worlds intersect with each other or with our own world.

An alternate world can be a carefully reasoned construct, based on principles that can be more or less justified by the findings of modern physics or historical examples. Or it can be built along the lines of purely imaginary science — a mythical kingdom or a dreamlike, surreal wasteland. In the area of alternate worlds, SF often seems to intersect with or even turn into high fantasy or horror. Roger Zelazny's *Amber* novels are an example of fantasies to which we are introduced through a rationale of imaginary science in which our own universe is possibly just an illusionary subset of a greater universe. Greg Bear's *Queen of Angels* has two characters immerse their minds into the subconscious of a disturbed poet/mass murderer, turning what had up to that point been an SF mystery into a gruesome horror story.

CHAPTER FIFTEEN
ALTERNATE
UNIVERSES

Because the concept of alternate universes lies on the border between existing and imaginary science, this final chapter will necessarily be different in tone from the rest of the book. There will be less reliance on "hard" science and more on examples from published science fiction. Even so, alternate universes are a popular setting in SF and may prove to be fertile ground for your own stories. Science can play a role in constructing these universes, but here, perhaps more than anywhere in SF, the imagination reigns supreme.

Alternate History

What would have happened had the Viking settlements in North America been successful, almost 500 years before Columbus? If the dinosaurs had never died out? If the British had crushed the American Revolution? If Hitler and the Axis forces had won World War II? If the young Hitler had emigrated to the U.S. after World War I? If the Spanish Armada had conquered Britain and executed Queen Elizabeth?

These and many other questions make up the branch of SF known as alternate history. They often rest on the concept of contingency—the notion, raised in chapter 7, that an alteration of small, seemingly insignificant factors can have dramatic long-range consequences. In *Wonderful Life*, Stephen Jay Gould's book about the 550-million-year-old Burgess Shale fossils (some of which may represent phyla with no living descendants), the author argues that evolution could have gone quite differently. Vertebrates, represented in the Burgess Shale fossils by a primitive, pre-vertebrate ancestor, *Pikaia*, might not have seemed the most promising creature of its day. It might have been Pikaia, and not exotic creatures such as *Anomalocaris*, that died out leaving no descendants. Possibly there would have been no fish, no amphibians, no reptiles, birds or mammals—no *humans*. Yet with all those available niches to fill, it might have been the arthropods or the mollusks or echinoderms who dominated the seas and then the land. Or it could have been the descendant of a creature stranger than we can imagine.

Harry Harrison's *West of Eden* is about what would have happened had the dinosaurs not died out. Most scientists believe that if this had happened, the mammals would not have been the great successes they were. But in Harrison's novel, mammals and even human beings evolve, thus pitting intelligent humans against a much older species of intelligent dinosaurs.

Contingency is a part of political history as well as natural history. In Norman Spinrad's *The Iron Dream*, Adolph Hitler emigrates to the United States after World War I. In Keith Robert's *Pavanne*, the Spanish Armada defeats the British fleet, so that Spain remains the most powerful nation on Earth for several centuries.

The Difference Engine by William Gibson and Bruce Sterling tells the story of a computerized Victorian England. Charles Babbage really did design an "analytical engine" in the 1830s, a computer that would have employed punch cards and memory elements, but the British government withdrew support in 1842.

In the novel, the engine is built, revolutionizing British society and beginning the computer age a century early.

In one of the most famous alternate history novels, *The Man in the High Castle*, Philip K. Dick uses an assassination of FDR in the early 1930s to change the course of history so that Germany and Japan win the Second World War. They split the U.S. down the middle and divide up the world, with Japan controlling the Pacific and the Far East and Germany controlling everything else.

If you are planning to write an alternate history, don't make the elementary mistake of placing it on another planet in our galaxy, where the Roman Empire or the Nazi Reich is still going on. The odds that a planet in *this* universe will exactly imitate Earth in all but one convenient respect are infinitesimal. Let your alternate world reside in an entirely different universe.

Parallel Universes

There is a paradoxical thought experiment in quantum physics known as "Schrödinger's Cat," named after Erwin Schrödinger, co-discoverer of quantum mechanics. A cat is inside a box, along with a Geiger counter, a single radioactive atom, and a bottle of poison. The radioactive atom stands a fifty-fifty chance of decaying within an hour. If the atom decays, the Geiger counter will tick. The box is set up so that a tick from the Geiger counter will break the bottle, releasing the poison and killing the cat. If the atom has a fifty-fifty chance of decaying within that hour, can quantum physicists predict whether the cat will be dead at the end of that hour? No, they can only calculate the probability. The quantum mechanical state of the cat is half-dead and half-alive, until the box is opened to find either a dead or alive cat. The problem, of course, is that the cat must be alive or dead, not some indeterminate state in between. And yet, this is what the most precise mathematical analysis tells us.

One solution is to say that quantum mechanics is designed to make predictions about large numbers of objects. If a billion cats, each in a separate box, are used in the experiment, it can be safely said that at the end of the hour, half of them will be dead. But what about the single cat?

Another resolution (suggested by physicists Hugh Everett and John Wheeler) was to imagine that at the end of the hour, the cat experiences both fates, but in different universes. If we open the box and pull out a live cat, then in a parallel universe prototypes of us are pulling out a dead cat. For every event that occurs in the universe, there is an alternate event occurring in a parallel universe. If there are an infinite number of alternatives to any event, then there must be an infinite number of alternate universes. Unfortunately, the theory may be impossible to prove, and the parallel universes, if they exist at all, may be separate and unbridgeable.

In SF, of course, the universes can and often are bridged. The geometry of a black hole can be mathematically extended to a counterpart of the black hole — the white hole, into which matter cannot fall, but only go out. This white hole would exist in a parallel universe. Using imaginary science, traveling through the black hole at faster-than-light velocity might be a way to reach a parallel universe.

But what would one find there?

In Isaac Asimov's *The Gods Themselves*, Earth scientists discover that samples of tungsten are mysteriously turning into a previously unknown radioactive isotope, Plutonium 186. The problem is the existence of such an isotope should be impossible, there being too few neutrons to hold its 94 protons together for even a trillion-trillionth of a second. In addition, it seems not to be decaying, but emitting *more* radiation as time goes on. Because the existence of such a substance defies the natural laws of the cosmos, it's suggested that it originates in a parallel universe with different laws, and that it is purposely being exchanged for tungsten across the barrier between the universes.

While the interaction between parallel universes may be as impossible as traveling back in time, it does offer SF writers ways to examine very similar and very dissimilar universes. Whether as a method of bridging SF with various types of fantasy or offering a slightly altered perspective on our own world through a skewed mirror, parallel universes provide SF writers with many valuable opportunities.

Microscopic Universes

One type of alternate universe not yet mentioned is that of the very small. Isaac Asimov's novelization of *Fantastic Voyage* is the classic example of a story set in a microscopic environment — the human body. As Asimov was the first to admit, there are scientific problems with such a story. In telling such a tale, you will either run into wrong science, or you will need to invent some imaginary science.

There are only three known ways in which a human being could be shrunk to microscopic size, and all of them have a serious drawback. If the matter in a body is compressed — squeezed down to a smaller size with high pressures — the process would kill him. Also, since the weight would remain the same, the tiny feet would cut through the ground like the point of a knife. The atoms themselves could be reduced in size, but they would become what is called degenerate matter, incapable of performing the chemical reactions on which life depends. The third alternative is to reduce the number of atoms in the body. However, this would reduce the number of atoms that make up the brain, making human intelligence impossible.

It was once popular to think of universes *within* universes, based on the observation that models of atomic structure resemble solar systems — with electrons acting as orbiting planets. But the beings on these electron-planets would be unable to see because photons of light would be larger than they were, and unable to breathe, because the atoms of gas would be larger than their entire planet.

There are limits to the kinds of worlds you can design in SF, but these limits are being stretched all the time. A mass-induced hallucination could turn the reality for everyone on a planet into one long, shared nightmare of unreality. A parallel universe might exist in which the laws of physics were altered just enough to make certain impossible concepts seem plausible. The science of some age far in the future could overturn all our notions of physical reality, putting the bridges between parallel universes, between present and past, between the microscopic and macroscopic all within reach.

Some of the speculations in SF are rooted in problems we are already experiencing: overpopulation, pollution, political tyranny and natural disaster. Others are rooted in problems and promises that lie almost within our reach: the commercialization of the solar system and the establishment of viable colonies on Mars and the Moon. SF examines our relationships with each other and with the life-forms with which we share this planet by showing us other kinds of life, from faraway planets, and scrutinizing the interactions. It can give us glimpses of the strange, awesome worlds on which our descendants may live thousands or millions of years in the future. It can also give us glimpses of worlds that would seem to defy all possibility, but exist in a universe strangely similar yet fundamentally different from our own.

As an SF writer, one of your purposes may be to educate your readers on matters of science or history, or to share your own social and political views. One of your purposes should always be to entertain the reader: with action and drama, with interesting characters or an original plot. But the SF audience nearly always demands a certain amount of plausibility. While a story can contain no science and still be SF, a story that contains a serious dose of wrong science will lose a lot of its credibility. SF is, more than anything else, an intense examination and manipulation of *knowledge*: scientific, historical and political. Every SF story idea you'll ever have will present its own set of problems and challenges. Every world you design will need to look and feel and behave like a *real* world. Reference materials will be your best friends: science journals, encyclopedias, nonfiction books of all kinds. To write good SF you can never stop learning, and you can never know enough.

○

Books

Abell, George O. *Exploration of the Universe,* 3rd ed. New York, NY: Holt, Rinehart and Winston, 1975.

Ashpole, Edward. *Search for Extraterrestrial Intelligence, The.* London, UK: Blandford Press, 1990.

Asimov, Isaac. *Asimov's New Guide to Science.* New York, NY: Basic Books, 1984.

Barlowe, Wayne Douglas. *Expedition.* New York, NY: Workman Publishing, 1990.

Barlowe, Wayne Douglas and Ian Summers. *Barlowe's Guide to Extraterrestrials.* New York, NY: Workman Publishing, 1979.

Beatty, J. Kelly, Brian O'Leary and Andrew Chaikin. *New Solar System, The.* Cambridge, MA: Sky Publishing Corp., 1982.

Card, Orson Scott. *How to Write Science Fiction and Fantasy.* Cincinnati, OH: Writer's Digest Books, 1990.

Dole, Stephen H. *Habitable Planets for Man.* New York, NY: Elsevier, 1970.

Dozois, Gardner, et al. *Writing Science Fiction and Fantasy.* New York, NY: St. Martin's Press, 1991.

Drexler, K. Eric. *Engines of Creation, The.* New York, NY: Anchor Books, 1986.

Edwards, Gabrielle I. *Biology the Easy Way.* New York, NY: Barron's Educational Series, 1984.

Goswami, Amit with Maggie Goswami. *Cosmic Dancers, The.* New York, NY: Harper & Row, 1983.

BIBLIOGRAPHY

Gould, Stephen Jay. *Wonderful Life: The Burgess Shale and the Nature of History.* New York, NY: W.W. Norton & Co., 1989.

Halberstam, David. *Next Century, The.* New York, NY: William Morrow, 1991.

Isaacs, Alan, et al. *Concise Science Dictionary,* 2nd ed. Oxford, UK: Oxford University Press, 1991.

Jackson, Steve and William A. Barton. *GURPS Space.*

Austin, TX: Steve Jackson Games, 1990.

Keeton, William T. *Biological Science*, 2nd ed. New York, NY: W.W. Norton & Co., 1972.

Lovelock, James. *Ages of Gaia, The*. New York, NY: Bantam Books, 1990.

McDonough, Thomas R. *Space: The Next Twenty-Five Years*. New York, NY: John Wiley & Sons, 1989.

McGraw-Hill Encyclopedia of Science & Technology, 6th ed. New York, NY: McGraw-Hill, 1987.

Miles, Frank and Nicholas Booth. *Race to Mars: The Harper & Row Mars Flight Atlas*. New York, NY: Harper & Row, 1988.

Minsky, Marvin. *Society of Mind, The*. New York, NY: Simon & Schuster, 1986.

Moché, Dinah L. *Astronomy: A Self-Teaching Guide*. New York, NY: John Wiley & Sons, 1989.

Nicholls, Peter, ed. *Science Fiction Encyclopedia, The*. New York, NY: Doubleday/Dolphin, 1979.

Nicholls, Peter, ed. *Science in Science Fiction, The*. New York, NY: Crescent Books, 1982.

Oberg, James Edward. *New Earths*. New York, NY: New American Library, 1981.

Pagels, Heinz. *Cosmic Code, The*. New York, NY: Bantam Books, 1981.

Pagels, Heinz. *Dreams of Reason, The*. New York, NY: Bantam Books, 1988.

Preiss, Byron, ed. *Planets, The*. New York, NY: Bantam Books, 1985.

Preiss, Byron, ed. *Universe, The*. New York, NY: Bantam Books, 1987.

Sagan, Carl. *Cosmos*. New York, NY: Random House, 1980.

Sagan, Dorion. *Biospheres*. New York, NY: Bantam Books, 1990.

Schell, Jonathan. *Fate of the Earth, The*. New York, NY: Avon Books, 1982.

Shipman, Harry L. *Space 2000: Meeting the Challenge of a New Era*. New York, NY: Plenum Press, 1987.

Stableford, Brian. *Future Man*. London, UK: Granada Publishing, 1984.

Stableford, Brian and David Langford. *Third*

Millenium, The. New York, NY: Alfred A. Knopf, 1985.

Toffler, Alvin. *Powershift*. New York, NY: Bantam Books, 1990.

Trefil, James. *1001 Things Everyone Should Know About Science*. New York, NY: Doubleday, 1992.

Voyage Through the Universe: Stars. Alexandria, VA: Time-Life Books, 1988.

Voyage Through the Universe: The New Astronomy. Alexandria, VA: Time-Life Books, 1989.

Voyage Through the Universe: Spacefarers. Alexandria, VA: Time-Life Books, 1989.

Voyage Through the Universe: The Sun. Alexandria, VA: Time-Life Books, 1990.

Voyage Through the Universe: The Near Planets. Alexandria, VA: Time-Life Books, 1990.

Periodicals

Analog Science Fiction/Science Fact. New York, NY.

Discover. New York, NY.

Futurist. World Future Society, Bethesda, MD.

Natural History. New York, NY.

New York Times, "Science Times" section. New York, NY.

Omni. New York, NY.

Scientific American. New York, NY.

Electronic Sources

Grolier's Academic American Encyclopedia, Online Edition (on CompuServe).

NASA Online Archive (on CompuServe).

SimEarth: The Living Planet. Orinda, CA: Maxis, 1991.

A

B

INDEX